Progress of the World's Women 2000

UNIFEM
Biennial
Report

UNIFEM

*United Nations
Development Fund
for Women*

Publication Team and Advisory Committee

Coordinator: Diane Elson

Consultants
  Isabella Bakker
  Radhika Balakrishnan
  Melika Hoodbhoy
  Hande Keklik
  Anita Nayar

Background papers
  Savitri Bisnath
  Jasmine Gideon

Editor: Karen Judd
Designer: Karen Kelleher

UNIFEM
  Nazneen Damji
  Interns
  Heather Clarke
  Meredith Anne Mishel
  Nadja Carolyn Schmeil

Production: Rosemary Kalapurakal, Joanne Sandler, Kirsten Gelsdorf, Tina Johnson

Advisory Committee

Dr. Irma Arriagada
UN Economic Commission for
Latin America and the Caribbean, Chile

Carmen Barroso
Director, Population Programme
John D. and Catherine T. MacArthur
Foundation, USA

Professor Lourdes Benería
Department of City and Regional Planning
Cornell University, USA

Nalini Burn
Consultant on Gender and Economics,
Mauritius

Dr. Marty Chen
John F. Kennedy School of Government
Harvard University, USA

Dr. Korkut Erturk
Department of Economics
University of Utah, USA

Dr. Maria Floro
Department of Economics
American University, USA

Dr. Renana Jhabvala
Self-Employed Women's Association
(SEWA), Ahmedabad, India

Rose Kiggundu
Council for Economic Empowerment
in Africa, Uganda

Kamal Malhotra
Senior Civil Society Advisor
UN Development Programme, USA

Professor Amina Mama
African Gender Institute
University of Cape Town, South Africa

Dr. Antonella Picchio
Dipartimento Economia Politica
University of Modena, Italy

Dr. Ewa Ruminska-Zimny
Warsaw School of Economics
Poland

Professor Gita Sen
Indian Institute of Management
Bangalore, India

Dr. Mariama Williams
Development Alternatives for
Women in a New Era (DAWN),
Kingston, Jamaica

The entire team wishes to thank Noeleen Heyzer, Executive Director of UNIFEM, for her support and guidance, and the many UNIFEM staff from regional offices and in New York who contributed insights, examples and comments on drafts of this publication. Special thanks go also to theWistat Database team of the UN Statistical Division in New York.

Contents

List of Tables

List of Charts

Preface

It is with great pride that I introduce the first edition of a new UNIFEM biennial report, *Progress of the World's Women*, to stand alongside other UN flagship publications: *The Human Development Report* (UNDP), *The State of the World's Children* (UNICEF), and *The State of World Population* (UNFPA). UNIFEM's decision to launch *Progress of the World's Women* responds to the need to inspire concentrated attention and action to address the opportunities and challenges that countries worldwide are facing in their effort to achieve greater equality in the lives of women and girls.

UNIFEM has been supporting innovative programmes of governments, NGOs and other actors in more than 100 countries to implement the Beijing Platform for Action. While the challenges are significant, we are encouraged by the advances that have been achieved in a number of critical areas. By focusing on strategic interventions, pilot initiatives, advocacy and the facilitation of new partnerships between United Nations agencies, governments, civil society and the media, we have made significant strides in critical areas, such as addressing violence against women. This includes changes in legislation and improvements in law enforcement, as well as increased allocation of resources to violence prevention, protection and rehabilitation services for women. Advances have also been achieved through innovative initiatives designed to engender governance and leadership, increase women's access to economic opportunities and improve understanding of the gender dimensions of HIV/AIDS.

This inaugural report, *Progress of the World's Women 2000*, assesses what has been achieved for women's economic empowerment and gender equality from the mid 1980s to the late 1990s. Launched at the UN Special Sessions to review progress in implementing commitments made at the Fourth World Conference on Women and the World Summit on Social Development, it focuses on the economic dimensions of women's progress in the context of globalization. Using a combination of statistical indicators and personal testimonies, it shows that while there has been progress in many countries, this progress is uneven. Even in the richest countries some forms of gender inequality persist. There is still a long way to go before the promise of the Beijing Platform for Action is fulfilled. This raises the need for greater accountability, calling for more concentrated attention to three areas: targets and indicators that are needed to track progress, individuals and institutions who need to be held accountable, and the measures that need to be taken towards accelerating progress for women.

While the Beijing Platform for Action and the programmes for action from other UN world conferences on women offer a resounding endorsement of the need for gender justice and equality, they provide a limited set of specific targets and indicators as tools for ensuring greater accountability. In essence, the countries of the world have agreed to a path but have neglected to create sufficient road signs that let us know how far we have come in our journey and how far we have to go.

The International Conferences of the 1990s have led to agreement on a range of targets and indicators for women's progress. The 1994 International Conference on Population and Development was especially instrumental in introducing targets and indicators that focus on women's health, education and reproductive rights. But we lack comparable targets and indicators for women's economic empowerment and economic rights. For instance, no targets and indicators are specified to address gender equality in the labour market, or in the time devoted to unpaid care work, or to measure the "feminization" of poverty. In June 2000, the world has an opportunity to link the review of the Fourth World Conference on Women to other UN world conference reviews, as well as to the goals set forth by the Millennium Report issued by the Secretary-General of the

United Nations. Integrated United Nations follow-up can serve to ensure that global development targets and indicators to address income poverty are specified in ways that take into account gender disparities in income poverty.

Policies to ensure that targets are met must be implemented in ways that promote rather than impede women's enjoyment of human rights. The discourse of rights has a powerful moral force, which the discourse of targets lacks. We must therefore explicitly link targets to the promotion and protection of women's human rights. The achievement of gender equality targets and protection of women's human rights require governments to make appropriate allocations of resources. Government budgets, both raising revenues and making expenditures, must be reshaped to ensure that they are fully supportive of women's empowerment and gender equality.

States have made national and international policy commitments to advance the status of women and by April 2000, 118 governments had adopted national action plans or policy directives on gender equality. However, with globalization, non-state institutions are increasingly becoming critical in promoting or hindering progress for women. The strengthened roles of civil society, the private sector, multilateral agencies, and international economic institutions in decision-making processes call for a shift of focus from governments to governance. Accountability has many dimensions, demanding synergetic partnerships, strategic alliances, and many more stakeholders. No single agent on its own can deliver the needed changes. Alliances and partnerships based on shared responsibility and common ground are crucial if we are to have progress for all.

The prospects for women's progress depend upon global, regional, national and local contexts. Currently, the major phenomenon shaping our world is globalization, the global integration of trade, finance, investment, and use of new technology. The gender effects of globalization are complex and uneven, with new risks and new opportunities for different groups. If globalization is to be pro-women and pro-poor people, it must be steered and shaped in accord with international human rights conventions and the development consensus and targets reached at various UN conferences. Women's capacity must be built to manage new risks and to take advantage of new opportunities, including new information and communications technologies. Women-friendly financial institutions based on greater participation and accountability must be created. At the same time, the elimination of gender bias as a "development distortion" must be a central objective of public policy if development gains

from new opportunities are to be maximized. Finally, business corporations must be encouraged to commit themselves to social responsibility and accountability in all their operations. Through a series of joint efforts, markets, technology and economic policy must be transformed so that they operate fairly, and deliver the potential fruits of globalization to poor women.

Equality, Development and Peace, the themes of the four UN conferences on women, are the bedrock upon which are anchored the aspirations of the UN system, its member states and its peoples. If equality, development and peace are to be the basis for organizing our social systems, then we need people in government, business and civil society to promote the right kind of values, policies, institutions and relationships to shape our world. Partnerships among governments, civil society and businesses for social responsibility are extremely important in a globalizing world. We need to give more attention to the norms, leadership and decision-making that can make globalization truly supportive of human development, economic and gender justice.

The stakes for women are high. Women want a world in which inequality based on gender, class, caste and ethnicity is absent from every country and from the relationships among countries. Women want a world where fulfillment of basic needs becomes basic rights and where poverty and all forms of violence are eliminated. Where women's unpaid work of nurturing, caring and weaving the fabric of community will be valued and shared equally by men. Where each person will have the opportunity to develop her or his full potential and creativity. Where progress for women is recognized as progress for all.

Noeleen Heyzer

Executive Director
UNIFEM

Overview
Progress of the World's Women 2000

This report examines the progress of the world's women from the mid 1980s to the late 1990s. It concentrates on the economic dimensions of gender equality and women's empowerment in the context of globalization. The report includes a discussion of women's visions, experiences and dilemmas about progress as well as benchmarks for progress established by internationally agreed-upon rights, standards, objectives and targets. It assesses women's progress using a variety of indicators and examines the issue of accountability, focusing in particular on government accountability for the gender impact of their policies and programmes, including national budgets, and on corporate accountability for the social impact of their operations. Finally, it explores ways in which globalization can be reshaped to promote the progress of poor women, including transforming microfinance, markets for goods and services, the development and use of new technology, and national and international economic policy.

The report presents national statistical indicators in tables and charts, and also presents the voices and faces of many individual women from around the world.

Chapter 1

The Progress of Women:
Empowerment and Economics

This report takes the human development approach to economic policy as a point of departure. But, recognizing that oppressed people may lack the courage to choose to develop and use their capabilities, it extends the idea of human development to encompass the process of empowerment. Women's empowerment includes:

- acquiring knowledge and understanding of gender relations and ways in which these relations may be changed;

- developing a sense of self-worth, a belief in one's ability to secure desired changes and the right to control one's life;
- gaining the ability to generate choices and exercise bargaining power;
- developing the ability to organize and influence the direction of social change to create a more just social and economic order, nationally and internationally.

Acquiring these capabilities requires both a process of self-empowerment, in which women claim time and space to re-examine their own lives critically and collectively, and the creation of an enabling environment for women's empowerment by other social actors, including other civil society organizations, governments and international institutions. It entails both the development of women's own agency and the removal of barriers to the exercise of this agency.

Conventional conceptions of the way in which economies operate offer limited guidance for policies to promote women's empowerment and ways to combine gender justice with economic justice. This because they leave out much of the work that women do, especially the unpaid care work that women do for their families and communities. This report draws upon recent work in gender-aware economics to present a more complete view of how economies work, including unpaid care work in the home as well as volunteer work and paid work in NGOs, and the often invisible "informal" paid work in small workshops, on the streets and in sub-contracted home-based work.

Looking at economies through a gender lens produces a different analysis of economic restructuring. Conventional economic indicators may signal that progress is being made, with more and more women entering into paid work, and economic reforms (including liberalization and privatization) producing increases in economic efficiency. But they may obscure a transfer of real costs (in people's time and effort) from the public sector, where such costs are monetized and show up in government accounts, to households (the "domestic sector"), where such costs are not monetized and therefore not visible. *Gender-aware economic analysis suggests the need for a more holistic definition of "efficiency" that directs attention beyond financial costs.*

The primacy of financial costs is intensified by globalization. International trade, investment and migration are not new phenomena; what is new is the accelerating speed and scope of movements of real and financial capital. This acceleration is due to the removal of state controls on trade and investment and to the rapid development of new information and communications technologies.

Women have experienced globalization in a number of different ways. Globalization intensifies some of the existing inequalities and insecurities to which poor women are subject, but for educated, professional women, it opens up new opportunities. Globalization does not so much create a problem in the unpaid provision of care where none existed before, as change the form of the problem. Before globalization, there was a care deficit, but mainly a deficit in the care provided to women, who spent much time caring for other people, but had little time to care for themselves. With globalization, men and children may also begin to experience a care deficit, if the pressures of the double burden of paid and unpaid work becomes too much for women and men do not take on more of this work. Solutions will require re-balancing responsibilities between private, public, domestic and NGO sectors of the economy; better ways of managing the global economy; and changes on the part of men as well as of women.

Among the negative consequences of globalization has been financial crisis in several regions in the 1990s. In times of crisis, women are called upon to act as the heroes of everyday life, providing the ultimate social safety net for their families when all other forms of social security have failed. Globalization creates an environment that allows many women to achieve greater personal autonomy but in an increasingly unequal and risky environment. *Women are faced with the dilemma of how to reconcile their demand for empowerment with their concern for a more just and equal economic order.*

One way forward is to promote the transformation of the institutional norms and values of business corporations, public agencies and NGOs, to reflect the patterns of women's as well as men's lives and to support not only individual choice but also economic justice. Gender mainstreaming should be understood as a process that brings about that kind of institutional transformation. In particular, it should change the expectation that

people who are decision-makers in economic and political life have no responsibilities for unpaid care work or can delegate them to others. Men need to take a larger share of the pains and pleasures of unpaid care work. Fortunately, there are men who are already thinking along these lines.

Women's diversity and the contradictory contexts in which they find themselves create great challenges for assessing and promoting the progress of women. Women have to defend their right to paid work in the private, public and NGO sectors in the face of familial and community opposition, their right to better terms and conditions of paid work in the face of global competitive pressures, and their right to more equal ways of sharing and supporting unpaid care work in the face of economic evaluations that do not recognize the costs and benefits of this work. This report is envisaged as a contribution to a global dialogue conducted in relation to the commitments made to women in human rights treaties and UN conferences and grounded in the efforts of women's organizations to humanize the world.

Chapter 2

Commitments to the Progress of Women: Rights and Targets

Governments have made many commitments to the progress of women, expressed internationally through UN human rights instruments, International Labour Organization Conventions and UN conference agreements. Chapter 2 reviews the jointly agreed norms, benchmarks and targets.

Women are actively working to use human rights instruments to address women's economic inequality in different parts of the world. For instance, women in Nepal and Tanzania have used the Convention on the Elimination of All Forms of Discrimination Against Women (CEDAW) to strengthen women's property rights. UNIFEM and International Women's Rights Action Watch Asia Pacific convene an annual training workshop on using the CEDAW convention.

In Canada, women's groups are among those who have appealed to the Committee on Economic, Social and Cultural Rights to request the government of Canada to explain how its 1995 Budget Implementation Act was consistent with the terms of the International Covenant on Economic, Social and Cultural Rights (ICESCR).

However, human rights instruments have some limitations as tools to advance women's economic progress. CEDAW, for example, outlaws discrimination against women but does not deal with the phenomenon of "equalizing down," when gender gaps narrow but the standard of living of both women and men falls. ICESCR includes the right of women and men to an adequate standard of living, but specifies that this right is to be "progressively realized," by each state, without setting out any kind of timetable or standards.

ILO Conventions, embodying standards agreed upon by recognized workers' groups, employers' groups and government representatives, offer another instrument for advancing women's economic progress. But until recently, ILO Conventions did not apply to workers in the "informal sector." The Convention on Home Work, adopted in 1996, has begun to correct this omission. It entitles paid workers who are based in their own homes to receive the same benefits and protections as those who undertake paid work outside their homes. Women's organizations such as HomeNet, an international network of home-based workers, and SEWA, the Self-Employed Women's Association, are campaigning, with the support of UNIFEM, to persuade governments to ratify the Home Work Convention and enact laws and develop policies to protect the rights of home-based workers in their countries.

Governments have reemphasized their commitment to human rights instruments and ILO Conventions in a series of UN conferences held in the 1990s. Some of these conferences identified specific targets and a timetable for reaching these targets. Chapter 2 summarizes those agreed upon at the International Conference on Population and Development (Cairo, 1994), the World Summit on Social Development (Copenhagen, 1995) and the Fourth World Conference on Women (Beijing, 1995). Some of these targets were subsequently incorporated into the International Development Targets (IDTs) first brought together by the Organisation for Economic Cooperation and Development and now widely used as a framework for development cooperation.

Looking at these targets from the perspective of the progress of women, this report identifies three key findings:

- **The prominent target:** The conferences at Cairo, Copenhagen and Beijing all agreed on a target of closing the gender gap in primary and secondary education by the year 2005. This target is identified in the International Development Targets as *the* target for progress towards gender equality and the empowerment of women.

- **The missing targets:** There are no targets for improving women's economic position or reducing the "feminization" of poverty.

- **The forgotten target:** The Beijing Platform for Action affirmed the target previously agreed upon by the UN Economic and Social Council that

women should have at least a 30 per cent share of decision-making positions. But this target is not included in the International Development Targets.

Targets can be a useful way of enabling people to monitor how far their governments are implementing international agreements. This report proposes some additional targets for consideration, of which the first is to end the disproportionate presence of women among the poor by 2015.

Women's organizations from all over the world pressed governments at Beijing and Copenhagen to address women's economic inequality and poverty, and to change macroeconomic policies that hindered women from enjoying secure and sustainable livelihoods. The agreements reached at both conferences include acceptance of the need to restructure and reformulate macroeconomic policies, but the main mechanism they recommend for reducing women's poverty is improving their access to credit. For example, the Beijing Platform for Action includes:

- 35 references to enabling poor women to gain access to credit;
- 17 references to employment creation and other strategies for poverty eradication.

The agreements at Beijing and Copenhagen recognized the importance of the private sector and called upon business corporations to support women in a number of ways, including increasing the participation of women in management and granting contracts to women's small businesses. Governments also agreed to encourage business corporations to observe national labour, environment, consumer, and health and safety laws and comply with international agreements. *But no mechanisms for corporate social accountability were identified.*

Running through the commitments that governments made at Beijing and Copenhagen is a paradox: *the commitments reflect an expectation that governments are responsible for implementing policies to improve the well-being of women, especially poor women, but they do not effectively address the ways in which market liberalization and privatization may undermine the capacity of governments to discharge these responsibilities, especially to poor women.* There is a need to refocus attention on gender equality and macroeconomic policy in the context of globalization.

Chapter 3

Assessing the Progress of Women: Linking Targets and Indicators

The process of evaluating how far commitments have been met requires gender-sensitive indicators. Chapter 3 reviews some of the indicators that have been proposed and presents tables and charts for countries, grouped by regions, using three indicators selected by the UN Development Assistance Framework (UNDAF) to track progress in reducing obstacles to gender equality and the empowerment of women, over the period between the mid 1980s and the late 1990s. *These are brought together with national-level economic data in a scoreboard of women's progress.*

The review of the indicators proposed by the OECD to monitor achievement of International Development Targets finds that:

- only two out of 24 indicators are specifically designed to measure progress towards gender equality and women's empowerment, and both are related to education;
- the indicators for measuring progress in reducing poverty are not specified in a way that shows the extent to which poverty is "feminized," in the sense of women being disproportionately among the poor;
- there are no indicators on the gender balance in decision-making or on gender equality in the labour market.

The UNDAF Indicator Framework, which will be used in conjunction with national partners to assess development progress at the national level, contains 37 indicators disaggregated by sex, covering income poverty, food security and nutrition, health and mortality, reproductive health, child health and welfare, education, employment, housing, environment and crime prevention. These indicators will be valuable for assessing progress on issues of concern to women. In addition, the framework includes three gender-sensitive indicators that specifically assess progress in achieving gender equality and women's empowerment:

- ratio of girls' enrolment ratio to boys' enrolment ratio in secondary school;
- female share of paid employment in non-agricultural activities (i.e., industry and services);
- women's share of seats in national parliament.

These indicators are best understood as measures of the extent to which there is an enabling environment in which obstacles to women's exercising agency are diminishing. They do not measure the subjective dimensions of women's empowerment, the extent to which women feel themselves able to speak out and take control of their lives.

As with all indicators, they are never unambiguous in their meaning, but they can be powerful tools for women to use in dialogue with governments and international institutions to press for more accountability in the meeting of commitments. Using data from UN databases, especially the Women's Indicators and Statistics database, the report shows progress in many areas, but deterioration in others.

Gender Equality in Secondary Education Enrolment

By 1999:

- 11 per cent of countries had achieved gender equality;
- 51 per cent of countries had a lower enrolment ratio for girls than boys;
- 38 per cent of countries had a lower enrolment ratio for boys than for girls.

Progress in Girls' Enrolment in Secondary Education

Between 1985 and 1997, there were improvements in a wide range of countries, but declines in:

- 11 out of 33 countries in Sub-Saharan Africa;
- 7 out of 11 countries in Central and Western Asia;
- 2 out of 21 countries in Asia and the Pacific;
- 6 out of 26 countries in Latin America and the Caribbean;
- 6 out of 9 countries in Eastern Europe;
- 1 out of 23 countries in Western Europe and Other Developed Countries.

Women's Share of Paid Employment in Industry and Services

Most paid employment today is in industry and services. People who work in agriculture are more likely to be self-employed or unpaid family workers. Women's share of paid employment in industry and services is an indicator of how far the obstacles to women holding paying jobs have crumbled.

In the late 1990s the share ranged from a high of 54 per cent in Ukraine and Latvia to a low of 5 per cent in Chad.

Women's share has increased in most regions from the mid 1980s to the late 1990s (with the exception of parts of Eastern Europe).

But the quality of employment has not increased in the same way, and may even have deteriorated. Women's jobs tend to enjoy less social protection and employment rights than do men's jobs.

Women's Share of Seats in Parliament

Only 8 countries have achieved a level of 30 per cent or more:

Sweden, Denmark, Finland, Norway, Iceland, Netherland, Germany and South Africa.

The share has increased in many countries in the period 1987-2000, most notably in South Africa,

Uganda, Mozambique (in Sub-Saharan Africa); Argentina, Bahamas, Barbados, Ecuador and El Salvador (in Latin America and the Caribbean), and Australia, Austria, Belgium, Canada, Iceland, Netherlands, New Zealand, Sweden and the UK (in Western Europe and Other Developed Countries). Progress is strongly related to the introduction of various kinds of quotas for women in politics. The share has fallen in some countries in all regions, but the most dramatic falls are in Eastern Europe.

Highest Levels of Achievement

Only a few countries have simultaneously achieved gender equality in secondary education at high levels of girls' enrolment (i.e., about 95% or above) plus at least 30 per cent female share of seats in parliament plus women's share of paid employment in industry and services of around 50 per cent:

> Sweden, Denmark, Finland and Norway

Four others come close:

> Iceland, Netherlands, Germany and South Africa

Developed as well as developing countries still have quite a way to go.

Macroeconomic Obstacles to Gender Equality and Women's Empowerment

Some of the shortfall may be due to macroeconomic obstacles. A scoreboard is presented in Chapter 3 which relates scores (positive, negative or no change) for gender equality in education, employment and parliament to scores for increases in per capita gross national income, equality in distribution of national income among households, and debt reduction.

Key points revealed by the scoreboard are:
- deterioration in the economic conditions faced by women in Sub-Saharan Africa and Eastern Europe;
- increased indebtedness:
    22 countries out of 48 in Sub-Saharan Africa;
    10 countries out of 28 in Asia and the Pacific;
- association between increased indebtedness and deterioration in girls' enrolment in secondary school: of the countries for which scores are available for both education and debt reduction, 16 experienced deterioration in girls' enrolment in secondary school, of which 12 also experienced an increase in indebtedness;
- household income inequality increased across a wide range of countries, particularly in Eastern Europe and Western Europe and Other Developed Countries, suggesting that poor women have not enjoyed much of the fruits of any progress.

Chapter 4

Assessing the Progress of Women: A Broader Picture

The assessment of women's economic progress is broadened in Chapter 4, with a focus on women's relative occupancy of decision-making in employment and women's earnings relative to those of men.

Women's Share of Decision-making Positions in the Economy

Women's share of decision-making positions in the economy has been rising in many countries — but there is still a long way to go before it reaches 30 per cent or more in all countries:
- women's share of positions as an employer or as a self-employed ("own-account") worker is higher in the 1990s than it was in the 1980s in 58 out of 72 countries for which data is available;
- women's share of positions as an employer or a self-employed worker was 30 per cent or more in 28 countries in the 1990s;
- women's share of administrative and managerial employment was higher in the 1990s than it was in the 1980s in 51 out of the 59 countries for which data is available;
- women's share of administrative and managerial employment was 30 per cent or more in only 16 countries in the 1990s.

The Gender Gap in Earnings

The gender gap in earnings persists but there has been progress in reducing it in some countries:
- around 1997, women employed in industry and services typically earned 78 per cent of what men in the same sector earned, though in some countries it was as low as 53 per cent and in others as high as 97 per cent;
- in 22 of the 29 countries where data was available to make comparisons over time, the gender gap in earnings in industry and services fell, comparing the 1980s to the 1990s;
- the data reflect mainly the experience of women in full-time "formal" employment in larger places of work and do not necessarily imply that the gap has narrowed for the majority of women who work in part-time or "informal" employment in small-scale places of work or at home.

Feminization of Poverty

Economic inequality between women is likely to have increased as well, although more research is needed to document such a trend. It is not clear whether the "feminization of poverty" has increased or declined because there are no reliable indicators of the extent to which women are over-represented among the population with incomes below the poverty line. None of the indicators commonly used to track the incidence and severity of income poverty are gender-sensitive. Raw data is available in household surveys that could be used to calculate how many women are below the poverty line, as compared to the number of men ("gender poverty ratios"). It should be a priority to make these calculations, since the widely quoted estimate that 70 per cent of the poor are women has no firm foundation.

Social Obstacles

Important social obstacles to women's empowerment are also considered in Chapter 4: violence against women, the growing number of women living with HIV/AIDS and the unequal sharing of unpaid care work. While more complete statistics are needed for all of these, what those currently available suggest is that:

- between 10 and 50 per cent of adult women have experienced violence against them by a husband or a boyfriend;
- 55 per cent of those living with HIV/AIDS in Sub-Saharan Africa are women;
- women typically provide about 70 per cent of the unpaid time spent on care for family members.

There are signs of considerable progress in measuring the time spent in unpaid care work. For example:

- since 1995 at least 24 developing and 18 European countries have begun to measure time spent in such work in a more systematic way.

Women's Empowerment and Public Expenditure

Different dimensions of women's empowerment can be brought together in a composite index, such as the Gender Empowerment Measure, presented in the Human Development Report from 1995 onwards. As shown in Chapter 4, countries with a higher score on the Gender Empowerment Measure also tend to have higher levels of non-military government expenditure as a per cent of GNP. Perhaps this is because societies in which women are more empowered choose to spend more on public services and income transfers. Or perhaps the higher expenditure gives support to women and creates an enabling environment for their empowerment.

Chapter 5

Accountability for the Progress of Women: Women Demanding Action

Accountability of governments for public expenditure is a major theme of Chapter 5, together with accountability of business corporations. The progress of the world's women is facilitated or constrained by the ways in which governments raise and spend money; and the ways in which businesses organize production and sales to make money.

Implementation of UN conference commitments depends upon re-prioritizing public expenditure and revenue to ensure that adequate resources are allocated in national and local budgets. Governments find it easiest to report on funding targeted specifically to women's programmes. An evaluation by the Women's Environment and Development Organization of plans for spending on women's programmes reported in the national plans of action prepared after the Beijing conference found that:

- 31 per cent of reporting countries planned to increase their budget for women's programmes;
- about the same percentage reported that the budget for women's programmes has stayed the same;
- 9 per cent reported a decrease;
- no information on budgetary allocations was provided by the rest.

However, expenditure targeted to women's programmes is typically a very small proportion of government expenditure. Even if expenditure on equal opportunities and gender mainstreaming activities within the public sector is added, the total will typically be no more than 5 per cent of government expenditure. The other 95 per cent of government expenditure is left out of account.

The Beijing Platform for Action called for "the integration of a gender perspective in budgetary decisions on policies and programmes" and governments committed themselves to adjusting budgets to ensure equality of access. However, the Review and Appraisal Document for Beijing +5 prepared by the UN Division for the Advancement of Women on the basis of reports submitted in 1996 by 133 member and observer states notes the absence of any discussion of the comparative impact of this 95 per cent of government expenditure on men and women.

It is important to look at the 95 per cent or more of government expenditure which is not targeted to women beneficiaries or to equal opportunities and gender mainstreaming initiatives within government. *This is because this expenditure is not gender neutral: it will typically have different impacts on men and women, boys and girls because of their different social positioning.* For instance, in countries where girls' enrolment in secondary school is less than that of boys, public expenditure on education will benefit boys more than girls. Cutbacks in public expenditure on health, social services, housing, water and sanitation will frequently mean that women have to provide substitute services for their families, increasing the time they must spend on unpaid care.

Gender Budget Initiatives

Women's organizations are already active in many countries in monitoring the impact of fiscal policy on women and men and in holding governments accountable for their budgets. Some governments have also now started to look at the gender implications of their mainstream public expenditure. In early 2000, gender-sensitive budget initiatives were underway in 18 countries in 4 regions, drawing their inspiration from two sources:

- women's budget statements produced by federal and state governments in Australia;
- the women's budget initiative organized by NGOs and parliamentarians in South Africa.

The Commonwealth Secretariat is supporting the governments of South Africa, Sri Lanka, Barbados, St. Kitts and Nevis and Fiji in piloting tools for gender-sensitive analysis of public expenditure for use by ministries of finance.

UNIFEM has been supporting initiatives to build capacity for gender budget initiatives in Southern Africa and the Indian Ocean Island states, among NGOs, parliamentarians, government officials and academic researchers. *The most effective way of holding governments accountable for the impact of fiscal policy on women is a combination of an inside government project and an outside government project.* An inside government project, based in the ministry of finance or planning has access to key officials and information. An outside government project organized by NGOs and academic researchers can provide cutting-edge critiques and independent monitoring. Parliamentarians have a vital role to play in relation to both.

Holding Corporations to Account

Government budgets are shrinking in many countries and business corporations have a growing impact on the lives of women. Women have been in the forefront of campaigns for greater corporate responsibility, as students, consumers, workers and advocates for economic justice. Among the conclusions they have reached are that corporate codes of conduct must be simple and easy to use and must:

- include all core ILO labour standards and state company responsibility in agreements with contractors, subcontractors and suppliers;
- establish a labour contract;
- ensure high-quality independent monitoring;
- involve workers and trade unions in implementation and monitoring;
- include reproductive rights protection and sexual harassment clauses.

Complementing the introduction of codes of conduct for existing businesses is the creation of new businesses organized from the outset along ethical lines, such as fair trade organizations and ethical investment funds. The UNIFEM National Committee in Singapore has created an ethical equities fund which will invest in publicly listed companies that support UNIFEM objectives by demonstrating a commitment to the empowerment of women. This has grown in a short span of time to $20 million and 75 per cent of the investors are women.

Effective accountability of governments and businesses to women requires:

- greater participation of women within national parliaments and ministries of finance, as well as on the boards of transnational corporations;
- greater access to the media by organizations working to challenge gender-blind policies of globalization and economic restructuring;
- resources for women to monitor governments and business and make independent assessments of the impact of their activities.

Chapter 6

Future Progress for Women: Reshaping Globalization

There is growing recognition that globalization needs renegotiating if information and communications technologies are to be used in equitable ways and markets are to be used to serve human ends. Chapter 6 examines progress towards reshaping globalization, highlighting the ways that women are organizing to *enter, challenge and change* the operation of markets, the use of new technologies and the formulation of economic policy at national and international levels.

Microfinance

Women have been engaging in a lively debate about the extent to which entry into financial markets via loans from microfinance institutions serves to empower women. Microfinance needs to provide complementary services that focus on women's empowerment and not merely provide loans.

Traditional savings and loan institutions which women themselves set up and control need greater recognition and support. The risks associated with microfinance need more recognition. Microcredit for women implies a need for more, not less, attention to social insurance and social protection, and a need for national and international financial institutions to operate according to social criteria as well as financial criteria.

Markets for Goods and Services

Women are very differently positioned in relation to markets in different parts of the world. In some places, where women are socially excluded from leaving their homes and going to market, the challenge is to find ways for women to participate. In other places the challenge is to create markets which are more women friendly through strategies such as:

- establishing local sales outlets under women's control;
- enabling women to participate in international trade fairs;
- enabling women to lobby for markets to be regulated in ways that are fair to women's small businesses;
- enabling women to bargain collectively for better prices;
- setting up women's desks in major regional intergovernmental bodies that deal with trade issues.

Information and Communications Technologies

Women are still very much in a minority among Internet users, but they are beginning to use the Internet in creative ways, both to communicate with other women who are online and also to disseminate information to women who are not online, via radio, newsletters, and videos. The Internet is being used by women for:

- e-inclusion, to overcome the constraints of seclusion;
- e-campaigns, to mobilize online for women's human rights and other objectives;
- e-commerce, to reach new markets;
- e-consultation, to get women's views made known.

But women still face huge imbalances in the ownership, control and regulation of these new information technologies, similar to those faced in other areas, such as new technologies of fertility control. Women are now seeking to participate actively throughout the agenda of knowledge for development, ranging from basic science to regulatory frameworks for technology development and use.

Transforming Economic Policy Making and Global Economic Governance

Women have been taking a variety of initiatives to promote different, more gender-sensitive approaches to economic policy and global governance, including:

- improving economic literacy of women's advocacy groups;
- securing more participation by women in economic policy processes;
- training policy makers to look at economic issues from a gender perspective;
- finding ways to "engender" economic analysis;
- pressing for changes in global economic governance, especially changes in the World Trade Organization WTO.

Ways have been identified of analysing links between economic policy and unpaid work. Suggestions have been made about how the process of taking decisions about macroeconomic policy could be made more participatory and could avoid biases which harm women, especially poor women. Gender issues in the WTO agenda have been identified. Women's groups are particularly concerned about the way in which the WTO and its rules and enforcement mechanism have enlarged the scope of policies that can be considered "barriers to trade" to include most of national economic and social policy.

The initiatives identified in Chapter 6 and others like them need to be gathered together in a global campaign for economic justice with a woman's face. Government and international organizations concerned with economic policy must make complementary changes so that ways of organizing the global economy recognize people as providers of care for one another and not just as producers of commodities, and subject markets to socially negotiated regulations, in which social values as well as prices are recognized. Only then will the conditions for the progress of all women be secure.

Chapter 1

The Progress of Women: Empowerment and Economics

Introduction:
Partnerships for Progress

Progress – the word conjures up images of purposeful movement towards a better life; of marking out and travelling a pathway to higher ground. But women have learned that it is not always easy to determine the direction in which to proceed, and whether the changes we are experiencing, and helping to bring about, take us forwards or backwards.

Women live their lives in many different ways, and different women have different ideas about what would make their lives better and how to achieve this. Many women fear that the world is changing in ways that destroy much that is valuable. They remind us that market liberalization entails the freedom to go hungry as well as opportunities for independent incomes. Others argue that a return to the past is impossible. They remind us that the protection of traditional ways of life perpetuates bonds of oppression as well as affection, and point to the ways in which women are constrained by family and community.

Cathy Cade

UNICEF/S.Paul

Suzette Mitchell

"For me, women's progress is when every woman can make and contribute to informed decisions about her rights, welfare, and general well-being of her society."

— Elsie Onubogu, ICTR sexual assault team, Nigeria

These positions represent opposite views of the complex process of change enveloping women. It is important to be open to a variety of viewpoints and to recognize that others will see things differently. A consensus about what counts as progress has to be negotiated, not assumed. But in order to take effective action in partnership with others, it is necessary to make strategic simplifications in a complex world.

The starting point for this report is that all human beings, in seeking to form and express their ideas and to preserve or to change their current ways of living, find their lives shaped by larger economic, social, political and cultural trends. Many of these trends, including environmental degradation, armed conflict and widespread violence and increasing inequality between and within nations — have the potential to undermine human rights and dignity, turning people into bodies to be violated, vessels to be used to preserve one or another ideology. A more complex trend is the increasingly global reach of market forces and transnational corporations, which have the potential to open new opportunities or close existing ones, depending on people's access to and control of resources. For the most part, women face greater constraints than men in their ability to take advantage of such forces, but this is changing as women demand the right to shape the process of change in ways that enable them to participate on a more equal footing.

All human beings experience to some degree the human pleasure of personal connection and intimacy with family, neighbours, friends, colleagues; and the human pain of disconnection, separation, ultimately the pain of death, one's own and that of loved ones. But societies position women and men differently in terms of their ability to manage such pleasures and pains. In most communities the time and effort needed to care for others is required mainly of women, and if men provide more of this time and effort they may risk being seen as "unmanly" rather than "unselfish."

"It is good to swim in the waters of tradition but to sink in them is suicide."

— Mahatma Gandhi

This report speaks about and for international partnerships and coalitions of diverse people, willing to negotiate both their difference and their connectedness, to promote women's dignity and rights as full and equal human beings (see Box 1 for examples). It

Box 1: Women's International Partnerships for Change

Women are increasingly organizing through international networks and coalitions which bring diverse women together to negotiate and pursue common objectives. Partnerships with which UNIFEM works include:

- DAWN (Development Alternatives with Women for a New Era), a network of women scholars and activists from the economic South who engage in feminist research and analysis of the global environment and are committed to working for equitable, just and sustainable development. Website: www.dawn.org.fj
- GROOTS International (Grassroots Organizations Operating Together in Sisterhood), a global network of women's groups committed to developing a movement giving voice and power for change to low-income and poor women's initiatives. Organizations within the network are active in areas such as credit, asset creation and small business development, sustainable agriculture, food processing, housing, popular education, health and bottom-up community development planning. Website: www.jtb-servers.com/groots.htm.
- WIEGO (Women in Informal Employment Globalizing and Organizing), a worldwide coalition of individuals from grassroots organizations, academic institutions and international development agencies concerned with improving conditions for women in the informal economy, through better statistics, research, programmes, and policies. Website: www.wiego.org
- HomeNet, an international network of women's groups, trade unions and other civil-society organizations advocating for the rights of home-based workers. HomeNet was pivotal in securing NGO and government support for the International Labour Organization Convention on Home Work, adopted in 1996, and campaigns to make governments aware of the need to ratify this and all other ILO Conventions. Website: www.gn.apc.org/homenet.

offers tools to clarify and deepen international dialogue about the progress of women. It emphasizes women as active, achieving, purposeful human beings. But it also recognizes that women face constraints not of their own making or choosing, and that many of these constraints can be weakened only by social choices, collectively made, and not through individual choices alone.

Dignity and Daily Bread

Women's ability to realize themselves as full human beings is complex and multifaceted. This report will pay particular attention to the economic dimension: to dignity and daily bread. In so doing it responds to the growing concerns of women in both the North and the South, concerns that were first expressed by women in developing countries in 1975 at the World Conference on Women in Mexico City and culminated in the 1995 UN Fourth World Conference on Women and parallel NGO Forum in Beijing. There, demands for economic justice were voiced by women of the South under pressure from World Bank and IMF-designed adjustment policies; by women of Eastern Europe plunged into insecurity with the break-up of the system of public ownership and state planning; and by women in industrialized countries facing economic restructuring, with cuts in public expenditure on health, education and welfare services, and privatization of public services and enter-

prises. Approximately 500 of the 3,000 panels at the Forum dealt with economic issues. Indeed, Indian feminist economist Bina Agarwal identified economic crisis as "the single most critical issue" at the NGO Forum.

Since then, the importance of economic issues has increased still further, with financial crises in East and South East Asia, Russia and parts of Latin America, and further deterioration of the prices that countries in Sub-Saharan Africa obtain for their exports. Indebtedness has continued to rise in many developing countries, while unemployment persists in many developed countries. Economic inequality has deepened both between and within countries (UNDP 1999). Thus Agarwal (1996) has drawn attention to the formation of a "strategic sisterhood" to confront a global crisis of economy and polity.

"The feminist movement and the demands of women in any particular country grow out of the reality of that country, and it is wrong to say that what we want is what everybody should want and what we do not want nobody should ask for."

— Wang Jiax'iang (1991)

Of course, the way in which a woman gets her daily bread (or bowl of rice, or beans or maize porridge) is influenced by and influences other aspects of her life. A woman who lacks economic independence is often more vulnerable to violence in the home: if she cannot obtain a living in her own right, it is all the more difficult for her to leave a home in which she is beaten and abused. However, if a woman's income depends entirely on selling her labour, and there is no social safety net for her to fall back on, she may be forced to work under exploitative conditions, even to endure sexual harassment in the workplace. If a woman is illiterate or lacks technical skills, she will be barred from more remunerative work. But if educated women are discriminated against in the labour market, and earn less than men, parents may be more likely to prioritize the education of boys rather than girls. A woman who lacks access to ways of effectively controlling her own fertility is more likely to find herself in a position of economic dependence. An impoverished woman in an impoverished society is less likely to survive childbirth. Health, education and enjoyment of liberty free from violence are all vital parts of a dignified life for a woman. But they are all related to the economic environment in which she lives, and the way in which decisions are made about the allocation of resources (see Box 2).

Women's Progress and Human Development

This report is based upon the belief that women's progress is facilitated by a "human development" approach to economic policy. Criticizing an "excessive preoccupation with GNP growth and national income accounts," the first UNDP Human Development Report declared that "we are rediscovering the essential truth that people must be at the centre of all development" (1990: iii), and launched the idea of human development as a focus for formulating policies to bring this about.

The first report defined human development as a process of "enlarging people's choices":

> Human development has two sides: the formation of human capabilities such as improved health, knowledge and skills and the use people make of their acquired capabilities for leisure, productive purposes or being active in cultural, social and political affairs. If the scales of human development do not finely balance the two sides, onsiderable human frustration may result (1990: 10).

The idea of expansion of human capabilities as the standard of progress was introduced into economic theory by Nobel prize winner Amartya Sen, who describes capabilities as what people can or cannot do: that is, "whether they can live long, escape avoidable morbidity, be well nourished, be able to read and write and communicate, take part in literary and scientific pursuits, and so forth" (1984: 497). He points out that focusing on the expansion of goods and services is inadequate, because "the conversion of commodities into capabilities varies enormously with a number of parameters, e.g., age, sex, health, social relations, class background, education, ideology and a variety of other interrelated factors" (1984: 511). This

---

Box 2: Reproductive Decision-making and Economic Empowerment

There is mounting evidence that women's ability to fully enjoy human rights – indeed, even to demand such rights - is integrally linked to their economic empowerment. A study of the circumstances in which women in poor communities feel entitled to make decisions about marriage and childbearing, contraception and sexuality was carried out by the International Reproductive Rights Research Action Group in seven countries: Brazil, Egypt, Malaysia, Mexico, Nigeria, the Philippines and the United States. Among its conclusions is that the ability to take such decisions requires a sense of personal autonomy, which develops in tandem with the knowledge that women can provide for themselves and their children. Their sense of personhood is sparked by motherhood and nurtured by participation in organized groups, but fundamentally depends on having incomes of their own.

For most of these women, livelihoods remain uncertain, and autonomy provisional, subject to factors outside their control, including the rising costs and care burdens they experience as a result of cuts in government spending and the privatization of social services. But for a few, those with a paid job or a small business and money they can call their own, economic empowerment conveys the right to imagine a different future. With it comes the courage to stand up against husbands and partners, parents and in-laws, to assert their rights to decide whether and when to have sex, or bear children, to resist violence, to make household decisions.

Source: Petchesky and Judd, eds. 1998.

Reuters/Str/Archive Photos

focus on expanding the activities that people are able to engage in rather than the extent to which they say they are satisfied avoids the problem that people's preferences are shaped by their experiences. Oppressed people may say that they are content with life because anything better seems inconceivable.

"The insecure sharecropper, the exploited landless labourer, the overworked domestic servant, the subordinate housewife, may all come to terms with their predicament in such a way that grievance and discontent are submerged in cheerful endurance by the necessity of uneventful survival. The hopeless underdog loses the courage to desire a better deal and learns to take pleasure in small mercies."

— Amartya Sen (1984)

From this viewpoint, a focus on fulfillment of basic needs is also inadequate, since it is a passive concept, emphasizing what can be done for a person, rather than what a person can do. Unlike the concept of capabilities, that of basic needs does not have a link with positive freedom ("freedom to").

A person's enjoyment of capabilities is linked to the exercise of entitlements. The ability to live a long life in human dignity depends on whether a person can establish sufficient command over resources. Amartya Sen points out that in a private ownership market economy, people's entitlement to resources depends primarily upon the resources they own (including their own skills and health and strength, as well as any natural resources or equipment) and how they can transform these resources through production and buying and selling (Dreze and Sen 1989). The problem is that there is no guarantee that a market economy will entitle a person to sufficient resources. Markets open up new opportunities. But they also open up new risks. So people in market economies always face the danger of "entitlement failure" – the inability to acquire enough resources to be capable of living in human dignity, because what they have for sale does not command a high enough price to buy the necessities of life.

Of course, there are other ways in which people can legitimately acquire resources in a market economy through transfers from the state, exchanges with family, neighbours and friends and charitable gifts. But these means are also subject to failure, and frequently do not have the status of legally enforceable claims. Moreover, the growth of market relations tends to undermine these non-market ways of transferring resources; partly by undermining their legitimacy, partly because market economies tend to be subject to periodic crises in which whole communities, indeed whole countries, are simultaneously subject to a loss of livelihood. So there is always a question mark over the security of people's enjoyment of their capabilities; and the poorer and less powerful the person, the bigger the question mark.

The issue of insecurity is particularly important to women, because women typically have the ultimate responsibility for the well-being of children. Women's ability to stretch diminishing resources further is the ultimate safety net for children and men often at the sacrifice of women's own well-being. Because of the risk of entitlement failure, the human development approach stresses that markets have to be socially regulated. This means establishing a framework of rules and norms that set limits to the market behaviour of firms and individuals and provide incentives for them to act in ways that support rather than undermine human development objectives. It requires the participation of civil society as well as government to create new social agreements on the scope of markets and on ways to pool risk and provide security when markets fail. The approach also calls for new forms of democratic accountability of governments to citizens in order to promote the restructuring of public expenditure to develop the capabilities of poor people.

Extending Human Development: Women's Empowerment and Gender Justice

There are some ambiguities in the definition of capabilities in terms of "what people can and cannot do." The courage to choose depends upon a person's sense of his or her own worth and of what he or she is entitled to demand, which in turn depends upon their personal experience and the social environment in which they live.

"If we do not have the courage to choose to live in a particular way, even though we could live that way if we so choose, can it be said that we do not have freedom to live that way, i.e., the corresponding capability?"

— Amartya Sen (1993)

Reuters/Dimitar dilikoff/Archive Photos

Gaining the courage to choose is part of what UNIFEM means by empowerment. UNIFEM's guidelines on women's empowerment (1997a) include:

- acquiring knowledge and understanding of gender relations and ways in which these relations may be changed;
- developing a sense of self-worth, a belief in one's ability to secure desired changes and the right to control one's life;
- gaining the ability to generate choices and exercise bargaining power;
- developing the ability to organize and influence the direction of social change to create a more just social and economic order, nationally and internationally.

Achieving this requires both a process of self-empowerment, in which women claim time and space to re examine their own lives critically and collectively; and the creation of an enabling environment for women's empowerment by other social actors, including other civil-society organizations, governments and international institutions (Gurumurthy 1998). This concept of women's empowerment goes well beyond women's participation in agendas set by others (Bisnath and Elson 1999). It entails both the development of women's own agency and the removal of barriers to the exercise of this agency.

A characteristic of women's successful self-empowerment is the ability to speak out on issues that concern women (see Box 3). Women speaking out is an important stimulus to governments, businesses and international financial institutions to make changes to economic, social and political conditions so as to widen the choices available to women. In this way, the internal and external dimensions of empowerment can be mutually reinforcing and women can develop both the capabilities and courage to use them.

Strengthening women's entitlements is a critical aspect of the external dimensions of empowerment. The concept of entitlement also has ambiguities. People may be able to acquire resources without breaking the law but in ways that demand self-abasement and are inconsistent with human dignity and the realization of women's human rights. Women are often treated, both in law and in social practice, as the economic dependents of men. Many women can only access the resources required to build and realize their capabilities through the goodwill of their fathers, brothers and husbands, who are supposed to protect them. Women without such protection are frequently at a disadvantage because economic and political institutions are constructed on the basis of the belief that men are the primary "breadwinners" and women need only earn a supplement. Women who are supposed to enjoy such protection are also at a disadvantage because of their lack of legally enforceable rights and real bargaining power. They are dependent upon the goodwill of male relatives—and too many discover, in the words of the popular American "blues" song that " A good man is hard to find."

"We had tongues but could not speak, we had feet but could not walk. Now that we have the land, we have the strength to speak and walk."

— Rural women in Bihar, India, late 1970s (Agarwal 1995)

Box 3: Speaking Out

Economic empowerment requires both personal determination and collective support, as shown by an analysis of grass-roots women in eight communities in South Asia. Together they give women the confidence to speak out: "to share problems, make demands, negotiate and bargain, and participate in public speaking and decision-making."

"Even if someone opposes me I can reply with confidence...Now I am going everywhere and am no longer afraid."
— Bibi Safida, Hussaini Women's Organization, Pakistan

"Before we organized ourselves in a Women's Organization we used to believe everything and agreed with everything our men told us. Now we have learned to state our opinions and views...."
— woman in northern Pakistan

"Previously, I never spoke to anyone on any subject. Now the strength of the members gives me the strength to speak to anybody."
— woman in southern India

"We do not fear authority. We can talk to officials, even police, because of the union."
— woman in the construction workers' union, southern India

Source: Carr et al. 1996.

Box 4: Women's Empowerment: Case Studies in South Asia

The empowerment of women requires both micro- and macro-level institutional changes, brought about in different ways at different levels. A study of women's day-to-day experiences of economic empowerment in South Asia, sponsored by UNIFEM and the Aga Khan Foundation, examines eight case studies where women organized to bring about improvements in their standard of living. The study defined economic empowerment as an "economic change/material gain plus increased bargaining power and/or structural change which enables women to secure economic gains on an on-going and sustained basis" (Carr et al. 1996: 203). The case studies showed that moving towards economic empowerment required changes in a whole series of institutions, some of which are usually labelled "economic" (like the market), some of which are usually labelled "social" (like the family) and some of which are usually labelled "political" (like the local and national state).

Each of these micro-level institutional changes required women's organizing. For example:

- where women had been secluded and not active in the market economy, economic empowerment involved women joining local support networks to defy strong patriarchal kinship norms and enter capital, labour and product markets;
- where women had been active in the market economy but were lacking in opportunities to sell their labour or their products, economic empowerment involved building alternative economic opportunities through grassroots women's organizations;
- where women had been active in the paid labour force and the local economy was strong, economic empowerment involved women organizing though a union to demand better terms and conditions of work.

None of these changes were possible without local-level organizing. But women's local-level gains would have been limited without their being able to bring about changes at the national level as well. By pursuing their concerns within organizations, women were able to make their voices heard by policy-makers and to get laws and policies changed in their favour:

- women construction workers in Tamil Nadu were able to get a Construction Workers Act passed that extended labour law protection, including maternity benefits, to construction workers, along with the provision of accident relief to workers' families;
- women in Andhra Pradesh secured a change in the laws on cooperatives to create a better environment for women's cooperatives;
- women in Gujarat persuaded the Forestry Department to modify trade liberalization policies that had been operating to the disadvantage of women gum collectors.

When women organize, the study concludes, whether to contest discrimination or demand access to resources, they shape the process of empowerment in ways that are "appropriate to their own needs, interests and constraints." Thus, "what may seem like shifts in women's status within their family, community or village often represents significant shifts in women's consciousness, perceptions, security and power."

Source: Carr et al. 1996.

Women, just as much as men, require clearly specified entitlements in their own right, enabling them to make independent claims that are both legally and socially recognized. Such claims should be enforceable by a legitimate source of authority that is external to the family, be it a village-level institution or a higher-level judicial or executive body of the state (Agarwal 1995). This kind of gender justice is a necessary foundation of democratic and egalitarian families whose members are genuinely mutually supportive, the kind of families that are needed if there is to be human development for all.

Extending the idea of human development to encompass women's empowerment and gender justice puts social transformation at the centre of the agenda for human development and progress of women. Choices for women, especially poor women, cannot be enlarged without a change in relations between women and men as well as in the ideologies and institutions that preserve and reproduce gender inequality

(see Box 4). This does not mean reversing positions, so that men become subordinate and women dominant. Rather, it means negotiating new kinds of relationships that are based not on power over others but on a mutual development of creative human energy (power to, based on power within and power with). It also means negotiating new kinds of institutions, incorporating new norms and rules that support egalitarian and just relations between women and men.

Commodities and Care

Conventional conceptions of the way in which economies operate offer limited guidance for policies to promote women's empowerment and gender justice. This is because these conceptions leave out much of the work that women do in all economies. Women have challenged conventional views and proposed new visions of economic life in which women's activities count, in several senses: counted in statistics,

UNIFEM

United Nations/Kay Muldoon

accounted for in representations of how economies work and taken into account when policy is made.

The conventional view of a national economy depicts it as a circular flow of labour, goods and services and money, operating to produce and distribute marketed commodities (both goods and services). This view is encapsulated in the System of National Accounts (SNA), which is used to measure economic activity in a country and summarize it in terms of Gross National Product (GNP).

"Every time I see a mother with an infant, I know I am seeing a women at work. I know that work is not leisure and it is not sleep and it may well be enjoyable. I know that money payment is not necessary for work to be done. But, again, I seem to be at odds with economics as a discipline, because when work becomes a concept in institutionalized economics, payment enters the picture .... No housewives, according to this economic definition, are workers."

— Marilyn Waring, former MP, New Zealand (1999)

The System of National Accounts and Women's Work

The SNA was designed to reflect the operations of a market economy in which people are remunerated financially for the work they do. It draws a line, called the production boundary, between the activities which are seen as constituting the economy and those that are seen as non-economic. The SNA has been revised several times since it was first established by the United Nations in 1953. It began from the idea that production is carried out exclusively by enterprises, while households merely consume. This was gradually modified to recognize a limited amount of subsistence production by households (INSTRAW 1995).

The latest version of the SNA, agreed in 1993, recommends the inclusion in the GNP of all production of goods, whether intended for sale or for consumption. Thus the GNP should in principle include the following types of household

Box 5: Overburdening Unpaid Care-givers

Irene van Staveren, an economist from the Netherlands, explored the issues of balancing unpaid care work and paid work with women in a focus group in Costa Rica. Their stories reveal the personal costs and undermining of women's own capabilities.

Thera says:
"It is not easy, because it requires superhuman strength. I get up at five in the morning, preparing the uniform, the breakfast, washing clothes, everything, go to work, come home in the evening at eight.... I think it would be very difficult for a man, well, he may do it but only when he develops the same mechanisms – but it requires a superhuman strength."

Not every woman can be superhuman. Lili says:
"I realise we are developing a whole series of symptoms, such as stress, or in my case, a chronic disease. This is how we women are really keeping up a rhythm of work in which we put other peoples' needs over our own priorities."

Martina agrees:
"I am a mother of two little daughters and an adolescent and I have two jobs. I could, without exaggeration, say that all the work I do in a day amounts to, I guess not less than fifteen hours. Sometimes one asks: how do we manage? Of course I know: at costs of our health, we do it at cost of our happiness, we do it at cost of ourselves...."

Exhausted women are not well placed to contribute voluntary labour to community NGOs or to spend time supervising their children's homework or to maintaining the networks of reciprocity with relatives and neighbours that economists now call "social capital." When stresses are very great, as they have been in many countries undergoing transition to the market, unpaid care cannot compensate for the withdrawal of state-provided support to care for children and the elderly and sick, and for the tearing of the social fabric of community. Ultimately, the social supports of the economy collapse, as they have in some parts of the countries in transition.

Source: van Staveren 1999; UNICEF 1999.

UNIFEM

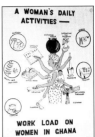

production, whether produced for the market or for consumption in the same household:

- production of all agricultural products and their subsequent storage, the gathering of berries or other uncultivated crops, foresting, wood cutting and collection of fuel wood, hunting and fishing;
- production of other primary products, such as mining salt, cutting peat, carrying water, etc.;
- processing of all agricultural and foresting products for own use or market;
- other kinds of processing, such as weaving cloth, dressmaking, production of pottery, footwear, utensils, etc.

This revision has the effect of including subsistence production within the SNA. In practice, however, the GNP often fails to include household subsistence production because questions in censuses and surveys do not cover it adequately.

As a matter of principle, the SNA continues to exclude the production of services for oneself and for other household members. It seems reasonable that eating, sleeping, washing and dressing oneself, taking exercise and engaging in leisure activities are not counted as part of production. But why exclude cooking and cleaning for family and community members, looking after children and sick and elderly people and tending to the emotional needs of family and community members by spending time listening and talking to them? All of these are productive activities which take up a large amount of time and energy on the part of those who perform them.

In 1934, American economist Margaret Reid suggested a different approach, proposing that if a third person could be paid to do the unpaid activity carried out by a household member, it should be counted as part of production. Arguments made by statisticians and economists for not treating such household services as production are open to many criticisms (Waring 1999; INSTRAW 1995). Their strongest argument is that the provision of such services has limited repercussions for the rest of the economy, since an increase or decrease will have little impact on the operation of public and private-sector enterprises. However, while this may be true in the short term, in the long term it is these services that sustain a supply of labour to the economy and make human societies possible, weaving the social fabric and keeping it in good repair. Taking these services for granted may have unforeseen costs in terms of deterioration of both human capabilities and the social fabric (see Box 5).

However, even when it is recognized that services produced within the household for other household members are an important and valuable form of production, there is still the dilemma of how to make these services visible and to make them count. It is possible to impute monetary values to these services. The monetary value of cooking for family members could be assessed in terms of what it would cost to hire a cook, or to purchase the food

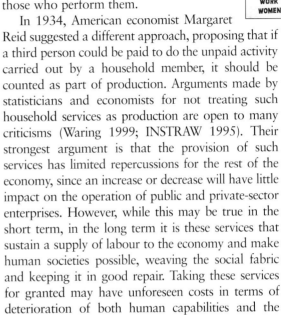

Box 6: Naming Women's Work

Names are needed to make visible women's provision of services within households for other household members. A variety of names have been used to call attention to the fact that this provision is:

- an obligation which has costs in terms of time and energy ("work");
- not remunerated by a wage ("unpaid");
- indispensable for the continuation of the entire society ("social reproduction").

Some of these terms can be ambiguous:

"Domestic labour": Does this refer to the work of family members to maintain the home or to the work of paid domestic help?

"Unpaid labour": Does this refer to what a woman does in taking care of her husband or the work she does without pay for the family business that he runs?

"Reproductive work": Does this refer to giving birth and breast-feeding or to maintaining the social fabric?

"Home work": Does this refer to unpaid housework or to paid work done in the home on subcontract from an employer?

The pros and cons of different labels have been discussed in *Feminist Economics*, a journal of the International Association for Feminist Economics: Website: www.facstuff.bucknell.edu/jshackel/iaffe

UNICEF/Nicole Tourounji

ready-cooked, or how much money could be earned if the food cooked for the family were instead to be sold in the locality or what the person doing the cooking could have earned if she had taken up some paid employment instead. However, there is a danger with the idea of obliterating the qualitative difference between work done on a commercial basis and care provided for members of the family. It may simply reinforce the tendency for more and more of life to be brought within the scope of the market and reduce the care that women provide their families to just another commodity.

Unpaid Care Work

An alternative to imputing money values is to measure the time taken to produce these non-SNA services and compare this total with that taken to produce goods and services that do get counted on the SNA. There are similar dilemmas about what name to give to services not included in the SNA. Women have used a variety of labels over the last 30 years, each with advantages and disadvantages (see Box 6, p.23). This report uses the term adopted by feminist economists during the 1990s, "unpaid care work." The word "unpaid" differentiates this care from paid care provided by employees in the public and NGO sectors and employees and self-employed persons in the private sector. The word "care" indicates that the services provided nurture other people. The word "work" indicates that these activities are costly in time and energy and are undertaken as obligations (contractual or social).

There is a risk that the use of the term "care" will mystify the relationship between the provider and the receiver. It must be recognized that care may be given unwillingly, extracted by psychological and social pressure or even physical violence, from women who can see no alternative but to provide care, even to those who oppress them. The lack of support for such care creates pressures on those who give it; thus caregivers may also visit their frustrations upon those in their charge, who are even more vulnerable to abuse. The advantage of the term is that it signals the fundamental importance of interpersonal attention to other people's needs in the maintenance of human societies.

"If there is less, we eat less. You have to feed men more, or they beat you."

— poor woman in Bangladesh (Neuhold 1998)

Revisioning Economies

Conventional accounts of how economies work do not bring out the centrality of care work and the particular way in which unpaid provision of care relates to the market and the state (Folbre 1994). They envision economies in terms of market flows between households and enterprises, with households supplying labour and consuming the goods and services produced by enterprises with that labour. The public sector appears as an employer of labour and provider of services and social security payments, financed by levying taxes and charges for some services. Labour is treated in this vision as if it were like land — an input that exists without having to be produced, a "primary factor of production."

Chart 1.1 (p. 26) shows a different picture of the economy, one drawn from women's perspective. It highlights production by a domestic sector (the realm of unpaid care work in households and neigbourhoods) and an NGO sector, as well as a public sector and a private sector. In principle, one could measure the size of the sectors by the monetary value of the services produced by them or by the total number of hours of time spent on the activities included in them. National time-use estimates, currently available for a limited range of industrialized countries (United States, Germany, Italy, United Kingdom, France, Canada, Australia, the Netherlands, Austria, Denmark, Finland and Norway), can be analysed to compare the unpaid time spent in the domestic sector and the voluntary part of the NGO sector with the paid time spent in the NGO, public and private sectors.

Time use measurements clearly have a potential for assessing the economic dimensions of human labour. Perhaps the most important indication they give is that, on average, the labour inputs into non-SNA activities are of the same order of magnitude as the labour inputs into SNA activities. Labour statistics however record only the latter; because of this enormous gap, labour statistics give a distorted image of how even industrialized societies utilise available labour resources to achieve their standard of living (Goldschmidt-Clermont and Pangnossin-Aligsakis 1995).

HomeNet

UN/John Isaac

Data on paid employment is available for all countries, but it is usually organized acording to industry and occupation. No international database presents employment data in terms of numbers of people employed in the private, public and NGO sectors. The private sector includes a variety of kinds of work, all of it included in the GNP, much of it directed towards generating profits for owners and managers of businesses (including the self-employed). The most visible form of private sector work is regular paid employment in registered businesses – often called formal sector employment. But the private sector also includes a large informal sector, including both paid and unpaid work.

The official international definition of the informal sector includes:

- unregistered enterprises below a certain size;
- paid and unpaid workers in informal enterprises (i.e., family farms and businesses);
- casual workers without fixed employment.

This definition embraces many wage-earners, including sweatshop workers and domestic servants; all those people who work on an unpaid basis for family farms and businesses producing for their own subsistence consumption and for the market (labelled in labour force surveys as "unpaid family workers"); and many "own-account" workers, the name given in labour force surveys to those who are self-employed or employers. It includes home-based paid workers working on subcontract and those whose workplace is the street. Estimates of the size and gender composition of informal sector employment vary widely, according to size of enterprise included and whether agricultural activities are included (UN 1999b: 27-30).

Estimates produced by WIEGO suggest that the informal sector accounts for well over half of urban employment in Africa and Asia, and a quarter in Latin America and the Caribbean. If agriculture is included, then three-quarters of total employment in Africa and Asia, and almost half in Latin America, is informal

(see Table 1.1). Informal work lacks the social protection afforded to formal paid work, such as job security or health insurance, and is often irregular and casual. Much of informal work is subcontracted from the formal sector and its low costs contribute to the profits of larger businesses. In principle, informal work as well as formal work in the private sector should be included in the GNP. But informal work is often under-counted, especially when it is unpaid.

Work in the public sector is both paid and formal. These jobs offer the highest social protection, though not always the highest financial returns. The point of this work is not to make profits, but to provide a public service. Financing via taxation means that the public sector can be organized to permit social considerations rather than private costs and benefit considerations to guide decisions. All public sector work is included in the GNP. While no international database contains data on the size of total public sector employment, data is available from the World Bank World Development Indicators Database for employment in state enterprises as a percentage of total employment for a very limited range of countries. In the period 1985-96, it ranged from a low of around 1 per cent to a high around 30 per cent. But these figures do not cover employment in public services, such as public administration, defence, health and education.

The non-governmental organization (NGO) sector has some similarities to the public sector, in the sense that it is not for profit, but unlike the public sector, it makes use of unpaid volunteers as well as paid workers and frequently engages in advocacy for change in public policy as well as service provision. Its income comes from payments from the public sector, which increasingly subcontracts service provision to large NGOs; from donations and grants from businesses, philanthropic foundations and the general public; and, increasingly, fees for their services.

A 1995 study of the NGO sector in 22 countries in North America, South America, Europe and Asia found that in total, the sector accounted for 10 per cent

Table 1.1: Size of the Informal Sector

Informal Sector	LAC (%)	AFRICA (%)	ASIA (%)
Total employment (excl. ag.)	45	31	19
(incl. ag.)	66	90	90
Non-agricultural employment	57	75	63
Urban employment	25	61	40-60
New jobs	83	93	na

na = not available

Source: Charmes 1998 (updated February 2000).

of employment in services in those countries, and was just over a quarter of the size of the public sector in terms of paid employment. Adding in volunteers raised the share of employment in services to almost 14 per cent. Taking both paid and volunteer labour into account, the size of the NGO sector was equivalent to just over 40 per cent of public sector employment (Salaman et al. 1999).

The domestic sector of unpaid care work is not appropriately measured in terms of numbers of people employed in it, since the majority of people engage in some work (paid or unpaid) in the other three sectors, in addition to the work they do caring for family and neighbours. The full-time housewife who works at nothing else besides providing care for her family seems to be very much in a minority.

The comparative size of the domestic sector, plus the volunteer part of the NGO sector in the late 1980s has been measured in terms of labour time for 12 developed countries. On average, adults spend just over 26 hours a week in unpaid domestic care work and voluntary work, compared to 24 hours per week in paid work. This means that the total volume of work each week is just over twice the work covered by the official employment statistics (Ironmonger 1996).

The four sectors are linked by both market and non-market channels. The domestic sector supplies people to work in all other sectors. The private sector sells goods to all the other sectors (see chart 1.1). The public sector levies taxes and user fees and makes income transfers to the other sectors, as well as providing them with public services. The NGO sector provides services, such as health, education, social services and cultural and recreational services to the domestic sector, sometimes free of charge, sometimes for a fee.

Chart 1.1: Revisioning the Economy Through Women's Eyes

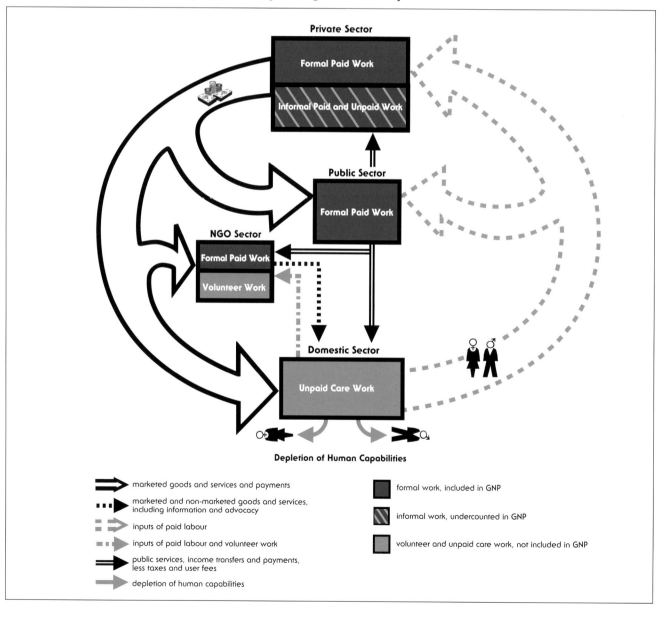

UNICEF/Jane Taylor

These channels are cultural as well as financial, carrying messages and values as well as goods, money and people. Commercial values flow from the private sector, emphasizing the importance of making money and creating a kind of equality - but only for those with sufficient money. Regulatory values flow from the public sector, emphasizing the importance of citizenship, rules and laws, but often failing to ensure the rules and laws are democratic rather than autocratic or bureaucratic. Provisioning values flow from the domestic sector, emphasizing the importance of meeting people's needs, but often meaning that adult able-bodied women meet everyone else's needs while remaining needy themselves. Values of mutuality and cooperation flow from the NGO sector but often in ways that remain hierarchical and exclusionary.

Division of Labour
Men and women work in all four sectors, but there are systematic variations in the gender division of labour. Unpaid care work, volunteer work and informal paid and unpaid work tend to be more female-intensive (with women having a relatively high share of employment) while formal paid work in private, public and NGO sectors tends to be more male-intensive (with men having a relatively high share of employment).

International databases are not organized to show these differences. However, it is reported that two-thirds to three-quarters of work in the domestic sector is done by women in developed countries (UN 1995a). The upper figure is likely to obtain in most countries in other regions, though there is little quantitative data. The female-intensive nature of the domestic sector is rivaled only by that of the informal sector, as shown in Table 1.2 for selected African countries, while by contrast, the formal sector is highly male-intensive, as shown by public sector employment in these countries.

An alternative way to look at the gender division of labour is to compare the ways that women and men allocate their working time between the sectors. The study of work in 12 developed countries referred to above found that while adult

women on average work for just over 35 unpaid hours in the domestic and NGO sectors, men contribute only half that time. In paid work in the public, private and NGO sectors, the position is reversed, with men spending on average just over 31 hours a week in paid work, and women spending just over half that time (Ironmonger 1996). Within paid work, women also allocate more time to the public sector than do men. In the European Union, for instance, the share of women's paid employment in the public sector is double that of men's: almost 44 per cent compared to almost 22 per cent (Rubery and Fagan 1998).

In the developing countries, the gender differences may be even greater. Information on the proportion of working time that men and women spend on market and non-market work for a group of nine developing countries indicates that men spend on average 76 per cent of their time in market work and 24 per cent in non-market work, while women spend 34 per cent of their time on market work and 66 per cent of their time on non-market work (UNDP 1999, table 27). In addition, research conducted as part of the WIEGO network found that the majority of women in employment in Asia and Africa are in the informal sector. In all developing regions, a larger share of economically active women than of men are in informal employment, and women's share of informal sector employment is higher than their representation in the total labour force in most countries.

The gender divisions in the patterns of work between the four sectors of the economy are a key factor in the relative weakness of women's entitlements as compared to men, which in turn perpetuates gender gaps in capabilities.

Table 1.2: Women's Share of Employment in Informal Sector, Industry and Services and the Public Sector, Selected Sub-Saharan African Countries

Country	Informal sector early 1990s (%)	Public sector 1986 (%)
Benin	61	na
Botswana	na	36
Burkina Faso	na	21
Burundi	na	38
Chad	53	na
Ethiopia	na	23
Malawi	na	13
Mali	59	na
Morocco	na	29
Swaziland	na	34

Sources: informal sector: Charmes 1998 (updated February 2000); public sector: Standing 1999.

Economic Restructuring

In all countries, the balance betweeen the amount of work done in the four sectors has been changing since the early 1980s as a result of neo-liberal economic reforms. Public-sector employment has been shrinking as a result of privatization, efforts to increase "efficiency" in the public sector and cuts in public expenditure. The private sector has been expanding – but through a process of "informalization," by which more and more jobs are low-paid, part-time, temporary, casual and lacking social protection. The NGO sector has also been expanding. In eight countries for which time series data are available, NGO paid employment grew by 24 per cent between 1990 and 1995, while overall paid employment in the same countries grew by 8 per cent (Salaman et al. 1999).

Concern has been expressed that this changing balance between the sectors adds to women's overall workload, especially that of poor women in poor countries. Women's rate of participation in the labour force has been increasing with their entry into the public, private and NGO (paid) sectors in greater numbers. But women still have overwhelming responsibility for the provision of care to family members. Better-off women with well-paid jobs are employing poorer women to work in the home, caring for their children or elderly relatives, cooking and cleaning for the household. But poorer women have to cope with a double burden of paid work and unpaid care work. There is pressure on the health of poor women and children; there is pressure on the education of daughters who may have to drop out of school to substitute for their mothers (see Box 7). But these pressures are slow to show up in the calculus of economic policy-makers.

The conventional sets of indicators considered by economic policy-makers may signal that progress is being made. More women are getting paid for the work they do and the efficiency of the public sector seems to be increasing. But there may be a hidden transfer of costs from the public sector, where costs are monetized, and therefore visible, to the domestic sector, where costs are not monetized and therefore not visible. For instance, health services are reorganized to improve efficiency by increasing the "throughput" of patients, discharging them more quickly to care in the community than would formerly have been the case. This increases health service efficiency by reducing its financial costs, but transfers costs of caring for convalescent patients to the domestic sector, where it is largely women who pick up the bill, in terms of demands on their time.

If too much pressure is put upon the domestic sector to provide unpaid care work to make up for deficiencies elsewhere, the result may be a depletion of human capabilities, as shown in Chart 1.1 (p. 26). To maintain and enhance human capabilities, the domestic sector needs adequate inputs from all other sectors. It cannot be treated as a bottomless well, able to provide the care needed regardless of the resources it gets from the other sectors. Lack of attention to the domestic sector in economic policy-making is particularly harmful to women, since they currently have the responsibility for managing this sector.

"Women's love in the family is expressed and demanded in terms of work. The difference in gender is related to this enormous mass of energy which women pour into others, to make them feel like human beings in a system that treats them like commodities."

— Antonella Picchio (1992)

Box 7: Economic Reform and Women's Work

The government of India took steps to try to protect expenditure on education when it introduced economic reforms in the early 1990s. But the impact of the reforms pushed some poor women to take on more paid work, which meant some poor girls had to drop out of school to substitute for their mothers.

Research in a village in Raisen District in Madhya Pradesh revealed that poor women had to do more work as casual wage labourers to keep up with rapidly rising prices of food, which had resulted in part from a reduction in subsidies and other reform measures. Many said:

"I do whatever work is available, whenever it is available."

In order to be available for work at a moment's notice, women had to keep their daughters at home. Women said:

"She goes to school but the days I go out of the house for wage work, she stays at home to do the domestic work and look after her brothers and sisters";

"If she goes to school, then who is going to do the housework?"

Their daughters agreed:

"Who would cook the food and look after the house and my younger brothers and sisters?"

Source: Senapaty 1997.

UNICEF/John Isaac

In managing the sector to meet the social needs for unpaid care, women frequently find themselves in a position with more responsibilities than resources. Their entitlements to inputs from the other sectors are frequently weak and ambiguous. Their entitlements to commodities acquired via markets are weak because their own earnings typically are low and irregular, and their access to men's earnings depends on how well they can negotiate the conflicts as well as the cooperation of household life. Their entitlement to the services of NGOs may depend on giving up their leisure time to participate in meetings or contribute their labour to the construction of community facilities.

Unpaid care work is the foundation of human existence, but it is overshadowed by the power of the state and increasingly, by the power of market forces. The NGO sector may offer opportunities to share responsibilities for care more widely in self-governing associations, but many NGOs themselves are under pressure to be competitive with private businesses (Ryan 1999). This may compromise their mission to act as advocates for social change as well as service providers. Globalization intensifies the pressure on the domestic, NGO and public sectors and increases the power of the private sector, even as it concentrates power in fewer private sector hands.

Globalization

International trade, investment and migration are not new phenomena. What is new is the accelerating speed and scope of movements of real and financial capital in the last two decades of the twentieth century, primarily due to:

- removal of state controls on trade and investment;
- new information and communications technologies.

These twin enabling processes have put businesses of all kinds in a position to treat the whole world as their field of operations and to redeploy their capital and move the location of their production at will. The private sectors of each national economy are well on the way to merging to create the global private

sector (see Chart 1.2, p. 30). Countries in every part of the globe have experienced greatly expanded markets and the commercialization of more and more aspects of life. The result has been the rapid growth of output and employment in some parts of the world, but at the cost of growing inequality within and between countries (see Box 8, p. 30), shattering financial crises in South East Asia and the collapse of the average standard of living in many parts of the former USSR and Sub-Saharan Africa (UNDP 1999b). There are MacDonalds hamburger restaurants in large cities all around the globe – but there is persistent malnutrition for millions of people, some of them in the very same cities.

The domestic, public and NGO sectors remain grounded in national economies. International links among them exist and they are increasingly using new information and communication technologies to share experiences and strategies. But their access to the "tools" of globalization is weak and fragmented compared to those among businesses. In particular, states retain detailed control over international migration. Moving a household to New York requires state-recognized documents (visas, work permits), while moving money to Wall Street does not. The private sector is the hub of the global economy; the other sectors remain distinct, though interlinked, national peripheries, differentiated by the fact that some states are much more powerful than others in setting the global rules for the private sector.

Stephenie Hollyman

Box 8: Increasing Inequality

Income inequalities between countries have been accelerating since the early 1970s. An analysis of trends in world income distribution shows that the distance between the richest and the poorest country was about 44 to 1 in 1973, and 72 to 1 in 1992. In 1999, per capita incomes in East Asia had grown to three times what they were in 1980, while in Sub-Saharan African and other least-developed countries per capita incomes had fallen to below their levels in 1970.

Income inequality has been increasing among individuals as well. The world's 200 richest people are getting richer. The net worth of the world's 200 wealthiest people moved from $440 billion in 1994 to $1,402 billion in 1998. Their assets are now more than the combined income of 41% of the world's people.

Source: UNDP 1999b.

Chart 1.2: Globalization

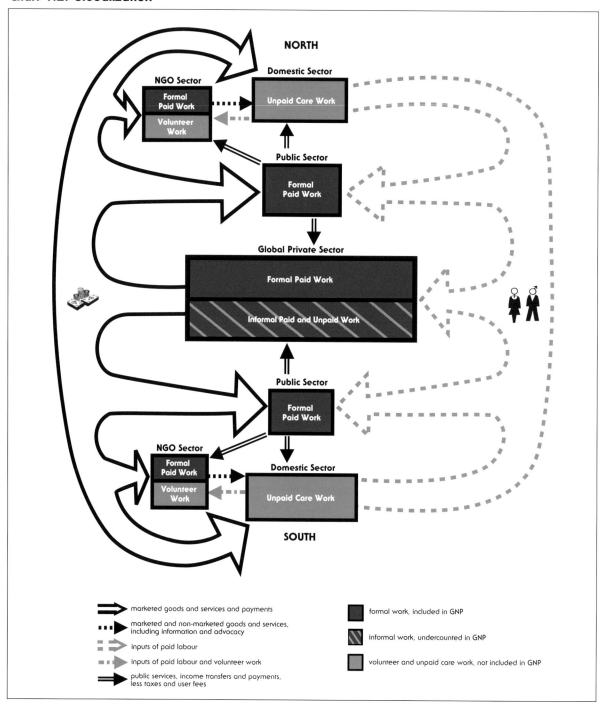

In addition to removing national controls on capital, states have endeavoured in a series of UN conferences and trade negotiations to agree on guidelines, rules and targets for economic, social and environmental policies (see Chapter 2). But these have lacked clear mechanisms of implementation and accountability, or have been tilted in favour of powerful countries and powerful companies. A case in point is the trade liberalization rules of the World Trade Organization, which are often applied asymmetrically, requiring developing countries to open up to imports from developed countries, while failing to sufficiently widen the markets for their exports to developed countries. Examples are the swift application of sanitary standards to restrict of exports of fish from Bangladesh, Mozambique, Tanzania and Uganda and the slow implementation the agreement to phase out the Multifibre Agreement that protects textile and garment industries in developed countries (Williams 1999).

Information and communications technologies have at the same time sustained a parallel globalization of social movements, bringing together civil-society organizations of all kinds — women's groups, trade unions, environmental activists, farmers associations, campaigners for social justice — in global networks to contest a one-sided and unequal globalization. Sometimes the networks have met in the virtual reality of the Internet, sometimes in the NGO forums of the UN conferences, and sometimes in the streets, as at the WTO meetings in Seattle in November 1999. But civil-society organizations cannot always agree on whether they want to promote a system of locally self-sufficient economies or to transform the new global economy into a more egalitarian system.

A critique of globalization has also come from many religious organizations. From women's perspective, however, such critiques are often compromised by an association with religious fundamentalism. Religious fundamentalism is itself a global phenomenon, premised on ideas of family values that deny women's human rights instead of building families on the basis of respect for the human rights of all their members. Fundamentalism, as Gita Sen (1997) points out, is especially dangerous because "it breeds on marginalization and loss of control among young men, and often encompasses a critique of globalization even as it intensifies the subordination of women to patriarchal control."

While fundamentalist movements may be the most extreme example, it is important to recognize the inequalities that sustain all "traditional" societies. Women may not be vulnerable to workplace discrimination if they remain at home. But their exclusion from participation in international markets as employees or self-employed workers or owners of small businesses tends to reinforce gender inequality

rather than narrow gender gaps. Paradoxes abound: the spread of entertainment consumer culture via TV and film and advertising that serves the interests of big businesses and erodes community norms and values also helps many women to develop a sense of a self with choices and desires (Balakrishnan 1999).

Experiencing Globalization

How have women experienced globalization? Globalization does not so much create difficulties for poor women where previously there were none as intensify some of the existing inequalities and insecurities to which poor women are subject. But for educated women with professional skills, it opens up new opportunities. For some unskilled women, it has meant loss of livelihoods, as the goods they produced were outcompeted by goods produced with cheaper labour or cheaper materials or in far less time on modern machinery. For others, it has meant loss of labour rights (such as social benefits and the right to organize) in the whirlwind of international competition. For still others, especially educated women, it has meant new, better paying employment, and opportunities previously undreamed of (UN 1999b; UNIFEM 1999b, 1998b).

For increasing numbers of women, globalization has meant international migration. Although men still outnumber women in the total number of adults who have migrated to another country, from 1985 to 1990, the number of women increased at a faster rate than the number of men (UN 1999b: table III.2). More and more women are migrating on their own, or as the primary earner in their household, but often as temporary workers in low-paid jobs. The opportunities for permanent migration and the acquisition of citizenship rights in other countries have declined since the 1970s, in large part because of increased restrictions on international mobility of unskilled people introduced by developed countries. In contrast to the dismantling of barriers to the international mobility of capital, barriers to the mobility of labour have remained strong, except for professional people with skills that are relevant to high-tech industries (UNDP 1999).

UNHCR

"Globalization is putting a squeeze on care and caring labour"

— Human Development Report, 1999

In an important step forward, the 1999 Human Development Report notes that globalization raises new issues about ensuring that all people preserve enough time to care for themselves, their families, neighbours and friends. Globalization demands women's time in the non-domestic sectors of the economy. It strengthens market relationships at the expense of non-market relationships. It puts pressure on paid care-givers in the non-domestic sectors to be "competitive" and judges competitiveness over a very short time span, so that the quality of paid care is likely to suffer.

But globalization does not so much create a problem in care provision where previously there were none, as change the form of the problem. Before globalization, the care deficit was more a deficit for women, who spent much time caring for other people but had little time to care for themselves. With globalization, men and children may also begin to experience a care deficit, if the "double burden" on women becomes too great. Pushing women out of paid work will not solve the problem – there will still be a care deficit, one borne largely by women themselves. Solutions will require rebalancing responsibilities among all four sectors of the economy and new ways of managing globalization.

Suzette Michell

UNICEF/Carolyn Watson

Managing Globalization

The top decision-making positions that govern globalization are still overwhelmingly occupied by men (mainly men from developed countries). Men hold about 90 per cent of the top positions in major Wall Street investment firms (New York Times, 27 October 1999). They overwhelmingly dominate the World Economic Forum (the annual meeting of global political and business leaders in Davos, Switzerland). Lists of speakers on the Website of the forum held in January 2000 indicates that out of 392 panelists, no more than 9 per cent were women.

Women are in a minority at the WTO. The World Bank does somewhat better: women constitute 36 per cent of key professional positions (such as economist) and almost 20 per cent of managerial and senior technical positions. But at the International Monetary Fund, a mere 11 per cent of economists are women and women occupy only 15 per cent of all managerial positions (www.imf.org). These are the international financial institutions charged with managing globalization so as to promote stability, growth and development. Criticism of the way in which they carry out this charge is growing dramatically everywhere, with women taking a leading role (see Chapter 6).

The East Asian economic crisis, which began in Thailand in July 1997 and rapidly spread to other countries in the region, gave these criticisms added weight. After a decade or more of rapid growth and improvements in human development indicators, the GNP of Korea and Malaysia fell by more than 8 per cent in 1998; in Thailand by nearly 8 per cent and in Indonesia by as much as 20 per cent. Poverty and unemployment rose substantially and real wages plummeted. According to the World Bank's own estimates, by the end of 1998, about 20 million people were added to the 30 million already below the poverty line in these countries; 18 million more people became openly unemployed in Indonesia, Thailand and Korea; real wages fell by 10 per cent in Thailand and as much as 40 to 60 per cent in Indonesia (World Bank 1998).

"The Korean government promoted a national slogan 'Get Your Husband Energized' that called on women to help offset the impact of the crisis on men, who on becoming unemployed or bankrupt were subject to depression."

— Ajit Singh and Ann Zammit (2000)

The public sector provided very little in the way of income transfers to cushion the blows. Many of the economies affected descended suddenly into social and political chaos. Mass unemployment, sudden rise in poverty levels, return migration to the small towns and rural areas, food shortages and riots, cutbacks in expenditure on education and health care, the pharmaceutical shortages, rising crime rates, severely damaged the prospects for human development. Mutual support systems were eroded or stretched to the breaking point as local communities tried to adjust to the demands of a volatile global financial market (Heyzer 1999). Women were expected to absorb the shocks (see Box 9).

The origins of the financial crisis are still debated. The view of the IMF is that domestic policies and practices were mainly responsible: weak supervision of financial institutions and poor corporate governance. Others locate the origins of the crisis in the liberalization of financial and capital markets and speculation by foreign investors. The depth of the crisis is frequently attributed to the austerity measures insisted upon by the IMF as a condition for loans to deal with it, measures such as cuts in public expenditure and increased interest rates (Singh and Zammit 2000; Lim 2000). These measures have been openly criticized by the former chief economist of the World Bank, Joseph Stiglitz, who says they were based on economic models that are out-of-date and out of touch with reality, and a policy process conducted in secrecy without open dialogue.

"If the people we entrust to manage the global economy – in the IMF and in the [US] Treasury Department – don't begin a dialogue and take their criticisms to heart, things will continue to go very, very wrong. I've seen it happen."

— Joseph Stiglitz, April 2000

WEDO/Rosa Lizarde

Box 9: Women, the Heroes of Everyday Life

Case studies conducted in 1998 by the United Nations Population Fund in Indonesia, Malaysia, the Philippines and Thailand show how women had to absorb the impact of the financial crisis in Asia.

In Jakarta: men get very frustrated when they lose their job. They stay around the house doing nothing instead of helping the wife with the household chores or looking after children. Expenses on cigarettes seem to increase. The burden of laid-off husbands is on the wife.

In Bangkok: women who had lost their jobs faced family conflict. Some suffered violence from their husbands and complaints about their inability to take care of their children and elderly relatives.

In the Philippines: farmers complain about the increased cost of labour and farming supplies, which oblige their wives to take jobs as domestic helpers in Metro-Manila and other urban areas and older children to drop out of school to take care of younger siblings. Husbands left behind are tempted to have extra-marital affairs.

In Malaysia: the recession has affected the lives of women who are single parents as well as those with heavy family commitments, forcing them into commercial sex, even though they know its perils. A single woman, 24 years old, supporting a sick mother said, "I earn about RM3,000 per month this way or more — I have to pay for my car, house installments [mortgage] and expensive medical treatment for my mother who suffers from chronic arthritis." A divorced mother of one said: "My parents know about my job and depend on my income. The crisis has affected me and is making my life miserable."

Source: UNFPA 1998.

Dilemmas and Transformations

Globalization creates an environment that allows many women to achieve greater personal autonomy, but allocates them a lowly place in an increasingly unequal global hierarchy, thus denying them their economic, social and cultural rights (see Box 10).

> These contradictions mean that women's struggles for greater personal autonomy (including among other things control over and access to familial or community resources, a fairer share in inheritance, rights in decision making, and sexual and reproductive rights) may not mesh simply or easily with their concerns for a more just and equal economic order (Sen and Correa 2000).

One approach to this dilemma is to promote the transformation of the values and practices of business corporations, public agencies and NGOs, to reflect the patterns not only of men's lives but also of women's lives and to support not only individual choice but also social justice. In fact, such institutional transformation is one of the primary objectives of gender mainstreaming, which the UN Economic and Social Council defines as follows:

Mainstreaming a gender perspective is the process and assessing the implications for women and men of any planned action, including legislation, policies and programmes, in all areas and at all levels. It is a strategy for making women's as well as men's concerns and experiences an integral dimension of the design, implementation, monitoring and evaluation of policies and programmes in all political, economic, and societal spheres so that women and men benefit equally and inequality is not perpetrated. The ultimate goal is to achieve gender equality (UN 1997b).

"Can women offer different voices as they become more integrated in the market and public life? Can 'difference' be maintained, and can it be a source of inspiration to those who work toward progressive social change?"

— Lourdes Benería (1999)

Box 10: Albanian Women: Change and Complexity

With the coming of democracy, Albanian people started to change their mentality, because they had the means of seeing the world and better opportunities. It is true that political change influenced changing attitudes [about] women issues. During 1992-96, Albanian women started gradually to gain control of their lives and to become economically independent, as well.

[Women had more opportunities] for better-paid jobs... which had good and bad results. On the one hand they were more independent, broadened their knowledge and started to think about themselves as having equal rights with men, but on the other hand it brought problems within Albanian families. Albanian men (in villages mostly) are not always open to letting their wives work, because [women] have to take care of the children.

Hopefully, this attitude has started to change in the main cities. [In] projects that we have dealt with, the role of men in the family, domestic violence, gender equality, etc., there is a new way of thinking, especially among the young people, but there is much to do in the villages and rural areas.

We have given our support for social services and for the need to raise the number of women in the political life. Our women want more women to represent them in Parliament, in the government, and all other fields where men are dominant. We use our capacities to train them and make them ready to find new jobs (confidence-building projects), because ... unemployment in Albania is very high and this effects every individual....

Women face economic discrimination concerning jobs because [although] there are some women managers or directors, they win these places with more difficulty than men do. The government has a lot to do on this issue and must treat women's issues with priority, because [with] economic difficulties, social issues are left somehow behind....

Source: Olsi Devoki, Albanian Women's Federation (Lajla Pernaska), Beijing +5 online forum on women's rights
http://sdnhq.undp.org/ww/women-rights/

A gender mainstreaming matrix applied to European Union countries shows how progress towards institutional change can be assessed (see Box 11). It should be complemented by detailed audits that show the extent to which institutions in the public, private and NGO sectors are governed by rules and norms based on men's lives only, and how these can be changed (Maddock and Parkin 1993). Such change will promote the breakdown of occupational segregation and encourage women to enter fields and occupations previously thought of as for men only, and vice versa.

A major barrier to the transformation of the public, private and NGO sectors is the expectation that major decision-makers either have no significant responsibilities for unpaid care work or can delegate them to someone else. Effective gender mainstreaming will change this expectation. A complementary transformation of the domestic sector is needed, so that men take on a larger share of the pains and pleasures of unpaid care work, and construct new masculine identities around the values of giving care and paying attention to the personal needs of others. There are men who think along those lines, with whom coalitions can be built to create a world in which diversity and difference are enriching rather than polarizing (see Box 12, p. 36).

Doranne Jacobson

UNIFEM

Box 11: Gender Mainstreaming in European Union Employment Policy

Gender mainstreaming requires more than policy statements. It needs to be embodied in operational measures. The matrix below presents an assessment of progress in gender mainstreaming in EU employment policy, and indicates that few countries have yet proposed changes in either law or taxation and public expenditure (fiscal policy).

Country	Policy commitments	Legislation	Fiscal measures	Positive action including special training	Institutional mechanisms	Collection of baseline and monitoring data
Belgium	X					X
Denmark	X	X				
Germany	X	X		X	X	X
Greece	X			X	X	
Spain	X					X
France	X			X	X	X
Ireland	X					
Italy	X			X	X	X
Luxembourg	X					
Netherlands	X	X		X		
Austria	X			X	X	X
Portugal	X			X		X
Finland	X			X		
Sweden	X		X	X		X
UK	X		X			

Source: Joint Employment Report 1999, Part I, table 9.

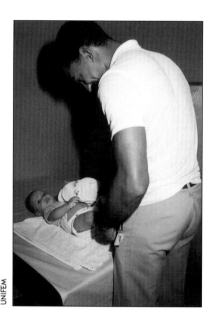

UNIFEM

"If society and particularly men do not assume with solidarity the responsibilities of caring for the family, we will be curbing the opportunities of half of humanity."

— Jose Antonio Ocampo (2000), Executive Secretary, ECLAC

Conclusion

Women's diversity and the contradictory contexts in which they find themselves create great challenges for assessing and promoting the progress of women. Women have to defend their right to paid work in the private, public and NGO sectors in the face of familial and community opposition; their right to better terms and conditions of paid work in the face of global competitive pressures; and their right to more equal ways of sharing and supporting unpaid care work in the face of economic evaluations that do not recognize the costs and benefits of this work. This report is envisaged as a contribution to a global dialogue conducted in relation to the commitments made to women in human rights treaties and UN conferences and grounded in women's organizations' own efforts to humanize the world.

Box 12: Men's Support for Gender Equality

More men are speaking out more actively in favour of gender equality and women's empowerment. The recently formed Men's Group for Gender Equality at UNDP, New York, brought some of them together in a roundtable discussion on Violence and Masculinities at the Preparatory Commission for Beijing +5 in New York, March 2000.

Mufti Ziauddin, a human rights lawyer from Pakistan, is working to reduce men's violence against women and girls. He explained: " I was very alone. It is a sensitive subject...I have been inspired by my mother. She taught me that I had to be a women's rights activist."

Captain Goran Lindberg, Chief of Police, Uppsala, Sweden, directs gender violence prevention training for police officers. He believes strongly in men's sharing responsibility for child-rearing and domestic life: "If you want to be police officer in a high rank in my department, you must show me you have nursed children...We must support new male role models."

Jackson Katz, American filmmaker, agreed: "We need to create a peer culture climate among men where they realize they will lose their status in their peer culture if they hit women."

The Men's Group for Gender Equality has established a Website to enable men around the world to strategize and discuss their efforts to secure gender equality in their own countries.

http://www.undp.org/gender/programs/men/men-csw.htm

Sources: Men for Gender Equality, UNDP; Miriam Zoll, American News Service, March 2000.

"A multinational feminism is likely to be stronger and certainly presents a richer tapestry than any insular version. Images of the other provide the warp and weft of dreams and possibilities."

— Chilla Bulbeck (1998)

Chapter 2

Commitments
to the Progress
of Women:
Rights and Targets

The Peace Torch was first lit in
Kwa Zulu Natal, South Africa, on
Pan-African Women's Day 1995,
and traveled to several war-torn
African countries on the road to
Beijing for the opening of the
NGO Forum of the Fourth World
Conference on Women. The torch
continues to travel and burn as
a symbol of women's quest for
peace, equality and development.

Yu Xiangjun

Introduction

The differences in the experiences, expectations and priorities of different groups of women mean that there is always scope for debate about exactly what constitutes progress for women. Nevertheless, international human rights instruments, beginning with the Universal Declaration of Human Rights in 1948, provide a common framework for defining and assessing the progress of women. These are supplemented by International Labour Organization (ILO) Conventions and by the blueprints for action agreed upon by governments at a series of United Nations (UN) conferences in the 1990s on a broad range of issues, such as education, environment, human rights, population, social development, women's empowerment, human settlements and food security.

The human rights treaties provide a set of principles that describe the inalienable and inviolable rights of all members of the human family. These international treaties require governments to respect, protect and fulfill the rights contained in

" By making national and international commitments for action, including those made at the Conference, Governments and the international community recognize the need to take priority action for the empowerment and advancement of women."

— Beijing Declaration, September 1995

them and they are legally binding on all states parties. While states are responsible for the realization of, as well as for violations of, the human rights guaranteed by the treaties, the enforcement of human rights law depends on political pressure, both nationally and internationally. In common with other social movements, women's movements worldwide have used the standards embodied in the treaties to hold their governments accountable for violations of women's human rights, and to press for progress in the realization of all human rights, including women's human rights.

During the 1990s, at a series of UN conferences (see Box 10, p. 45), governments reaffirmed these human rights principles and agreed to take action on a broad range of social and economic issues in order to enable women to realize them in practice. Though not legally binding, these agreements do provide a framework for national and international actions, monitoring and accountability. The UN conferences provided a dynamic arena for action by non-governmental organizations (NGOs), including women's groups, at several interconnected levels — national,

> ### Box 1: Targets and Benchmarks: What Do They Do?
>
> Patricia Flor, Chair of the UN Commission on the Status of Women, suggests that targets and benchmarks are useful in the following ways:
>
> - They make progress visible and measurable. Since agreements such as the Platform for Action are expressed in general terms, they provide means to its goals.
> - They allow monitoring of trends, to see if there is progress.
> - They translate idealistic, ultimate goals into realistic stages or phases of sub-objectives.
> - They provide incentives for sustained and strengthened efforts.
> - They help determine responsibility for achieving targets.
> - They allow progress to be rewarded by general recognition.
>
> Source: NGOs for Women 2000, 1999.

regional and international. Such activism was central to both the process and the outcomes of each conference, but the agreements reached do not encompass all NGO priorities, and reflect compromises made during government negotiations.

Like the human rights treaties, the operational usefulness of the UN conference agreements is increased if they are linked to specific targets and indicators that can be used to define and monitor progress in compliance. This is particularly important in the case of economic and social rights, which are subject to different interpretations in different countries. The UN conference agreements of the 1990s do contain a number of relevant quantitative, time-bound targets. Many of these have been brought together in the vision for development cooperation in the 21st century issued by the Organisation for Economic Cooperation and Development (OECD) in 1996. These targets have been endorsed by the UN system and the World Bank and are widely used to inform development cooperation. (Some advantages of targets are summarized in Box 1.)

Targets should always be specified and interpreted in a human rights framework, in order to guard against the danger that they will be pursued in ways that violate human rights. Provided this is done, internationally agreed upon targets can provide useful ways to focus and crystallize commitments to the world's women and provide standards against which the progress of women may be assessed.

In keeping with the overall emphasis of this report, this chapter examines the ways in which the economic dimensions of women's progress have been specified in the norms set out in human rights treaties as well as in the goals and measures called for in UN conference agreements, paying particular attention to the scope of internationally agreed-upon time-bound targets.

Human Rights Instruments

The cornerstone of international human rights law, the Universal Declaration of Human Rights, adopted in 1948, expressed standards of human dignity for all nations to aspire to. A series of human rights instruments, based on the standards contained in the Declaration, have been created over the years by various UN bodies and have progressively been incorporated into national legal systems (see Box 2). Within the UN system, UNIFEM, in partnership with the Office of the High Commissioner for Human Rights, works to provide a gender perspective on human rights and conducts training and capacity-building activities on the gender dimensions of human rights.

The primary forum for political debate on human rights within the UN system is the Commission on Human Rights, a functional body of the UN Economic and Social Council. Special Rapporteurs of the Commission are appointed to conduct independent investigations on thematic or country-based violations as they arise. For example, there is a Special Rapporteur on Violence Against Women. Each of the core human rights instruments has a committee that monitors its implementation. The committees meet in special sessions on a regular basis to review reports submitted by states parties to the relevant convention. The committees also clarify the meaning of provisions contained in the conventions and make recommendations about their implementation.

Some human rights conventions are accompanied by so-called Optional Protocols, which set up complaint mechanisms to allow individuals in those countries that ratify both the convention and the related optional protocol to submit complaints about violations of the convention directly to the committee that oversees implementation of the convention. The committee then reviews these petitions and responds to them.

In most cases, individuals first look for redress of human rights violations at the national level, through local courts, commissions or judicial bodies. Some countries have established Human Rights Commissions to handle such complaints. In many countries, petitioners who cannot receive redress for human rights violations at the national level can turn to regional human rights mechanisms, notably

Box 2: Core UN Human Rights Instruments

Universal Declaration of Human Rights
Adopted in 1948

International Covenant on Economic, Social and Cultural Rights
Adopted in 1966/entered into force 1976
Monitored by the Committee on Economic, Social and Cultural Rights (CESCR)

International Covenant on Civil and Political Rights
Adopted in 1966/entered into force 1976
Monitored by the Human Rights Committee (HRC)

International Convention on the Elimination of All Forms of Racial Discrimination
Adopted in 1965/entered into force 1969
Monitored by the Committee on the Elimination of Racial Discrimination (CERD)

Convention on the Elimination of All Forms of Discrimination Against Women
Adopted in 1979/entered into force 1981
Monitored by the Committee on the Elimination of Discrimination against Women (CEDAW)

Convention against Torture and Other Cruel, Inhuman or Degrading Treatment or Punishment
Adopted in 1984/entered into force 1987
Monitored by the Committee against Torture (CAT)

Convention on the Rights of the Child
Adopted in 1989/entered into force 1990
Monitored by the Committee on the Rights of the Child (CRC)

United Nations

the European System and the Inter-American System. (Human rights advocates in Asia are pressing for a similar mechanism in that region.) These systems vary with regard to how and on what topics a complaint can be filed as well as the means by which complaints are examined and resolved. Finally, in states that have ratified both the treaty covering the alleged violation and its optional protocol, individuals seeking redress also use the UN-based international human rights system.

Over the last two decades, women have effectively used the human rights framework to draw attention to violations of women's human rights, especially violence against women. In 1993, at the World Conference on Human Rights in Vienna, they succeeded in enshrining women's rights into the heart of the human rights framework, with the recognition that "women's rights are human rights." Since then, women have worked at different levels — national, regional and international — to integrate gender into all aspects of human rights.

International Covenant on Civil and Political Rights (ICCPR)

The International Covenant on Civil and Political Rights, which took effect in 1976, guarantees that all individuals shall enjoy civil and political rights, without distinction on the basis of sex or other grounds. Article 3 establishes states parties' obligation to ensure women's and men's equal rights to the enjoyment of all other rights in the Covenant, including:

- the right to life and liberty, freedom from arbitrary arrest and detention;
- freedom from torture or cruel, inhuman or degrading punishment;
- freedom from slavery or servitude;
- freedom of thought, conscience and religion;
- freedom of expression;
- freedom of assembly and association, including the right to join a union;
- equality of rights to both parties within a marriage and upon its dissolution;
- the right to equal protection of the law.

States that ratify the Covenant are required to submit a report to the Human Rights Committee, which monitors implementation, within one year, and thereafter at five-year intervals. Since 1995, ratifying states have been requested to include information on factors affecting equal enjoyment of rights by women under each of the articles, including practical matters affecting women's status and the human rights of women. While there is no formal provision

for NGO input on government reports, the Committee may accept information from NGOs or invite them to comment on the reports.

The Human Rights Committee publicly reviews the reports and submits its concluding observations and recommendations for improvement to the government. In reviewing reports, the Committee regularly raises issues of inequality and discrimination in employment, including equal remuneration, as well as access to public services and participation in public affairs. In a significant milestone for gender equality, the 56th Session of the Commission adopted, in April 2000, a strong resolution on "women's equal ownership of, access to, and control over land and the equal rights to own property and to adequate housing." Currently the Committee is updating its general comment on Article 3, giving it an opportunity to link women's equal rights to all other substantive provisions and to explain the gender dimensions of these provisions. Such linkages might include the relationship between freedom of religion and religious expression and women's right to equality. In addition, the Optional Protocol of the ICCPR, which entered into force in 1977, has been the most visible and effective of the complaint procedures administered by human rights treaty committees.

International Covenant on Economic, Social and Cultural Rights (ICESCR)

More directly relevant to women's economic status is the International Covenant on Economic, Social and Cultural Rights. ICESCR's provisions deal with working conditions, social protection, standard of living, physical and mental health, education and the enjoyment of the benefits of cultural freedom and scientific progress.

States that ratify the Covenant are expected to submit an initial report on their implementation efforts to the Committee on Economic, Social and Cultural Rights within two years of ratification, and thereafter once every five years. The Committee reviews the report and makes recommendations for further action.

The ICESCR provides a legal framework in which to enforce three fundamental economic rights that apply equally to women and men:

- the right to work (Articles 6–10);
- the right to an adequate standard of living (Article 11);
- workers' rights, such as the right to freely chosen employment, to fair wages and equal remuneration, to form and join trade unions and to social security and other benefits.

In some places, the ICESCR uses outdated language that assumes a model of employment based on a male breadwinner and thus fails to reflect the many forms of remunerated and unre-munerated work that women perform. There is a potential contradiction between Article 3, which specifies that women and men are entitled to equal enjoyment of provisions contained in the ICESCR, and Article 11, which presumes a male head of house-hold, stating that there is a right to an adequate stan-dard of living for "himself and his family." However, the Committee has clarified in its comment on the right to housing that this language, which reflects usage and assumptions at the time the Covenant was adopted, cannot be interpreted in a way that infringes on women's right to equal treatment.

Article 2 (1) states that the rights contained in the Covenant are to be "progressively realized." The process envisioned here is not clearly defined, which makes it difficult to monitor progress in implementation. However, not all of the provisions in the ICESCR are subject to "progressive realiza-tion." In several areas states parties can make legislative and/or judicial changes that could have immediate effect, such as passing laws to secure trade union rights (Article 8).

States parties are required to ensure the satisfac-tion of minimum essential levels of each of the rights contained in the Covenant and a state's failure to meet this minimum would be considered a violation. However, what constitutes the minimum essential level in most cases is not specified, other than to cite examples of deprivation of essential food, essential primary health care, basic shelter and basic forms of education (General Comment 3, 1997).

Box 3: Poor People's Economic Human Rights Campaign in the Americas

In 1999, to raise the issue of poverty as a human rights violation, the Poor People's Economic Human Rights Campaign organized a March of the Americas that brought together families from Canada, the United States and several Latin American countries. The march was led by poor and homeless women, men and children of all races, many of whom travelled by foot for 30 days through 5 states, covering some 400 miles. At the closing Rally to Demand Economic Human Rights, marchers presented evidence of US failure to adhere to economic human rights standards and norms regarding the provision of basic human needs. Since 1997, the campaign has mobilized poor and homeless individuals and families to bring economic rights violations to the attention of the UN in New York. Prior to arriving in New York, advocates travel through poor urban and rural communities to hold public discussions and collect testimonies of economic human rights abuses.

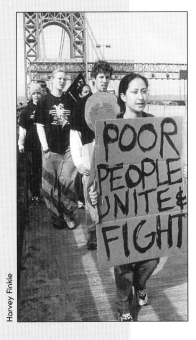

Harvey Finkle

The Poor People's Campaign, spearheaded by the Kensington Welfare Rights Union in North Philadelphia, includes over 40 organizations of poor people from across the country, including residents protesting the demolition of public housing in Chicago, welfare recipients facing cut-offs from public assistance in Philadelphia, farm workers working for subsistence wages in Immokalee, Florida and workfare workers organizing in San Francisco.

In an effort to get legal redress for these violations, in October 1999 the campaign filed a petition with the Inter-American Commission on Human Rights of the Organization of American States (OAS) on behalf of all US citizens, focusing on the changes in social welfare law and policy wrought by the 1996 Personal Responsibility and Work Opportunity Reconciliation Act. The petition asks the Inter-American Commission on Human Rights to rule that US policy is in violation of the OAS Charter, and by extension the ICESCR, with respect to several economic and social rights, including the right to an adequate standard of living, the right to health, the right to protection for familial relations, the right to work under just and reasonable conditions, the right to education, the right to food, the right to housing, the right to social security, and the right to be free from discrimination. The petition states:

"Despite a growing economy, increasing wealth and federal budget surplus, US law and policy has nonethe-less steadily eroded the economic and social rights of its poor citizens and residents. The working poor, the unemployed and those who need assistance from the state face increasing economic insecurity and desper-ation, threatening the health and well-being of countless individuals and families across the country."

Given that the United States has not ratified the ICESCR, an OAS ruling in favour of the petitioners would be the first time an international human rights body finds the United States to be in violation of its obligation to promote economic and social rights. This would open up doors for activists in the United States who have long been frustrated by the lack of a forum to raise concerns about economic human rights abuses.

Sources: Kensington Welfare Rights Union 1999; Cheri Honkala et al. v. The United States of America, 1999.

Box 4: Budget Legislation and the ICESCR in Canada

In Canada, the National Action Committee on the Status of Women, together with the Charter Committee on Poverty Issues and the National Anti-Poverty Organisation, appealed to the ICESCR Committee to request the government of Canada to explain how the 1995 Budget Implementation Act (BIA) was consistent with the terms of the Covenant.

The Canadian budget act swept away a system of common standards that gave a basic entitlement to all persons in need, based on an income test for eligibility. Previously, claimants were entitled to appeal against decisions about the level of payments to be made to them. The system also provided critical social services to those in need and those who give care. Its elimination was presented in terms of the need to reduce the government budget deficit. But the result was to severely weaken women's economic and social rights.

In November 1996, the NGO coalition stated that the budget act represented "the most serious retrogressive measure ever taken in Canada with respect to the legislative protection of the right to an adequate standard of living." It had transformed Canada from a country in which the right to adequate financial assistance was "a legal requirement, enforceable in court," to one with "no federal legislation recognizing this right or providing any means of enforcing it."

The ICESCR Committee subsequently called upon the Canadian government to provide an account in its third periodic report in 1998. The Committee concluded that the Budget Implementation Act, by replacing the Canada Assistance Plan (CAP) with the Canada Health and Social Transfer, "entails a range of adverse consequences for the enjoyment of Covenant rights by disadvantaged groups in Canada" and noted with concern that "the replacement of the CAP and grave cuts to social assistance rates, social services and programmes have had a particularly harsh impact on women."

Sources: Elson and Gideon 1999; Day and Brodsky 1998.

In 1997, the UN Division for the Advancement of Women convened an expert group meeting to think through how women's economic and social rights could be better addressed. Some of the important recommendations for states included taking steps to:

- incorporate guarantees of economic and social rights in national constitutions and guarantee a gendered interpretation of these rights;
- reflect key gender policy objectives and priorities in national budgets;
- incorporate time-bound targets to promote women's enjoyment of economic and social rights in national plans of action for implementation of the Beijing Platform for Action.

In addition, the expert group meeting urged the ICESCR Committee to:

- define a gender-sensitive "minimum core content" in relation to each right protected by the Covenant;
- encourage the Commission on Human Rights to appoint a Special Rapporteur on women's economic and social rights;
- urge the international financial institutions and the World Trade Organization (WTO) to integrate human rights and gender impact assessments into their procedures and policies.

As international recognition of the importance of human rights grows, some of the state-level recommendations have begun to be addressed, at least by some states. The Human Rights Commission has appointed a Special Rapporteur on Education, including education for the girl child. And the ICESCR Committee is currently preparing a General Comment on ensuring gender equity in the implementation of economic, social and cultural rights.

With regard to international financial institutions and the WTO, the ICESCR Committee stated in May 1998 that the realms of trade, finance and investment are in no way exempt from human rights principles and called upon the WTO to find ways to systematically consider the impact of particular international trade and investment policies upon human rights, especially upon economic, social and cultural rights (UNHCR 1998).

A major constraint on improving the capacity of governments to uphold the ICESCR is the lack of an operational human rights-based approach to economic policy-making. Currently governments, courts and international financial institutions tend to think of economics strictly in terms of allocating resources efficiently, balancing budgets or reducing inflation, treating economic and social issues merely as optional policy objectives rather than matters of fundamental human rights (see Box 3 and Box 4 on NGO protests in the United States and Canada).

Convention on the Elimination of All Forms of Discrimination against Women (CEDAW)
CEDAW is the only human rights convention that is gender-specific. It provides the basis for realizing equality between women and men through ensuring women's equal access to, and equal opportunities in political and public life, as well as education and employment. It is a groundbreaking document in that it "recognizes the inextricability of subordination and the economic and social structures that perpetuate it" and requires states to take steps to modify culturally based gender bias, however deeply entrenched (UN 1993a).

"The existence of a positive legal framework for women's rights does not automatically confer rights on women. However, it does legitimize women's claims for rights and makes possible women's transformation from passive beneficiaries to active claimants. It creates the space for women's agency."

— Shanthi Dairiam, Director, International Women's Rights Action Watch, Asia Pacific (UNIFEM 1998a:9)

The CEDAW Convention's great strength is that it requires that governments take positive actions to promote and protect the rights of women, noting that the absence of overtly discriminatory laws and policies alone is not sufficient. The provisions that are most relevant to advancing women's economic equality relate to employment, including the right to work and receive equal pay for work of equal value (Article 11), equal access to credit (Article 13) and land (mentioned in Article 16 and clarified with respect to marital property and inheritance in General Recommendation 21). In order to clarify the intent of the Convention, the CEDAW Committee has issued General Recommendations, including several related to women's economic equality. These call on states to:

- ratify ILO Convention 100 concerning remuneration and undertake comparable worth studies (No. 13, 1989);
- report on the social and legal situation of unpaid women working in family enterprises (No. 16, 1991);
- include women's domestic work in the calculation of gross national product (No. 17, 1991);
- clarify women's rights to marital property and inheritance (No. 20, 1992);
- collect gender-specific data (No. 9, 1989).

Box 5: Activists Use CEDAW

Implementing CEDAW in Brazil: The 1992 Paulista Convention
In 1992, the São Paolo Council of Women passed the Paulista Convention on the Elimination of All Forms of Discrimination Against Women to push state and local governments to take legislative action to implement CEDAW. Following consultations between NGOs and government institutions to identify gaps between CEDAW requirements and the living conditions and legal discrimination faced by women, the Paulista Convention specified detailed obligations for state and local governments regarding the enhancement of women's human rights in the areas of public administration (including budgets), child care, education, health care, employment and the prevention of violence against women. Within one year of its passage, municipalities representing about 45 per cent of the population had become signatories.

Amending Inheritance Laws in Nepal
In Nepal, where CEDAW has the status of national law, women activists used the Convention to persuade the Supreme Court that a section of Nepal's National Code, banning unmarried women under age 35 from inheriting property and requiring that the property be returned when the woman did marry, was discriminatory. In response, the government enacted a less-than-ideal inheritance law, allowing daughters to inherit from birth but still requiring that property be returned after marriage. Women's NGOs in Nepal have called for this law to be amended, and in 1998 held a demonstration to demand that parliament discuss the inheritance law.

Demanding Land Rights in Tanzania
In Tanzania, women drew upon the government's ratification of CEDAW to buttress their claim that a law prohibiting women from selling clan land was unconstitutional, even though the constitution's Bill of Rights does not specifically refer to women. In 1990, ruling on a challenge brought by a woman who wanted to sell land inherited from her father, the Tanzanian High Court declared that the rules of inheritance outlined in the Declaration of Customary Law, which allowed women to inherit land but not to sell it, were unconstitutional and violated the international conventions that Tanzania had signed. Rights pertaining to the sale of clan land are thus the same for women and men.

Source: UNIFEM 1998a.

Box 6: "Global to Local" Training on CEDAW

Each January, at the time of the CEDAW session at UN headquarters in New York, UNIFEM and the International Women's Rights Action Watch Asia Pacific convene an annual training workshop on using the CEDAW Convention called "Global to Local." The workshop provides training to women advocates whose countries are reporting to the CEDAW Committee during its January or June sessions. Over 75 women's human rights advocates from more than 35 countries have received training to strengthen their understanding of the Convention, the Committee's working process and CEDAW's potential application to their national-level advocacy efforts. Participants have used the opportunity to provide valuable information to the Committee about the status and concerns of women in their countries. UNIFEM continues to support these annual training workshops, utilizing the experience to conduct national and regional-level trainings on CEDAW and facilitate the connection between global and local advocacy efforts.

Ratifying states are required to prepare an initial report within a year after signing the Convention and submit follow-up reports every four years. Reports are reviewed by the CEDAW Committee, which meets twice a year. Typically, some eight to ten country reports are reviewed during each Committee session, which makes concluding comments outlining priority areas for improvement and recommendations for action.

Government reports to the CEDAW Committee are prepared in various ways, and increasingly, women's NGOs are asked to participate in their preparation. NGOs are also invited to prepare their own "shadow reports," giving them an opportunity to put forward alternative perspectives on government policies and practices. The CEDAW Committee is open to input from NGOs and often uses this input to question governments during the review process. Women activists have also used CEDAW as the basis for drafting or modifying provisions in national constitutions, to persuade courts to interpret national legislation in the context of CEDAW, to make changes to legislation that discriminates against women and to improve government policy (see Boxes 5 and 6 on using CEDAW).

CEDAW came into effect in September 1981. However, for a long time it lacked an Optional Protocol, allowing individuals and groups in countries that ratify the protocol to bring complaints directly to the CEDAW Committee. In response to a concerted effort by NGOs as well as

UN agencies, an Optional Protocol was finalized in March 1999. Opened for ratification in October 1999, by May 2000 it had been signed by 35 countries. In addition, the CEDAW Committee is authorized to invite states parties to the Convention to report on widespread or systematic violations of women's rights and conduct investigations into these allegations. This was done, for example, following widespread allegations of the systematic rape of Bosnian women by Serbian forces during the civil war in former Yugoslavia.

A further problem with CEDAW concerns the issue of government reservations. CEDAW is the second-most widely ratified UN human rights treaty and, at the same time, the one to which countries have entered the greatest number of substantive reservations, which tend to undermine the essential objective of gender equality. Yet CEDAW contains no mechanism to reject reservations, even those that are inconsistent with its objects and purpose.

Another limitation of the convention is its silence with regard to gender-based violence, which can seriously impede the ability of women to fully enjoy human rights, including economic rights. For women, as human rights advocates point out, "a division between rights to economic security and rights to personal liberty is purely artificial. In the circumstances of women who have violent or psychologically abusive male partners, for example, the indivisibility of economic issues from violence issues is clear" (Day and Brodsky 1998). Responding to such comments, the CEDAW Committee agreed to examine the matter, and in 1992 issued General Recommendation 19, which specifically defines gender-based violence as a form of discrimination against women.

With regard to economic equality, CEDAW is limited in that, by focusing on discrimination between men and women, it does not directly address the impact of economic policies on women's standards of living. Although its preamble acknowledges that "in situations of poverty women have the least access to food, education, training and opportunities for employment and other needs," it does not directly address what states should do to improve women's living standards. CEDAW relies on evidence that compares the status of women with that of men, rather than demonstrating that women are able to achieve an adequate standard of living. For example, if the incomes of both men and women have declined, but men's incomes have fallen more than women's, the gender-based income gap may be narrowing, but this will be overshadowed by the fact that the standard of living for both women and men has decreased. The Convention's discrimination-based approach cannot adequately deal with this phenomenon of equalizing down.

International Labour Organization (ILO) Conventions

The ILO, founded in 1919, was established to improve living and working conditions by developing a comprehensive code of law and practice through the joint efforts of governments, employers and workers. Over 182 conventions and 190 recommendations have been adopted by the International Labour Conference, a world forum for the discussion of social and labour questions (see Box 7). Each national delegation to the conference is composed of two government delegates, one employers' delegate and one workers' delegate, accompanied by technical advisers. To date there are 174 member states of the ILO.

ILO Conventions are legal instruments that cover a wide field of social concerns, including basic human rights such as freedom of association, abolition of forced labour, and elimination of discrimination in employment, as well as minimum wages, labour administration, industrial relations, employment policy, working conditions, social security and occupational safety and health. A number of these deal specifically with women workers, some approved during the first half of this century, including:

- maternity protection, No. 3 (1919)
- underground work, No. 45 (1935)
- night work, No. 89 (1948)
- equal remuneration, No. 100 (1951)
- discrimination, No. 111 (1958)
- workers with family responsibilities, No. 156 (1981)
- part-time work, No. 175 (1994)
- home work, No. 177 (1996).

Conventions, once they have been ratified by a government, involve a dual obligation: both a formal commitment to apply the provisions and a willingness to accept a measure of international supervision. (See www.ilo.org for a list of ratifying states.) In June 1998 the ILO adopted a Declaration on Fundamental Principles and Rights at Work, which reiterated the protections in each of these Conventions.

Setting international standards of labour and employment practice is one of the principal functions of the ILO. Its constitution specifies that these standards be developed through negotiation among recognized workers' groups, employers' groups and government representatives from ILO member states in what is known as a Tripartite Consultation process. Conventions and recommendations can be proposed by any of the three groups and also evolve through ILO conferences and technical meetings. A recommendation differs from a convention in that it is not subject to ratification but provides specific guidelines for national legislation and practice.

A limitation of the ILO system is that the standard-setting, implementation oversight and complaint processes and procedures are not accessible to unrecognized unions or unorganized workers, especially in the informal sector. However, the recently passed Convention on Home Work (No. 177) has begun to change this. Article 2 of the Convention entitles home-based workers who work for remuneration to treatment on a par with wage earners, not only as regards wages and workplace conditions but also in relation to forming associations and collective bargaining (see Box 8 on the Home Work Convention).

Consistent with the language of most ILO standards, that used in the Home Work Convention is not gender specific and does not recognize that women comprise the majority of home-based workers. Greater representation of women is needed in the tripartite

Box 7: Core ILO Conventions

Convention	Ratifications as of April 2000
Forced Labour Convention 29 (1930)	153
Freedom of Association and Protection of the Right to Organize Convention 87 (1948)	128
Right to Organize and Collective Bargaining Convention 98 (1949)	146
Equal Remuneration Convention 100 (1951)	146
Abolition of Forced Labour Convention 105 (1957)	144
Discrimination - Employment and Occupation, Convention 111 (1958)	142
Minimum Age Convention 138 (1973)	89

Source: ILO Website: www.ilo.org.

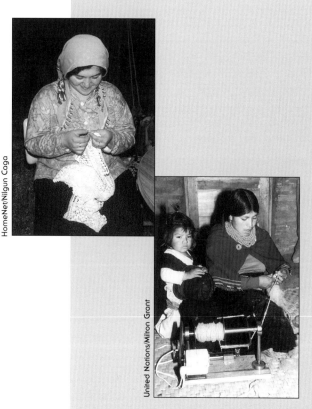

HomeNet/Nilgun Caga

United Nations/Milton Grant

NGOs and independent advocates in both the North and the South. The campaign was led by HomeNet, an international network of home-based workers set up in 1994 to coordinate the efforts of organizations working to make the issues of home-based workers visible and to advocate for their rights. HomeNet in turn is the result of the organizing efforts of the Self Employed Women's Association (SEWA) of India, which has worked for over two decades to bring visibility and recognition to work done by women, especially poor women, in their homes. In 1988, SEWA won the support of the International Confederation of Free Trade Unions (ICFTU), which agreed to make protection for home workers an organizing issue and to take it before the ILO.

Critical to HomeNet's success in securing government support were regional organizing meetings. In May 1996, an Asian Regional Consultation on Home-based Work, convened by SEWA and supported by UNIFEM, brought together high-level policy-makers and NGOs from over ten countries in the region and focused on lobbying governments to support the Convention. Organizers credit this workshop, which was held in Bangkok, Thailand, with contributing to the strong support by the Government of India at the conference.

Since the adoption of the Convention, HomeNet has been working to make governments aware of the need to ratify this and all ILO Conventions. UNIFEM support is coordinated in the South Asia office, working with HomeNet, unions, and NGOs to collect and disseminate information, and to build and strengthen grassroots organizing networks to pressure governments throughout the world to ratify the ILO Convention and develop national policies to protect the rights of home-based workers.

In a complementary effort begun in July 1998, the Committee on Asian Women, a regional women workers' organization based in Hong Kong, initiated a campaign to generate public awareness of the ILO Convention on Part-time Work (No. 175) as well as the Home Work Convention. The aim is to encourage governments to ratify the conventions and revise national labour laws in conformity with the ILO Conventions in order to protect the rights of part-time and home-based workers. A total of 4,630 individual signatures and 110 organizational endorsements were collected from 24 countries and sent to the relevant government and intra-governmental representatives in February 1999.

Box 8: ILO Convention on Home Work

In June1996, delegates to the ILO's 83rd Conference adopted the Home Work Convention (No. 177) setting minimum standards regarding pay and conditions, and Recommendation No. 183 outlining how these standards should be applied. Delegates included one employer and one worker representative along with two government representatives from each country. Arguing that the Convention would create obstacles to job creation, the employers' group endeavoured to prevent a quorum by collectively abstaining. However, governments were more concerned with the situation of home workers, who earn low piece-rates, work long hours, and have no job security or legal protections. Government delegates from both North and South spoke in favour of the Convention, with particularly strong support from the Indian and South African delegations as well as a majority of countries within the European Union. The Convention ultimately passed with 246 in favour, 14 against and 152 abstaining. As of April 2000 it had been ratified by Finland (1998) and Ireland (1999).

Adoption of the Home Work Convention was the result of a concerted organizing campaign by women's groups together with trade unions,

Sources: Committee for Asian Women (CAW) 1998; HomeNet Newsletter, July 1996; Winter 1996/97; HomeNet Website: www.gn.apc.org/homenet/ilo.html.

decision-making structures of the ILO to ensure that policies better reflect women's concerns, including:

- the irregular and vulnerable employment opportunities created for women as a result of the globalization of the economy;
- the double burden for women who continue to perform unpaid domestic work;
- the increase in women's work in the informal sector, either through self-employment or through sub-contracting that is not protected by labour regulations.

Nevertheless, the ILO Conventions can be used in countries that have ratified them to challenge practices that discriminate against women. In countries where constitutional guarantees of equal rights do not specifically mention sex as a basis for outlawing workplace discrimination, for example, they can be used to change existing laws or pass new ones establishing equal rights and protections for women workers (see Box 9).

Commitments and Targets at UN Conferences

In the year 2000, the UN is coordinating reviews of the implementation of international and national level commitments made at the World Summit on Social Development (WSSD) in Copenhagen and the Fourth World Conference on Women (FWCW) in Beijing. At these conferences, previous commitments to the implementation of international human rights treaties and ILO Conventions were restated and a number of specific targets were agreed upon. The international women's movement was a major force not only in ensuring that the conference agreements were infused with a gender perspective, but also in reminding governments of the need to build on the agreements reached at earlier UN conferences in the 1990s (see Box 10).

The 1992 UN Conference on Environment and Development (UNCED) in Rio de Janeiro was the first milestone conference of the 1990s. NGOs formally participated for the first time, and national and international women's groups had a tremendous impact on the document that emerged from UNCED: Agenda 21. Initial drafts had only two references to women, but due to intensive advocacy efforts, the final draft had over 172 references to women and an entire chapter on women's role in the environment.

The 1993 UN Second World Conference on Human Rights in Vienna resulted in further gains for the international women's movement. Prior to Vienna, women's rights were often viewed as separate from human rights. Through the advocacy of women's groups, women's rights were fully recognized as human rights in the Vienna Declaration and Programme of Action (see Box 11, p. 49).

At the 1994 International Conference on Population and Development (ICPD) in Cairo, women's advocates from both North and South collaborated in successfully moving the overall objective of population policy away from one focused on reducing population growth to one focused on women's sexual and reproductive health and rights. Preparatory meetings for ICPD strengthened women's NGOs and often revealed links between reproductive health and economic opportunities and constraints.

In 1995, women's NGOs were pivotal at the World Summit on Social Development (WSSD) in Copenhagen, where they persuaded governments to recognize the gendered implications of macroeconomic policies, especially the negative impacts of structural adjustment and the crippling effects of debt. Heads of state agreed upon ten concrete commitments, all of which addressed the important links between macro-economic and social development issues (UN 1995c).

Box 9: Women Workers' Rights in the Caribbean: UNIFEM/ILO Handbook

A joint publication by UNIFEM-Caribbean and the ILO aims to inform women workers about their workplace rights as outlined by CEDAW and ILO Conventions.

Caribbean laws for the most part fail to incorporate the rights of women workers laid down by CEDAW and ILO Conventions. Throughout the region, women are typically clustered in the lowest paid sectors and positions; they are often paid less for the same work and are usually the first to be laid off and last to be employed, particularly during periods of structural adjustment. Efforts to apply broad equal rights guarantees in constitutions to women's rights in the workplace have generally failed, owing to the fact that articles that deal with workplace rights do not specifically include sex as a category of discrimination. Courts have been reluctant to oblige states to implement principles that impose a cost obligation.

However, all countries in the Caribbean have ratified CEDAW as well as many of the ILO Conventions regarding workplace equality. Accordingly, their governments are supposed to implement these Conventions by passing new laws or reforming existing laws to guarantee workplace equality on the basis of sex. In line with CEDAW, case law in the region is increasingly treating these rights as enforceable.

The Handbook identifies innovative litigation strategies for the short and long terms. It can be used by NGOs, trade unions, employers concerned to adopt gender-sensitive employment policies, government officials and women workers.

WEDO

Box 10: Women Organizing at UN Conferences

The Women's Caucus, a democratic vehicle for consensus building, has enabled women's NGOs from around the world to develop an advocacy agenda and infuse a gender perspective into the process and outcomes of nine world conferences and their preparatory processes. The Caucus was organized primarily by the Women's Environment and Development Organization (WEDO), an international women's organization founded by a visionary feminist and former US Congresswoman, Bella Abzug. At daily meetings during each preparatory meeting leading up to the final conference, Women's Caucus members exchanged information, jointly prepared amendments to the official documents and developed advocacy strategies at every stage in the inter-governmental process. The Women's Caucus was successful in persuading many governments to adopt these amendments, resulting in the incorporation of hundreds of women's recommendations in the final agreements.

Members of the Women's Caucus addressed economic issues to varying degrees at each of the major UN conferences. The first caucus, organized in preparation for the Earth Summit in Rio, was based on a meeting in Miami of 1500 women from 83 countries, which outlined a holistic agenda emphasizing economic justice issues such as poverty, over-consumption, debt burdens, unfair trade, and over-reliance on the market. In Vienna, at the World Conference on Human Rights, the Global Campaign for Women's Human Rights succeeded in getting recognition of women's rights as human rights and of violence against women as a human rights violation.

At the Population and Development conference in Cairo, the caucus shifted its focus to sexual and reproductive rights, partly due to the large representation of NGOs working on women's

health issues. Some development NGOs felt that broader economic constraints affecting women's lives and health were not sufficiently addressed and were concerned that the 'D' was dropped from ICPD. At the Social Summit in Copenhagen, where the focus was on the links between economic and social issues, women's NGOs were able to better articulate an economic justice agenda with a gender perspective.

Prior to the Women's Conference in Beijing, UNIFEM also created a forum through which women could effectively articulate their agenda at the conference. In collaboration with the UN Non-Governmental Liaison Service (UN-NGLS), which also seeks to increase NGO participation at UN conferences, UNIFEM prepared a set of practical guidelines about how UN conferences work. This handbook, "Putting Gender on the Agenda: A Guide to Participating in UN World Conferences," was used with NGOs in a series of training workshops conducted at the regional preparatory meetings, which enabled women to familiarize themselves with the procedures and processes through which the UN conferences work.

As a result of these experiences, women's NGOs from all over the world worked together to advocate on economic issues at the Women's Conference in Beijing. This was continued by the women's caucus at Habitat II in Istanbul and the World Food Summit in Rome. The momentum generated at all of these conferences led to international organizing by women to increase awareness of the policies and practices of the World Bank and the World Trade Organization and to demand greater accountability by both organizations.

1990s UN Conferences
1990 World Conference on Education for All, Jomtien
1992 UN Conference on Environment and Development (UNCED), Rio de Janeiro
1993 World Conference on Human Rights (WCOHR), Vienna
1994 Global Conference on the Sustainable Development of Small Island Developing States (SIDS), Barbados
1994 International Conference on Population and Development (ICPD), Cairo
1995 World Summit on Social Development (WSSD), Copenhagen
1995 Fourth World Conference on Women, (FWCW), Beijing
1996 Second UN Conference on Human Settlements (Habitat II), Istanbul
1997 World Food Summit (WFS), Rome

Earth Times

Women's groups around the world mobilized for the Fourth World Conference on Women (FWCW) in Beijing (see Box 12). At the Conference, they stressed the importance of incorporating a gender perspective in all areas of policy and action. Governments agreed to a Platform for Action that consolidated and built on the gains made by women in each of the previous conferences. Under the three main themes of the Conference, equality, development and peace, the Platform outlined goals and recommendations that addressed twelve critical areas of concern and specified that the primary strategy for implementation should be by means of gender mainstreaming (UN 1995b).

NGOs at Beijing:

- 3000 NGOs were accredited to the UN Conference at Beijing and 30,000 people attended the parallel NGO Forum (UN 1996b);

- NGO representatives made one-third of the plenary speeches at the UN Conference at Beijing and the Platform for Action incorporated almost 90% of the NGO Caucus recommendations (Davis 1996).

At each of these conferences, in addition to commitments, governments agreed to a number of specific time-bound targets to serve as benchmarks for progress (see Box 13). In the Cairo, Copenhagen and Beijing agreements, however, the major focus of these targets is on education and health. The only reference to closing a "gender gap" is in relation to education. The Beijing Platform for Action reiterated a target regarding the representation of women in positions of power and decision-making endorsed by the UN Economic and Social Council. However, the Beijing Platform contains no targets related to two critical areas of concern – women's poverty and women's economic equality.

Box 11: Global Campaign for Women's Human Rights

In preparation for the 1993 World Conference on Human Rights in Vienna, a coalition of hundreds of groups and individuals worldwide, including UNIFEM, mounted a Global Campaign for Women's Human Rights. Coordinated by the Center for Women's Global Leadership, the campaign launched a petition drive that called for the Vienna conference to "comprehensively address women's human rights at every level of the proceedings" and to recognize gender violence as "a universal phenomenon which takes many forms across culture, race, and class" and as "a violation of human rights requiring immediate action."

By the time of the Vienna conference, over 1,000 sponsoring groups had gathered nearly half a million signatures from 124 countries, and the slogan "women's rights are human rights" had become a rallying call all over the world. At the NGO Forum in Vienna, the campaign held a Global Tribunal on Violations of Women's Human Rights, bringing attention to violations of women's human rights in relation to political and economic rights and violence against women in the family and in situations of armed conflict. The Vienna Declaration for the first time recognizes violence against women as a human rights abuse (UN 1993b).

Following hearings at the UN conferences in Cairo and Copenhagen, the Global Campaign petition initiative had accumulated over 1 million signatures from 148 countries and was translated into 26 languages, calling for a UN report on implementation of the commitments in the Vienna Declaration and their incorporation into the Beijing Platform for Action.

The Beijing Platform for Action reiterated the universal and holistic nature of women's human rights and called on governments to promote and protect women's human rights, including freedom from violence, sexual and reproductive health free of discrimination and coercion, and equal rights to inheritance. The Global Campaign continues to advocate for the integration of women's human rights into international and regional human rights systems.

celebrate & demand
women's human rights
1998 global campaign

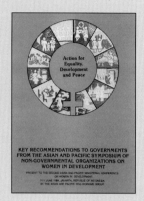

Box 12: Regional NGO Advocacy in Preparation for Beijing

NGO preparation for the Beijing Conference and parallel NGO Forum began in 1993. Under the leadership of Thanpyuying Sumnalle Chartikavanij and Noeleen Heyzer, a group of NGOs in Asia and the Pacific formed a coalition called the Asia and Pacific Non Government Organisation Working Group. The primary objective of the group was to articulate a regional NGO position on issues confronting women in the region and ensure that these views were reflected in the final document, the Platform for Action. Over 500 women activists attended the first official regional NGO meeting in Manila.

The Working Group opened opportunities for greater NGO participation in the Beijing process and helped bring about a shift in the nature of NGO engagement in that process. Group members identified substantive critical issues, including the need to quantify women's work and reflect their contribution to the economy, both paid and unpaid, in national accounting systems. They articulated the rationale for an ILO Convention on the rights of home based workers and highlighted the issue of state responsibility for the elimination of gender-based violence. These and other major issues were summarized in the "Yellow Book," which informed preparatory activities in other regions.

The ideas and recommendations in the Yellow Book were disseminated throughout the region in a series of meetings in 1994. The next year, the Working Group played a leading role in NGO activities at Beijing, convening caucuses, lobbying governments and drafting alternative language for the Platform. Consequently, most of the issues and recommendations in the Yellow Book were included in the final document.

After Beijing, the Working Group was formalized as the Asian Pacific Watch and the South-East Asian Watch, both of which have taken the lead in the regional follow-up process, including the Beijing +5 Regional Preparatory Meeting in Thailand in September 1999. The recommendations from this meeting have been compiled in a publication titled "Asia-Pacific Women 2000: Gender Equality, Development and Peace for the Twenty-First Century," which will inform the Beijing +5 Session in June 2000.

In 1999, at the five-year review of the International Conference on Population and Development (known as "ICPD +5"), 177 Member States adopted "Key actions for the further implementation of ICPD." This reaffirmed the Programme of Action and called on governments to ensure that the human rights of women and girls, particularly their freedom from coercion, discrimination and violation, including harmful practices and sexual exploitation, be protected and promoted through the implementation and enforcement of gender-sensitive legislation and policies. It called for greater efforts in the areas of reproductive and sexual health, maternal mortality, prevention of HIV/AIDS and gender issues in education, and adopted several new benchmarks in each of these areas (UN1999c). In addition, recognizing the need for adequate resources to achieve the desired targets, the session urged developed countries to increase efforts to mobilize funds to agreed-upon levels and reiterated the need for the international community to provide financial and technical assistance to developing countries and those with economies in transition.

The ability of governments to achieve many of the agreed targets is greatly influenced by the macroeconomic environment, including the rate of growth of national economies, the extent to which they provide adequate livelihoods for the people of the country, the extent to which there is a system for redistributing income and the type of macroeconomic policies introduced by governments and promoted by international trade and finance institutions.

Gender and Macroeconomic Policies

Both the Copenhagen Programme of Action and the Beijing Platform for Action address macroeconomic issues to some extent. The Copenhagen document discusses policies necessary to achieve the three themes of the conference, the eradication of poverty, promotion of full employment and social integration, but does not discuss the differential impact of macroeconomic policies on men and women. The Beijing Platform includes such a discussion, noting that macroeconomic policy is not

Box 13: Targets agreed at Cairo, Copenhagen and Beijing

Targets	Cairo (ICPD)	Copenhagen (WSSD)	Beijing (FWCW)
Governments reiterated the target for women in decision-making positions endorsed by ECOSOC: 30% of decision-making positions to be held by women by 1995			PFA 182
Eradicate absolute poverty by a date to be specified by each country		POA 25	
By the year 2000, governments committed themselves to meet basic needs:			
Universal access to basic education and completion of primary education by at least 80% of primary school-age children	POA 11.6	POA 36a	PFA 80b
Gender equality for girls in primary education			PFA 81b
Life expectancy not less than 60 years in any country		POA 36b	
Mortality rates of infants and children under 5 reduced by one-third of the 1990 level, or 50 to 70 per 1,000 live births, whichever is less	POA 8.16	POA 36c	PFA 106l
Maternal mortality reduced by one half of the 1990 level	POA 8.21	POA 36d	PFA 106i
Severe and moderate malnutrition among children under 5 by half of the 1990 level		POA 36f	PFA 106w
Primary health care for all, reducing malaria mortality and morbidity by at least 20% from 1995 levels in at least 75% of affected countries		POA 36g	
Eradication or control of major diseases constituting global health problems		POA 36j	
Greater availability of affordable and adequate shelter for all		POA 36m	
By the year 2005, governments promised to:			
Close the gender gap in primary and secondary education	POA 11.8	POA 36a	PFA 80b
Remove all programme-related barriers to family-planning	POA 7.19		
Countries with intermediate mortality rates aim for infant rate below 50 deaths per 1,000 and under-5 rate below 60 deaths per 1,000 births	POA 8.16		
Countries with highest maternal mortality rates aim for a rate below 125 per 100,000 live births; those with intermediate rates aim for a rate below 100	POA 8.21		
Countries with highest mortality rates to achieve life expectancy greater than 65; all countries, a life expectancy greater than 70	POA 8.5		
By the year 2015, governments promised to:			
Provide universal primary education in all countries	POA 11.6	POA 36a	PFA 80b
Achieve an infant mortality rate below 35 per 1,000 live births and under-5 mortality rate below 45 per 1,000	POA 8.16	POA 36d	PFA 106l
Make reproductive health care accessible to all individuals of appropriate ages through the primary health-care system	POA 7.6	POA 36h	PFA 106i
Achieve equivalent levels of education for boys and girls	POA 11.6		
Reduce maternal mortality rates by a further one-half	POA 8.21		
Countries with highest maternal mortality rates aim for a rate below 75 per 100,000 live births; those with intermediate rates aim for a rate below 60	POA 8.21		
Countries with highest mortality rates to achieve life expectancy greater than 70; all countries, a life expectancy greater than 75	POA 8.5		

United Nations

designed in ways that recognize such differences, but does not spell out the changes required, particularly at the international level, to ensure women's equality and equity. The Platform also emphasizes the importance of a gender analysis and the full and equal participation of women in rethinking, reformulating and monitoring macroeconomic policies and strategies for the eradication of poverty.

Commitment to Providing Secure and Sustainable Livelihoods

At Copenhagen, governments committed themselves to creating full employment and providing "secure and sustainable livelihoods" through freely chosen productive employment and work. The main difficulty with this agreement is that the concept of full employment does not recognize the unpaid work that women do in caring for families and communities and the double burden women carry as a result of their entry into paid employment. The problem for women is often one of too much work rather than too little work.

The means emphasized in the document to ensure full employment were the liberalization of trade and investment. However, there was some recognition that the impact of liberalization may not always be positive. Governments therefore committed themselves to:

- regulate markets and mitigate "negative impacts posed by market forces";
- monitor the impact of trade liberalization on progress in meeting basic needs in developing countries;
- disseminate information on the impact of trade and investment liberalization on the economy.

Recent UN agreements reveal contradictory notions about the role of market forces in development, with both an expectation that they will deliver prosperity and a growing concern with their adverse effects, as seen in references to international and regional trade agreements and the World Trade Organization. At Beijing, governments committed themselves to ensuring that trade agreements do not have an adverse impact on women. This was reiterated at the World Food Summit two years later in Rome.

Commitment to Minimize Negative Effects of Structural Adjustment Programmes

At both Copenhagen and Beijing, NGOs challenged the growing role of the international

financial institutions in development. Their critique was directed primarily at World Bank policies, particularly structural adjustment programmes (SAPs). Women's NGOs grounded their critique on feminist research on gender and structural adjustment that showed how male bias in orthodox macroeconomic analysis resulted in the potential costs of adjustment to women being overlooked, along with the barriers to women gaining benefits. They called for a thorough policy review and reformulation to mitigate the adverse effects on women. This led to the launching of an international campaign called "Women's Eyes on the World Bank," which raised women's concerns directly with the World Bank president at the Beijing conference and pursuaded the Bank to set up an External Gender Consultative Group (see Chapter 6).

At both Cairo and Beijing, governments recognized that the burden of foreign debt, stabilization and structural adjustment programmes had led to a reduction in social expenditures, which had adversely affected women, particularly in Africa and the least developed countries. They committed themselves to include social development goals in SAPs; to protect basic social programmes and expenditures; and to review the impact of SAPs on development, using gender-sensitive social impact assessments to develop policies to reduce women's disproportionate burden.

The international financial institutions were called upon to ensure that:

- SAPs are designed to minimize their negative effects on vulnerable and disadvantaged groups;
- marginalized communities benefit from the positive effects of SAPs by taking actions to "reduce inequality and economic disparity."

Though governments committed themselves to minimizing the negative effects of structural adjustment policies, particularly on women, the link between these policies and the increased unpaid work of women that results was not made. Since women typically absorb the adjustment costs by working more both inside and outside the household to provide social services no longer delivered by the state, it is essential to measure work in the unpaid sector to assess the true impact of such policies.

Women and Poverty

Poverty was a key theme at both the Copenhagen and Beijing conferences. Women drew attention to the structural causes of poverty, particularly the macroeconomic framework, including policies of the international financial institutions, and the inherent problems of a market-based economy. Their analysis informed the intergovernmental debates and was an important factor in governments linking the increased poverty of women to macro-economic policies in their diagnosis of the reasons for poverty. Governments agreed that poverty is a problem in both the North and the South and that its eradication requires democratic participation and changes in economic structures in order to ensure more equitable distribution of productive assets, wealth, opportunities, income and services.

Commitment to Eradicating Poverty

In Copenhagen, poverty was one of three core issues along with employment and social integration The goal of eradicating poverty was highlighted as the second of ten commitments and governments agreed upon numerous actions under this broad goal "as an ethical, social, political and economic imperative of humankind." Governments specifically committed themselves to:

- develop national policies to reduce overall poverty by the year 1996 and "eradicate absolute poverty by a target date to be specified by each country in its national context";
- develop a precise definition and assessment of absolute poverty, preferably by 1996.

However, by 1998, only 39 out of 130 countries surveyed by the UNDP had set specific national targets for the eradication of poverty (UNDP 1998b). Although there are repeated references in the Copenhagen commitments to more women than men living in absolute poverty, no attention is paid to the need to measure poverty in a gender-specific way.

The feminization of poverty was noted in the Beijing Platform for Action. Governments agreed that over the past decade the number of women living in poverty had increased disproportionately to the number of men, particularly in the developing countries, and committed themselves to address the needs of women living in poverty under four broad strategic objectives:

- adopt and maintain macro-economic policies and development strategies that address the needs of women in poverty;
- revise laws and administrative practices to ensure women's equal rights and access to economic resources;
- provide women with access to savings and credit mechanisms and institutions;
- develop gender-based methodologies and conduct research to address the feminization of poverty.

Both agreements include increasing credit access as a key strategy for the eradication of poverty. A range of actors are called upon to strengthen

UNICEF/Nicole Tourounji

women's access to capital, with the assumption that secure livelihoods will follow:

- governments are to promote and strengthen microenterprises, new small businesses, cooperative enterprises, expanded markets and other employment opportunities and facilitate their transition from the informal to the formal sector;
- governments, central banks and private banking institutions are to encourage regulatory reforms that support financial institutions' efforts to meet the financial needs of enterprises run by women;
- commercial banks and the private sector are to reduce transaction costs, redefine risk, open lending to women, simplify banking practices, and ensure the participation of women clients in the decision-making process of credit and finance institutions;
- international development organizations are to provide credit for women' enterprises.

There is a basic disjuncture between what are identified as the causes of poverty and the solutions proposed. While governments accept that there is a need to restructure and reformulate macroeconomic policies for poverty eradication, the main solution put forward is microeconomic: enabling poor women to gain access to credit for entrepreneurial activities. There are 35 references to such strategies in the Beijing Platform compared with 17 references to employment creation and other strategies for poverty eradication (for a discussion of microenterprise, see Chapter 6).

A fundamental problem with the Copenhagen and Beijing commitments on poverty is the underlying assumption that sustained economic growth will indeed benefit the poor.

"Growth cannot be assumed to automatically 'trickle down' to the poor. It can in fact trickle up to create greater inequalities."

— Noeleen Heyzer, Executive Director, UNIFEM (1994)

Suzette Mitchell

Women's Economic Equality

Women at both Copenhagen and Beijing pressed governments to address the inequalities that women face in their access to economic resources such as land or other natural resources, credit, technology and training and the discrimination they face in labour markets. Three important areas in which governments committed themselves to take actions are land and other property, employment rights and recognition of women's unpaid work.

Commitment to Women's Equal Access to Land and Other Property

Women's success in securing a commitment to their equal right to own, control and inherit land and other property, especially in rural areas, is particularly significant. This was a contentious issue, owing to the existence in some countries of laws and practices that assign land ownership and control to men. Nevertheless, governments agreed:

- to make legislative and administrative reforms to give women equal rights with men to economic resources, including access to ownership and control over land and other forms of property;
- to "remove all obstacles...to their ability to buy, hold and sell property and land equally with men."

These rights to own and control land and other property are essential for women's economic security. The ability to lease, mortgage or sell the land can prove critical in an economic crisis, and is important even in non-crisis situations where land can be used as collateral for a loan. These rights can also give women some bargaining power in relation to relatives and potential heirs. However, the role of the state in enforcing laws related to these rights is often hampered by local customs, particularly concerning marriage and inheritance.

Commitment to Women's Employment Rights

In both Copenhagen and Beijing, governments confirmed their commitments to the core International Labour Organization (ILO) Conventions. Governments that had ratified these and other ILO Conventions agreed to fully implement them. Others were urged to take into account the principles embodied in the ILO Conventions and consider ratifying and fully implementing them.

In separate paragraphs, the final documents of both conferences emphasized ILO Convention No. 100 on Equal Remuneration for men and women for work of equal value as a basic right. This Convention requires that governments evaluate comparable jobs performed by women and men, to ensure that the jobs performed by women are not undervalued. Governments further agreed to:

- enact and enforce laws and measures to eliminate discrimination against women employees on grounds of sex, age, marital or family status, regarding access to and conditions of employment, training, promotion, maternity leave and social security, as well as legal protection against employers requiring proof of contraceptive use or sexual and racial harassment or dismissal due to pregnancy;
- extend labour standards and social protection and create social security systems for part-time, temporary, seasonal and home-based workers without destroying the ability of the informal sector to generate employment;
- change policies that reinforce the gender division of labour to promote equal sharing of family responsibility for unpaid domestic work.

The ratification and implementation of ILO standards is increasingly critical to counter the "race to the bottom" brought about as countries compete for advantage in the global economy on the basis of availability of cheap labour. Although some new employment opportunities have been created for women as a result of economic globalization, some of its consequences have exacerbated inequalities between women and men workers. More women have been recruited into the labour market, particularly in developing countries, but this often reflects the fact that women can be hired for low pay, poor working conditions and irregular and vulnerable employment in comparison with men (UN 1999b).

"When my husband died, my neighbours wanted my land. They beat me on any pretext, they tried to chase me out. Then they started to say I was having an affair with my brother-in-law, that was why I wouldn't leave despite their harassment. My homestead is like a jungle. I cannot grow any crops on it because my neighbours let their goats graze on my land. When I go to the bazaar, they steal what few crops I have."

— Bangladeshi Widow (Agarwal 1994)

Moreover, women's entry into paid work results in their taking on a double burden, as they continue to perform unpaid work in caring for their families and communities. The agreement to extend labour standards to informal sector workers is crucial, given the increase in women's work in that sector, either through precarious forms of self-employment or employment in home-based, part-time, casual and seasonal work.

Compared with the Copenhagen commitments, the Beijing Platform for Action more directly addresses the gender disparities in economic power-sharing within families and the need for policies to enable women and men to reconcile work with family responsibilities. However, such policies will remain flawed if they are not linked to concerted national efforts to measure and value unremunerated work, performed largely by women.

Commitment to Measuring and Valuing Unpaid Work

In 1985, the Third World Conference on Women in Nairobi included a call to recognize and measure the unremunerated economic contributions of women and to reflect these contributions in national accounts, economic statistics and gross national products. Ten years later, at both Copenhagen and Beijing, governments affirmed the need to:

- devise statistical means to "recognize and make visible" women's unpaid work;
- develop methods to reflect the value of such work in quantitative terms for "possible reflection" in core national accounts;
- examine the "relationship of women's unremunerated work to the incidence of and their vulnerability to poverty."

In Beijing, governments acknowledged that women's unremunerated work in market-oriented family farms or businesses remains undervalued and under-recorded even though it is included in principle

in the UN System of National Accounts. On the other hand, women's unremunerated domestic and community work is by definition excluded from the system of national accounts because it is not market-oriented. The Platform for Action commits governments to develop a methodology to measure unremunerated work but does not specify how to use such data in macroeconomic policy-making or how to redress the inequities uncovered by the data.

Role of the Private Sector

In a climate of diminishing development assistance, the private sector was viewed as a key player in the implementation of Beijing and Copenhagen conference commitments. Both documents emphasize developing partnerships with the private sector especially in the provision of social services, particularly health and education. The Beijing Platform calls upon the private sector to:

- cooperate with the government in the development of a comprehensive national strategy for improving health, particularly women's health, education and social services so that girls and women of all ages living in poverty have full access to such services;
- develop skills and create opportunities for women to access market opportunities;
- help provide credit for poor women;
- adopt policies and mechanisms to grant contracts on a non-discriminatory basis;
- recruit women for leadership and increase the participation of women in decision-making and management.

The emphasis on the role of the private sector in the delivery of basic social services runs the risk of weakening states' capability to do so. Further, neither of the final conference documents addresses the structural changes necessary to hold accountable the most influential actor in the economy, the private sector. Private-sector accountability is especially important in view of the increasing emphasis on creating an enabling environment for private savings and investment, including the reversal of capital flight and promoting the full participation of the private sector in the growth and development process.

"Planning, development programmes, employment policies, training and educational programmes, and introduction of technological change at all levels (including the household) must be based on accurate information on women's work if they are to be fully relevant to about 50 percent of the world's population."

—Lourdes Benería (1982)

Karen Judd

Commitment to Corporate Responsibility

At both Copenhagen and Beijing, NGOs called for strong regulation of transnational corporations to ensure social responsibility. However, the final conference documents contain only a few references to such regulation. No regulatory mechanism was identified to ensure the accountability of transnational corporations, despite the acknowledgment of the importance of transparent and accountable governance and administration in all public and private national and international institutions. It was merely suggested that transnational corporations should be monitored by national and international NGOs and women's groups. At Copenhagen and Beijing, governments specifically agreed to encourage transnational and national corporations to:

- observe national labour, environment, consumer, health and safety laws, particularly those that affect women;
- comply with social security regulations, applicable international agreements, instruments and conventions and other relevant laws.

One year later, at the Second UN Conference on Human Settlements, members of the Women's Caucus succeeded in getting governments to agree to "promote socially responsible corporate investment and reinvestment in, and in partnership with, local communities." This commitment provides the basis for activists to hold corporations accountable to the communities in which they operate.

International Development Cooperation

NGOs at both Copenhagen and Beijing demanded that international development assistance and debt relief be given high priority, and governments committed themselves to:

- strive for the "fulfillment of the agreed target of 0.7 per cent of gross national product for overall official development assistance (ODA) as soon as possible, and increasing the share of funding for social development programmes," and "conduct a critical analysis of their assistance programmes so as to improve the quality and effectiveness of aid through the integration of a gender approach";

- encourage "interested developed and developing country partners" to allocate, on average, 20 percent of ODA and 20 percent of the national budget, respectively, to basic social programmes" (the so-called 20-20 initiative) and "take into account a gender perspective."

Earth Times

In Copenhagen, women activists staged a dramatic four-day hunger strike to demand debt cancellation and governments committed themselves to:

- "debt reduction, including cancellation or other debt relief measures and develop techniques of debt conversion applied to social development programmes";

Box 14: Shaping the 21st Century: International Development Targets

Economic well-being:
- a reduction by one-half in the proportion of people living in extreme poverty by 2015.

Social development:
- universal primary education in all countries by 2015;
- demonstrated progress toward gender equality and the empowerment of women by eliminating gender disparity in primary and secondary education by 2005;
- a reduction by two-thirds in the mortality rates for infants and children under age 5 and a reduction by three-fourths in maternal mortality, by 2015;
- access through the primary health-care system to reproductive health services for all individuals of appropriate ages as soon as possible and no later than 2015.

Environmental sustainability and regeneration:
- the implementation of national strategies for sustainable development in all countries by the year 2005, so as to ensure that current trends in the loss of environmental resources are effectively reversed at both global and national levels by 2015.

Source: OECD 1996.

- "alleviate the debts of the poorest and heavily indebted low-income countries at an early date";
- invite the international financial institutions to examine new approaches to multilateral debt, including debt swaps for social development;
- invite creditor countries, private banks and multilateral financial institutions to address the commercial debt problems of the least developed countries and of low and middle-income developing countries.

NGOs remained concerned about linking such debt-relief measures with International Monetary Fund and World Bank requirements that emphasize fiscal austerity and often adversely affect social sector spending. They also point out that the 20-20 initiative requires effective monitoring and data gathering of donor spending and national expenditures, in which they should be allowed to participate.

International Development Targets

One year after the Copenhagen and Beijing conferences, 21 donor governments, all members of the Development Assistance Committee of the Organisation for Economic Cooperation and Development (OECD), adopted a framework for development cooperation in the 21st century based on seven international development targets (see Box 14). "It is time to select," they said, "taking account of the many targets discussed and agreed at international fora, a limited number of indicators by which our efforts can be judged. We are proposing a global development partnership effort through which we can achieve together the following ambitious but realizable goals." These targets include a firming up of the commitment for poverty eradication agreed upon at Copenhagen and the inclusion of an environmental target. They have been endorsed by the major global development institutions, including the World Bank and the UN system.

Time-bound targets can be useful in two ways:

- as a tool to mobilize people and governments into action;
- as a benchmark to measure progress and hold governments accountable.

However, past experience with international development targets has been sobering. It is already clear that some previous targets have been missed (see Box 15). Moreover, it is not enough to hit a target once – success has to be sustained into the future. Sustained success tends to require wider systemic changes and not just a momentary inflow of resources directed towards a particular target. In addition, hitting a particular target can set back progress on dimensions of development that have not been targeted. For instance, school enrolments are easier to measure than quality of education (which is multidimensional) and therefore easier to target. But enrolments are merely a necessary condition, not a sufficient one, for ensuring that all children enjoy their right to education.

Further, it is important to interpret development targets in the context of ILO Conventions and human rights treaties. Targets can have a beneficial role in focusing efforts on SMART – Specific, Measurable, Achievable, Relevant and Time-bound – objectives and thus promote the progressive realization of human rights. But measures to achieve these targets must respect human rights. For example, it is important that strategies to halve the proportion of people living in extreme poverty do not simply focus on policies to increase the employment of the poor without regard for the conditions under which they earn their income. The right to an adequate standard of living entails the right to work in healthy and decent conditions. It also entails the right to freedom of association and collective bargaining, as is emphasized by the UN Secretary-General's report on the Role of Employment and Work in Poverty Eradication (UN 1999d).

Box 15: Shaping the 21st Century: Targets Already Missed

Basic education for all children by 2000
- goal agreed at World Conference on Education for All, 1990;
- need for additional international funding agreed;
- in real terms total aid for education sector lower in mid 1990s than before goal was agreed;
- target date for achieving the goal put back to 2015.

Development Assistance as a share of donor GNP
- UN target: 0.7%;
- G7 countries (major OECD donor countries): 0.19% in 1997;
- average of other OECD donor countries: 0.45% in 1997.

Source: McGee, Robinson and van Diesen 1998.

"We are determined to promote women's economic independence, including employment, and to eradicate the persistent and increasing burden of poverty on women."

"The involvement of women's organizations in participatory mechanisms and the role of women within relevant organizations should be emphasized to ensure that women's voices are heard in deciding policies on employment and work" (UN 1999e).

The OECD document, "Shaping the 21st Century," which sets out the international development targets, does little to relate the targets to specific human rights; and where it does mention the protection of human rights, it lists them as one of a number of "qualitative factors" which are "essential to the attainment of these measurable goals." This appears to see human rights as a way to achieve targets, rather than viewing targets as a way to achieve human rights.

In addition, the process of achieving targets should be participatory. In particular, there should be active social dialogue with poor people's and women's groups, and the effective organization of such groups should be promoted, as recommended by the UN Secretary-General's report on the Role of Employment and Work in Poverty Eradication. There is a danger that targets will be used in a top-down, mechanistic way without sufficient voice for the people that they are supposed to help. It is important to focus not just on the ends but on the means used to promote the ends. A rise in the contraceptive prevalence rate brought about by intimidation or force, or medical intervention undertaken without full consent, for example, may signal greater use of reproductive health services, but is hardly consistent with human rights.

International Development Targets and Women's Empowerment

There is only one target in the OECD document that specifically refers to progress towards gender equality, that regarding eliminating the gender disparity in primary and secondary education. This objective is to be operationalized in terms of the ratio of girls to boys in primary and secondary education and in the ratio of literate females to males in the 15-24 age group. Thus a complex and multidimensional objective is narrowed down to one target and two indicators. The OECD Website in January 2000 states that "All other indicators will be broken down by gender wherever possible, in order for a more in-depth analysis of gender inequality in the future." But no timetable is given. There is no recognition in "Shaping the 21st Century" of the continuing gender disparity in returns to education in those countries that have eliminated the gender gap. Indeed, as will be discussed further in Chapter 3, in a substantial number of countries, enrolment of girls in secondary education now outstrips enrolment of boys. But gender disparities persist in labour markets everywhere, in earnings and occupation of positions with greater decision-making responsibility.

It is also noteworthy that while all of the other targets are presented as important ends in themselves, the only target for progress towards gender equality is justified in instrumental terms: "Investment in education for girls has been shown repeatedly to be one of the most important determinants of development, with positive implications for all other measures of progress. Achieving gender equality in education will be a measure of both fairness and efficiency."

Of course, women are likely to benefit from progress towards achieving these other targets. But it is unclear how far priority is attached to women being able to shape the process of trying to achieve them. It is inconsistent that the same governments that endorsed the Beijing Platform identified development targets that make no mention of the objective, endorsed at Beijing, that 30 per cent of decision-making positions should be occupied by women. It is also notable that these targets do not include any specific goals for reducing women's poverty and economic inequality, given the widespread concern that women are disproportionately among the poor. The economic, political and social empowerment of women is not currently emphasized as an objective by this set of targets.

Despite their shortcomings, the international development targets are now well entrenched in the planning of development cooperation. They would be more useful to women if action were taken to:

- include the objective of reducing women's poverty and economic inequality;
- widen the range of targets for progress towards gender equality to include progress in reducing the gender gap in decision-making;
- interpret the targets, and strategies to achieve them, in the light of human rights obligations;
- link the process of monitoring and evaluation of progress in reaching targets to the monitoring and evaluation of progress in implementing the Platform for Action;
- press for participatory monitoring and evaluation at the country level, making use of qualitative as well as quantitative indicators, to relay women's experiences from the village, or township or city neighbourhood to national and international policy arenas.

UNICEF/Roy Witlin

From Rio to Beijing to Rome

In Rio they told us
Women play an important role in
protecting the environment

In Vienna we applauded
That women's rights are human rights

In Cairo they told us
That reproductive rights and safe
motherhood was assured to women

In Copenhagen it was said
That women's contribution to national
development would be considered

In Beijing we highlighted the themes
Of equality, development and peace

And reminded all to see the world through
women's eyes

In Istanbul we were assured
Of the right to shelter

At the World Food Summit in Rome
Women's role in food security
was recognized

Rio, Vienna, Cairo, Copenhagen,
Beijing, Istanbul and Rome
To all we have been

And now what next?

Ruth Mubiru, Uganda Women Tree Planting Movement,
Online Working Group 3, 1999
www.un.org/womenwatch

Conclusion

Many of the intergovernmental commitments at the Beijing and Copenhagen conferences to women's progress in the economy came about as a result of NGO demands for attention to distressing economic conditions in both the North and the South. Women eloquently voiced the social and economic concerns resulting from privatization and economic restructuring programmes promoted by the policies of the International Monetary Fund, the World Bank and, more recently, by the World Trade Organization. The commitments, while valuable in their recognition of the need to address structural inequalities, are fundamentally contradictory. They reflect the expectation that governments are accountable for implementing policies designed to improve the equality and well-being of their people, while at the same time, they do little to challenge the international, regional and national market forces that undermine the ability of states to implement such policies. For example:

- There is a commitment to poverty eradication and an acceptance of the need to revise macroeconomic policies to achieve this, but the actions and targets agreed by governments remain at the micro level, do not tackle the structural problems underlying the feminization of poverty, and over-emphasize poor women's access to credit for micro, small and medium-scale enterprises.
- There are commitments to ensure that international financial institutions' policies integrate social development and gender-equity principles, but there are no proposals for national and international mechanisms to monitor the practices of these key institutions, and ensure they are in compliance with human rights obligations.
- There are strong commitments to uphold women's economic and social rights, but no recognition of the erosion of state power to do so in the context of privatization.
- There is a recognition of the social problems associated with market forces, but also a continuing commitment to market-based solutions.
- There is an emphasis on promoting partnerships with the private sector, but there is hardly any reference to regulating the private sector, particularly corporations, and holding them accountable to social development goals and human rights standards. Indeed the only action specified is for national and international NGOs to establish monitoring mechanisms aimed at promoting accountability of the private sector.
- There is a commitment to people-centred sustainable development, but it is based on the assumption that economic growth will trickle down to the poor and will be sustainable.

UNICEF/John Isaac

To promote discussion, and encourage agreement on further targets, here are some possible targets for consideration:

- end the disproportionate presence of women among the poor by 2015;
- close the gender gap in the enjoyment of leisure by 2015;
- introduce schemes of social protection for informal sector workers by 2015;
- raise women's share of administrative and managerial positions to at least 30 per cent by 2005 and to 50 per cent by 2015;
- raise women's share of seats in elected assemblies at the local level to at least 30 per cent by 2015;
- ensure that all women employees earn a living wage by 2015.

- There is a commitment to the goal of full employment, but the means emphasized to achieve it are trade and investment liberalization. The role of governments in generating employment is limited to investment in human resources and entrepreneurial activity.
- There is a recognition of the importance of gender equality in development, but there is a tendency to simply add women on to inherently male-biased economic analyses and policies. For example, the concept of full employment is based on a male breadwinner model and does not address the role that women play in providing unpaid care for their families and communities and the double burden that women carry as a result of their entry into paid employment.
- There is a recognition of the links between women's unremunerated work and their increasing poverty, but the solution proposed is to develop a methodology to measure unremunerated work without specifying how to redress the inequities uncovered by the data and to use such data in macroeconomic policy-making.

Five years after the Copenhagen and Beijing agreements, there is a need to address these inconsistencies. An important step forward would be to identify further specific targets against which progress in implementing the Platform for Action can be judged. Even if all the data are not currently available, new targets will act as a stimulus for countries and international development agencies to produce them.

Box 16: Web-Based Sources of Information

Women's Human Rights

- Women's Human Rights Net: www.whrnet.org
- UN High Commission for Human Rights: www.unhchr.ch/
- UN CEDAW: www.un.org/womenwatch/daw/cedaw
- UN Division of the Advancement of Women: www.un.org/womenwatch/daw
- UNIFEM: www.undp.org/unifem/Beijing+5
- International Women's Rights Action Watch: www.igc.org/iwraw
- International Women's Rights Action Watch Asia Pacific: www.women-connect-asia.com/iwraw/index.htm

Monitoring Conference Commitments

- ILO: www.ilo.org/public/english/10ilc/ilc87/reports.htm
- OECD: www.oecd.org/dea/indicators
- Social Watch: www.socwatch.org.uy
- Women's Environment and Development Organization: www.wedo.org
- Women'sNet: www.womensnet.org.za
- Asian Women's Resource Network: jca.ax.apc.org/aworc or www.sequel.net/~isis
- Canadian Research Institute for the Advancement of Women: www.sympatico.ca

Chapter 3

Assessing the Progress of Women: Linking Targets to Indicators

Daranne Jacobson

Introduction

There are many ways to assess the progress of women. One way is through women's personal stories; another is through statistics and indicators. A complete picture requires both narratives and numbers. A global assessment, however, can tell only a limited number of stories. Moreover, numerical indicators have proven to be powerful advocacy tools when linked to the fulfillment of specific commitments regarding women's progress. As Patricia Licuanan, of South East Asia Watch, explains:

> *The extent to which a country has been able to impact on women's specific issues and to narrow the existing gender gap is what may be called progress. 'Progress' indicates distance from or nearness to specific outcomes or targets desired/aimed for in each of the critical areas of concern* (1999).

This report therefore emphasizes statistical measures, following the precedent of the Human Development Reports and Social Watch in presenting indicators derived from statistics in existing international databases (see Box 1). It also presents at least part of the underlying complexity of women's experiences in brief personal stories, which form a counterpoint to the tables and charts.

The indicators include both those that are gender-sensitive (i.e., constructed so as to compare the position of women and men at a point in time and over time, and therefore focus on gender gaps) and those that are women-specific, recording the absolute position of women at particular points in time (see Box 2). The indicators are all quantitative, as qualitative indicators are not readily available for global comparisons and are more appropriate for local-level assessments (see Box 3 for definitions and examples).

"Statistics in the hands of activists have power."

— Ela Bhatt, SEWA, 1999

Box 1: Social Watch

"The good news is that social indicators are showing significant progress in over 60 countries" – this was the conclusion of Social Watch, an organization set up to evaluate progress towards fulfillment of commitments made at Copenhagen and Beijing at the end of five years. "The bad news is that progress is too slow to reach the goals in another 70 countries. Thirteen countries are in the same shape or worse off today than they were in 1990, and for almost 40 countries, the data is insufficient to say anything, which probably reflects an even worse situation."

Through its Annual Report, Social Watch contributes to a process of citizen oversight of governments, UN agencies and multilateral organizations in their implementation of the Beijing and Copenhagen agreements. In 1999 this report stated, as it had the previous year:

"While the goals targeted are feasible, many countries have failed to make a sufficient effort. The assistance promised has yet to materialize, the participation of citizens is paltry, and globalization is not benefiting those who need it most."

Source: *Social Watch* 1999.

Box 2: Gender-Sensitive and Sex-Specific Indicators

Gender-sensitive indicators compare the situation of males to that of females, and show an aspect of their relative advantage (disadvantage). They can be constructed in several ways:

- Female share of a total (when it is evident that the total comprises the female share and the male share): 50% indicates gender equality.
  Example: Women's share of seats in legislative bodies.

- Ratio between a female and a male characteristic: 1 indicates gender equality.
  Example: The ratio between girls' and boys' school enrolment rates.

- Female characteristic as percentage of male characteristic: 100% indicates gender equality.
  Example: Average female weekly earnings as percentage of male weekly earnings.

- Difference between the female characteristic and the male characteristic: 0 indicates gender equality.
  Example: Average number of hours women spend on housework minus average number of hours men spend on housework.

Sex-specific indicators are also needed:
- Some conditions are experienced only by one sex.
  Example: Maternal mortality.

- Knowledge is needed about absolute levels of achievement as well as gender gaps.
  Example: Women's average real earnings; men's average real earnings.

Box 3: Quantitative and Qualitative Indicators

Quantitative indicators can be defined as measures of quantity, such as the number of people in a village who have obtained loans.

Qualitative indicators can be defined as people's judgements and perceptions about a subject, such as the extent to which loans have enabled them to improve their standard of living or bargaining power within the household.

Quantitative indicators focus on areas that are easier to quantify, such as employment rates or education levels. Because of this, quantitative indicators are usually constructed from formal surveys, such as censuses, labour-force surveys or administrative records. Quantitative indicators are useful for showing how typical an outcome is or what the average outcome is. Qualitative indicators, because they focus on attitudes and perceptions, are typically constructed from less formal sources, such as public hearings, attitude surveys, interviews, participatory rural appraisal, participant observation and sociological or anthropological fieldwork. Qualitative indicators are useful for understanding processes, but frequently do not show how typical or widespread are the views expressed.

Source: Adapted from Canadian International Development Agency 1996.

Time Frame for Assessment

Progress implies change over time. In this report, the time frame is from the mid-1980s to the latest year for which data is available (generally 1997). The aim is to cover the period since the Third World Conference on Women in 1985 in Nairobi. The period since the Fourth World Conference on Women in 1995 is too short, given the time lags in the availability of statistics, which means that for most indicators 1997 is the latest year available. Within this time frame, long-term structural changes and cyclical changes and one-off changes are all interwoven. During this period, globalization intensified; there were financial crises in a number of countries in East Asia and elsewhere; countries in Eastern Europe and the former Soviet Union made the transition to market economies; and many countries in Sub-Saharan Africa were embroiled in armed conflict and burdened by increasing levels of debt.

Women will want to make assessments at different levels of aggregation and in different contexts.

- At the *local* level, women can conduct context-specific participatory assessments with an emphasis on the use of qualitative indicators. The smaller the locality, the easier it is to select a reasonably representative group.

- At the *national* level, women can draw upon nationally representative surveys such as censuses and household, enterprise and labour-force surveys, and press for statistics that are disaggregated not only by sex but also by age, class, ethnic group and location.

- At the *regional* level, women can prioritize indicators that reflect regional social, economic and political characteristics and use regional databases.

- At the *global* level, women can focus on a few key indicators for a wide range of countries.

A global assessment cannot capture the rich diversity of local-level and national-level assessments, but it can put each country into a global context. A global assessment also relies on global databases, which have some limitations, including differences in the ways in which data is collected in different countries (definitions, coverage, quality of enumeration) and uneven coverage (much more data is available for richer countries than for poorer countries). This report uses the Women's Indicators and Statistics Database (Wistat) compiled by the UN Statistical Division from data collected by UN agencies and other international bodies, and data from UNESCO and ILO databases and the Human Development Reports (see Annex: Technical Notes).

What Does This Report Try to Measure?

Measuring the empowerment of women is difficult, because the concept itself is complex and multidimensional, with both tangible and intangible dimensions. There is no universally agreed method for identifying and measuring its components. A recent study of micro-level attempts to measure women's empowerment for the UN Research Institute for Social Development highlights many of the problems and dangers (Kabeer 1999). The study distinguishes between resources available to women, the agency they are able to exercise in using these resources, and the achievements that are the outcome. It recommends that all three dimensions be considered simultaneously in assessments of women's empowerment.

A global assessment requires a different approach, since it is not possible to do an in-depth case study of the whole world. As discussed in

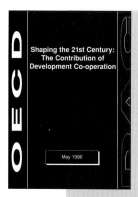

Box 4: OECD Working Set of Core Indicators

Economic well-being

- Incidence of extreme poverty: population below $1 per day
- Poverty gap ratio: incidence times depth of poverty
- Inequality: poorest fifth's share of national consumption
- Child malnutrition: prevalence of underweight under 5 year-olds

Social development

- Net enrolment in primary education
- Completion of 4th grade of primary education
- Literacy rate of 15-24 year-olds
- Ratio of girls to boys in primary and secondary education
- Ratio of literate females to males (15-24 year-olds)
- Infant mortality rate
- Under 5 mortality rate
- Maternal mortality ratio
- Births attended by skilled health personnel
- Contraceptive prevalence rate
- HIV prevalence in 15-24 year-old pregnant women

Environmental sustainability and regeneration

- Countries with national sustainable development strategies
- Population with access to safe water
- Intensity of freshwater use
- Biodiversity: land area protected
- Energy efficiency: GDP per unit of energy use
- Carbon dioxide emissions
- Forest area as % of land area
- Mangrove areas
- Urban air pollution

Source: OECD Website: www.oecd.org/dac/indicators.

Chapter 1, this report is informed by the idea that progress for women requires a twofold empowerment of women: the creation of conditions (by a variety of social actors) to enable women to enjoy autonomy and exercise their human rights; and women themselves engaging in a process of critical and collective re-examination of their lives that changes their perceptions of who they are, what rights they have and what they can and should do. The report does not attempt to try to measure the second aspect of empowerment. It does not try to assess the extent to which women are experiencing increases in their self-esteem, their sense of their capacity to change their lives or their sense of being able to take greater control over their lives. Instead it focuses on measuring obstacles to women's ability to enjoy autonomy and exercise their human rights and the extent to which such obstacles are increasing or diminishing. It thus follows the Human Development Reports in focusing on women's capabilities, on what women are actually doing and being.

The aim is to provide indicators not of the extent of women's self-empowerment but of the conditions in which their self-empowerment takes place, along with indicators that self-empowered women can use to hold governments, business corporations and international institutions accountable for the fulfilment of their commitments.

A number of indicators have already been proposed for monitoring the follow-up on UN conference commitments, including:

- OECD Development Indicators;
- Regional Initiatives to Monitor the Beijing Platform for Action;
- UN Common Country Assessment Indicators.

OECD Development Indicators

The OECD Development Assistance Committee has identified a set of 24 core indicators to measure progress in achieving the international development targets (see Box 4). While this indicator set is the most widely used in international development cooperation, it has a number of shortcomings in terms of accounting for women's progress. For example:

- Only 2 of the 24 are designed to measure progress towards gender equality and women's empowerment, both related to education.
- The indicators for measuring progress in reducing poverty are not specified in a way that addresses the extent to which poverty is "feminized," in the sense of women being disproportionately among the poor.
- There are no indicators on the gender balance in decision-making or on gender equality in the labour market.
- They are being applied to monitor progress only in recipient countries, not in donor countries.

Regional Initiatives to Monitor the Beijing Platform for Action

In 1999, two regional menus of potential indicators were designed to follow up on Platform for Action commitments. Neither included actual measurements, but both provide numerous ideas for governments and NGOs to draw upon. The Economic Commission for Latin America and the

UNICEF/Maggie Murray-Lee

Caribbean (ECLAC) produced a booklet identifying one or more gender-sensitive indicators for each of the Platform's twelve areas of concern, including a precise specification of the indicator and the type of instrument required to collect the data. Altogether just over 60 potential indicators are suggested, all of them quantitative and chosen on the basis of current availability of information and official statistics.

Eight countries in the region are already using this framework and have identified priority indicators from it to use in future monitoring of their performance. Constraints in the availability of statistics in the region mean that it will be much easier to monitor progress in urban areas than in rural areas. (For more information, see www.eclac.cl).

The Economic and Social Commission for Asia and the Pacific invited Patricia Licuanan, chair of South East Asia Watch, to produce a paper on Monitoring and Evaluation Strategies for the Empowerment of Women for the 1999 regional meeting to review implementation of the Platform. Licuanan suggests over 100 potential indicators, in the context of a framework for policy monitoring and evaluation, and the ways in which women's NGOs can make use of data to monitor and evaluate women's progress. For each critical area of concern, she presents examples of potential gender-sensitive indicators, which are divided into three types – input indicators, performance or process indicators and outcome or progress indicators (Licuanan 1999). She does not indicate the extent to which data is currently available in the region to actually operationalize these indicators.

Licuanan also recommends a qualitative approach to assessing women's empowerment, designed to reveal the extent to which a woman has a sense of control of her life, greater autonomy and independence, through a set of open-ended questions, such as: Looking at your life in the past few years, what has changed? What difference have laws and programmes introduced to implement the Platform made in your life? How do you feel about these changes? Focus groups can be used to discuss these questions at local and national levels. But it is a complex undertaking to collect qualitative data of this kind on a representative basis, even at a national level. And given the lack of national-level data, it was not feasible for UNIFEM to attempt to collect information of this kind for each country. Moreover, unless women have experienced a process of self-empowerment and are well-informed

about the content of the Platform, their answers may reflect resignation to constraints and impoverishment, a lifetime of "making the best of a bad job."

UN Common Country Assessment Indicator Framework

In 1999, the United Nations agencies selected a set of 40 indicators to guide the Common Country Assessments, made in partnership with countries in which UN development cooperation takes place, and to assist in monitoring follow-up to the UN conferences. The indicators cover income-poverty, food security and nutrition, health and mortality, reproductive health, child health and welfare, education, employment and sustainable livelihoods, housing and basic household amenities, environment, drug control and crime prevention and gender equality and women's empowerment (see Box 5, p. 66). This indicator framework measures progress towards gender equality and women's empowerment, in terms of political and economic as well as education indicators, and includes a commitment to disaggregate other indicators by sex. The framework is not designed to measure women's self-empowerment, and the selection of indicators was constrained by availability of national-level statistics. But it does contain many indicators for assessing the extent to which obstacles to women's ability to enjoy a range of ways of living their lives are diminishing.

Obstacles to Gender Equality and Empowerment of Women: Three UN Indicators

This report presents the first global assessment of obstacles to gender equality and women's empowerment using three key indicators identified in the UN indicator framework: the ratio of girls' enrolment ratio to boys' enrolment ratio in secondary education; women's share of parliamentary representation; and women's share of paid employment in industry and services (i.e., non-agricultural activities). It compares achievements across countries at one point in time, as well as progress within countries over time. Other organizations, such as UNFPA and UNICEF, are using other indicators in the UN framework to track improvements in women's and girls' health, reproductive rights and primary education.

To assess current achievements, the latest available data (usually 1997) is used, with countries in each region listed in tables of figures according to their level of achievement. (Ranking should be interpreted only as approximate, because data is not always strictly comparable). To assess progress over time, comparisons are made between the latest available data and data for 1985 (or the mid-80s, more generally). Information on progress is presented in a variety of charts and in relation to targets (where they exist).

Box 5: UN Common Country Assessment Indicators: UN Development Assistance Framework

Indicators (disaggregated by sex)

Income-Poverty
- Poverty headcount ratio (% of population below $1 dollar a day)
- Poverty headcount ratio (% of population below national poverty line)
- Poverty gap ratio
- Poorest fifth's share of national consumption

Food Security and Nutrition
- % of children under age 5 suffering from malnutrition
- % of population below minimum level of dietary energy consumption (caloric intake in context of food balance sheet)
- % of household income spent on food for the poorest quintile

Health and Mortality
- % population with access to primary health care services
- Estimated HIV adult prevalence rate
- HIV prevalence in pregnant women under age 25 who receive antenatal care in capital cities/major urban areas
- Infant mortality rate
- Under 5 mortality rate

Reproductive Health
- Maternal mortality ratio
- % of births attended by skilled health personnel
- Contraceptive prevalence rate

Child Health and Welfare
- % of 1-year-old children immunized against measles
- % of children under age 15 who are working

Education
- Net primary enrolment or attendance ratio
- % of pupils starting grade 1 who reach grade 5

- Adult literacy rate
- Literacy rate of 15-24 year-olds

Gender Equality and Women's Empowerment
- Ratio of girls to boys in secondary school enrolment
- Female share (%) of paid employment in non-agricultural activities
- % of seats held by women in national parliament

Employment and Sustainable Livelihood
- Ratio of employment to population of working age
- Unemployment rate
- Informal sector employment as % of total employment

Housing and Basic Household Amenities and Facilities
- No. of persons per room, or average floor area per person
- % of population with (sustainable) access to safe drinking water
- % of population with access to adequate sanitation

Environment (Indicator specification under review)
- Carbon dioxide emissions (per capita)
- Biodiversity: land area protected
- GDP per unit of energy use
- Arable land per capita
- % change in km^2 of forest land in past ten years
- % of population relying on traditional fuels for energy use

Drug Control and Crime Prevention
- Area under illegal cultivation of coca, opium poppy and cannabis
- Seizures of illicit drugs
- Prevalence of drug abuse
- No. of crimes per 100,000 inhabitants

Source: UN Website: www.dgo.org/index2.html.

Lagging School Enrolment

Education is essential for improving women's living standards and enabling women to exercise greater "voice" in decision-making in the family, the community, the place of paid work and the public arena of politics (see Box 6). Literacy and other basic skills are absolutely vital to women's empowerment; and without the skills acquired in secondary education, women cannot obtain better paid employment. As noted in Chapter 2, a target to close the gender gap in primary and secondary education by 2005 was adopted at both the Social Summit and the Beijing Women's Conference and has also been incorporated into the international development targets. The right to education is also one of the rights specified in the Covenant on Economic, Social and Cultural Rights.

In general, enrolment ratios tend to give an over-optimistic picture of the degree to which young people are educated, and the distortion is probably greater for girls than for boys. In particular, data on enrolment ratios:

- show how many students enrol but not how many attend. Drop-out rates can be high, especially for girls, and tend to increase when economic conditions worsen;
- do not show whether the education girls and boys receive is free of gender stereotypes that perpetuate gender inequality;
- do not show how well-qualified young people are when they leave school.

Box 6: Girls' Education in India

Manju Senapaty carried out research on the implications of economic reform in India for the education of poor girls. She spent some time in Naktar village in Madhya Pradesh, where she talked with poor women about the education of their children. She reports:

"They all said that they wanted to educate both their daughters and their sons. But the reasons for educating a son and a daughter were different. They wanted to educate their daughters so that 'she will get some intelligence' and many mothers said that 'we do not want them to suffer as we did, she can at least write a letter when she is mistreated in her (in laws') house' [i.e., the house where she lives after marriage with her husband and his parents]. These reasons suggested clearly that women were reflecting on their own lives and the suffering they may have experienced because of their inability to even write to their own families in times of distress. For questions on their reasons for educating a son, the standard answer given by most women was that 'if he is educated, he might get some job,' with an implication that this would provide them with security in their old age."

Source: Senapaty 1997: 314.

Nevertheless, it is important to monitor enrolment ratios as an indicator of the strength of the barriers that keep girls out of school (including structural adjustment policies and family poverty as well as social and cultural norms).

As shown in Chart 3.1 (p. 68) the most serious gender gap in terms of secondary education enrolment is in Sub-Saharan Africa, where the relative disadvantage of girls has been eliminated in only 5 out of 34 countries listed. In Northern Africa the number is slightly higher, 1 out of 5 countries, while in Central and Western Asia it rises to 4 out of 11, and in Asia and the Pacific it is much the same, at 8 out of 21 countries. The Latin America and Caribbean region has a much higher success rate, with 18 out of 26 countries reporting a ratio of 100 or more. Eastern Europe appears to do best, with 8 out 9 countries reaching a ratio of 100 or more, while Western Europe and Other Developed Countries are somewhat lower with 19 out of 23 countries reaching this level.

Chart 3.1 also shows a disparity to the disadvantage of boys (ratio greater than 100) in numerous countries, including some in every region except Northern Africa. In all, 38 per cent of the countries listed have a female/male ratio of more than 100. In 11 per cent of the countries there is equality with a ratio of 100, and in 51 per cent girls

are still at a disadvantage. This "reverse gender gap" is particularly pronounced in Latin America and the Caribbean, where 18 out of 26 countries for which data is available have ratios greater than 100. It appears that in some countries, especially more rural countries, boys may be called upon to join the labour force at an earlier age than girls, while recent studies in some more urbanized countries suggest that cultural factors — such as prevalent cultural ideas of masculinity — are encouraging boys to drop out at greater rates (Kimmel 2000).

Table 3.1 (p. 69) presents the absolute level of girls' net enrolment in secondary school in 1997 where available, and otherwise uses the gross enrolment ratio in 1996. (For a few countries neither type of data was available from the UNESCO database.) It shows that within each of the developing regions, some countries have achieved a high level of enrolment, comparable with that in the developed countries. This is true even in Sub-Saharan Africa, where levels are for the most part very low.

Comparing enrolment levels in Table 3.1 with girls' enrolment ratios in Chart 3.1 shows that in some countries, the gender gap has been almost eliminated but at very low levels. Examples include Haiti, where the girls' to boys' enrolment ratio is 95 but the girls' net enrolment ratio is only 33.2; Cape Verde, where the girls' to boys' enrolment ratio is 94 but the girls' net enrolment ratio is only 35.5; and El Salvador, where the girls' to boys' enrolment ratio is 102 but the but girls' net enrolment ratio is 36.7.

Chart 3.2 (pp. 70-71) shows progress in female enrolment at the secondary level. While the majority of countries have made progress, some report deterioration. In fact, the data suggest that the only region where there has been no deterioration is Northern Africa. In every other region female enrolment ratios have declined: in 10 out of 33 countries in Sub-Saharan Africa; 7 out of 11 in

Chart 3.1: Secondary Net Enrolment Ratio, female/male, 1997

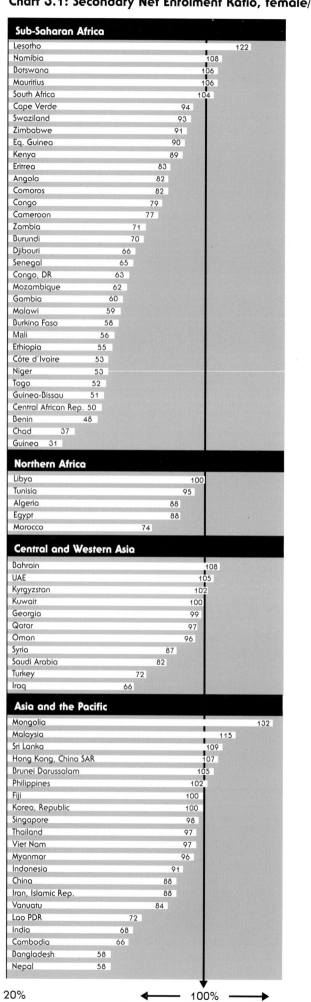

Sub-Saharan Africa

Lesotho	122
Namibia	108
Botswana	106
Mauritius	106
South Africa	104
Cape Verde	94
Swaziland	93
Zimbabwe	91
Eq. Guinea	90
Kenya	89
Eritrea	83
Angola	82
Comoros	82
Congo	79
Cameroon	77
Zambia	71
Burundi	70
Djibouti	66
Senegal	65
Congo, DR	63
Mozambique	62
Gambia	60
Malawi	59
Burkina Faso	58
Mali	56
Ethiopia	55
Côte d'Ivoire	53
Niger	53
Togo	52
Guinea-Bissau	51
Central African Rep.	50
Benin	48
Chad	37
Guinea	31

Northern Africa

Libya	100
Tunisia	95
Algeria	88
Egypt	88
Morocco	74

Central and Western Asia

Bahrain	108
UAE	105
Kyrgyzstan	102
Kuwait	100
Georgia	99
Qatar	97
Oman	96
Syria	87
Saudi Arabia	82
Turkey	72
Iraq	66

Asia and the Pacific

Mongolia	132
Malaysia	115
Sri Lanka	109
Hong Kong, China SAR	107
Brunei Darussalam	105
Philippines	102
Fiji	100
Korea, Republic	100
Singapore	98
Thailand	97
Viet Nam	97
Myanmar	96
Indonesia	91
China	88
Iran, Islamic Rep.	88
Vanuatu	84
Lao PDR	72
India	68
Cambodia	66
Bangladesh	58
Nepal	58

20%   ⟵   100%   ⟶
       Gender gap   Gender gap   Reverse
                     closed   gender gap

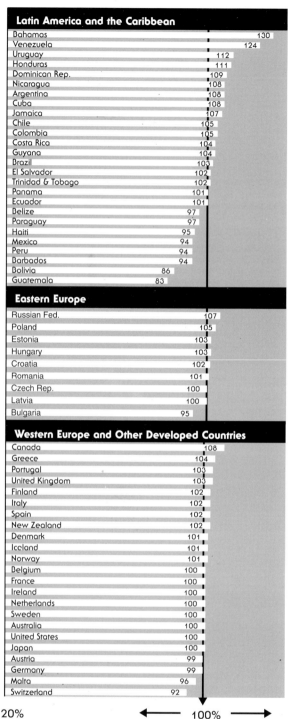

Latin America and the Caribbean

Bahamas	130
Venezuela	124
Uruguay	112
Honduras	111
Dominican Rep.	109
Nicaragua	108
Argentina	108
Cuba	108
Jamaica	107
Chile	105
Colombia	105
Costa Rica	104
Guyana	104
Brazil	103
El Salvador	102
Trinidad & Tobago	102
Panama	101
Ecuador	101
Belize	97
Paraguay	97
Haiti	95
Mexico	94
Peru	94
Barbados	94
Bolivia	86
Guatemala	83

Eastern Europe

Russian Fed.	107
Poland	105
Estonia	103
Hungary	103
Croatia	102
Romania	101
Czech Rep.	100
Latvia	100
Bulgaria	95

Western Europe and Other Developed Countries

Canada	108
Greece	104
Portugal	103
United Kingdom	103
Finland	102
Italy	102
Spain	102
New Zealand	102
Denmark	101
Iceland	101
Norway	101
Belgium	100
France	100
Ireland	100
Netherlands	100
Sweden	100
Australia	100
United States	100
Japan	100
Austria	99
Germany	99
Malta	96
Switzerland	92

20%   ⟵   100%   ⟶
       Gender gap   Gender gap   Reverse
                     closed   gender gap

Source: Based on tabulations prepared by
UNESCO for the Human Development Report Office,
Human Development Report 1999, table 25, pp. 229-32.

Table 3.1: Female Enrolment in Secondary Education, 1997, 1996

Sub-Saharan Africa

Net Ratio, 1997

South Africa	96.9
Botswana	91.3
Namibia	83.9
Lesotho	80.3
Swaziland	78.8
Congo, Republic	74.3
Mauritius	69.9
Eq. Guinea	64.8
Kenya	57.4
Zimbabwe	56.3
Malawi	53.9
Togo	40.0
Cape Verde	35.5
Zambia	34.9
Cameroon	34.7
Eritrea	34.3
Comoros	32.2
Congo, DR	28.6
Angola	28.0
Gambia	25.1
Côte d'Ivoire	23.6
Benin	18.3
Ethiopia	17.5
Mozambique	17.1
Guinea-Bissau	16.4
Djibouti	15.6
Senegal	15.5
Burundi	14.1
Mali	12.9
Central African Republic	12.7
Chad	9.6
Burkina Faso	9.4
Guinea	6.9
Niger	6.5

Gross Ratio, 1996

Nigeria	31.1
Ghana	24.1
Sudan	19.1
Madagascar	12.7
Sierra Leone	12.1
Rwanda	11.5
Mauritania	11.0
Uganda	8.7
Liberia	8.1
Tanzania, UR	4.9
Somalia	3.5

Northern Africa

Net Ratio, 1997

Libya	99.9
Tunisia	72.4
Egypt	70.1
Algeria	64.0
Morocco	31.9

Central and Western Asia

Net Ratio, 1997

Bahrain	90.8
UAE	79.9
Kyrgyzstan	78.7
Georgia	75.3
Qatar	72.0
Oman	65.1
Kuwait	63.2
Saudi Arabia	52.9
Turkey	48.5
Syria	39.4
Iraq	33.8

Gross Ratio, 1996

Turkmenistan	111.1
Kazakhstan	88.9
Uzbekistan	87.6
Israel	87.4
Armenia	85.9
Lebanon	85.5
Azerbaijan	81.1
Tajikistan	71.7
Yemen	14.3

Asia and the Pacific

Net Ratio, 1997

Korea, Republic	99.0
Fiji	84.4
Brunei Darussalam	83.9
Sri Lanka	79.3
Philippines	78.5
Iran, I.R.	75.8
Singapore	74.8
Hong Kong, China	71.5
Malaysia	68.5
China	65.1
Mongolia	63.7
Viet Nam	54.2
Indonesia	53.4
Myanmar	53.0
Lao, PDR	52.9
India	48.0
Thailand	46.9

Net Ratio, 1997

Nepal	39.7
Vanuatu	38.8
Cambodia	30.9
Bangladesh	15.6

Gross Ratio, 1996

Samoa (Western)	65.8
Maldives	64.9
Pakistan	21.0
Afghanistan	11.4
Papua New Guinea	11.2

Latin America and the Caribbean

Net Ratio, 1997

Bahamas	95.9
Uruguay	88.7
Chile	87.2
Barbados	83.1
Dominican Rep.	82.1
Peru	81.1
Argentina	79.8
Colombia	78.2
Guyana	76.4
Cuba	72.6
Trinidad & Tobago	72.2
Jamaica	72.1
Panama	71.7
Brazil	67.0
Mexico	64.0
Belize	62.6
Paraguay	60.1
Costa Rica	56.9
Venezuela	54.2
Nicaragua	52.6
Ecuador	51.3
Honduras	37.9
Bolivia	37.1
El Salvador	36.7
Haiti	33.2
Guatemala	31.7

Eastern Europe

Net Ratio, 1997

Czech Rep.	99.9
Hungary	98.2
Russian Fed.	90.7
Poland	88.5
Estonia	87.4
Latvia	80.5
Romania	76.3
Bulgaria	75.4
Croatia	73.0

Gross Ratio, 1996

Slovakia	96.0
Ukraine	95.6
Belarus	95.4
Slovenia	93.9
Lithuania	87.5
Moldova, Republic	80.7
Macedonia, FYR	51.1
Albania	35.7

Western Europe and Other Developed Countries

Net Ratio, 1997

Sweden	99.9
Netherlands	99.9
Japan	99.9
Ireland	99.9
Belgium	99.9
France	98.6
Norway	98.0
Austria	97.1
United States	96.2
Finland	96.2
Italy	96.0
Australia	96.0
Denmark	95.4
Germany	94.9
Canada	94.4
New Zealand	94.0
United Kingdom	93.2
Greece	93.1
Spain	93.0
Portugal	91.0
Iceland	88.1
Malta	83.3
Switzerland	80.3

Sources: Net enrolment data is based on tabulations prepared by UNESCO for the Human Development Report Office, *Human Development Report, 1999*, table 25, pp. 229-32; gross enrolment data: UNESCO Website:http://unescostat.unesco.org/.

Chart 3.2: Change in Secondary Level Female Net Enrolment Ratio, 1985-1997 (1985=100)

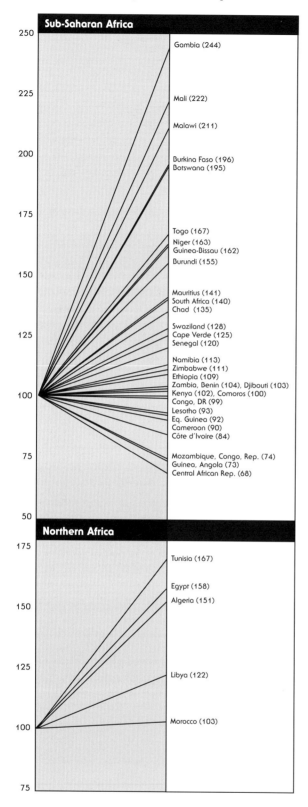

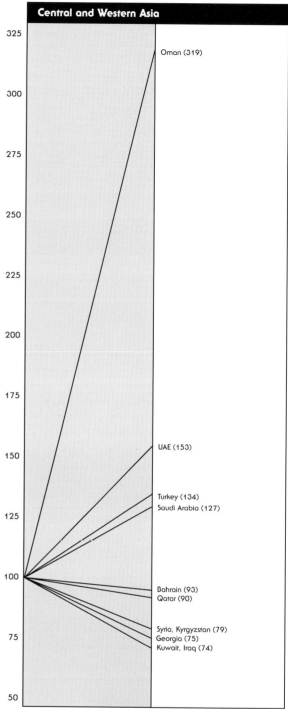

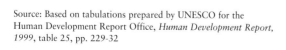

Source: Based on tabulations prepared by UNESCO for the
Human Development Report Office, *Human Development Report,
1999*, table 25, pp. 229-32

Suzette Mitchell

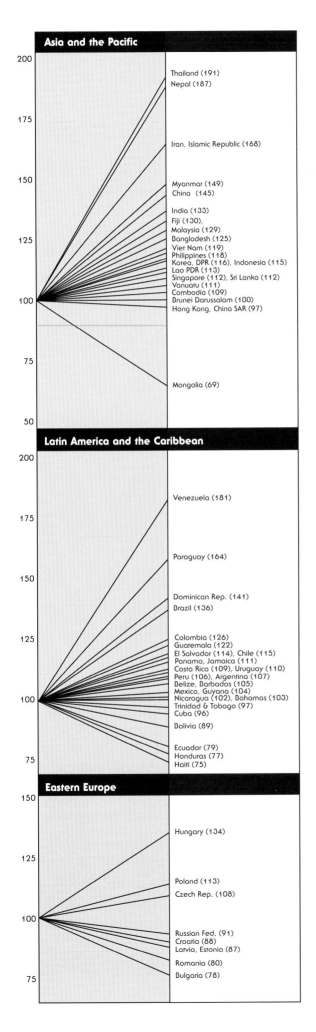

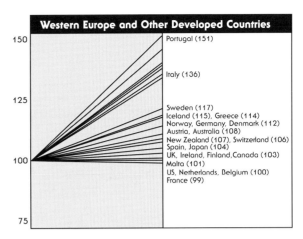

Central and Western Asia; 2 out of 21 in Asia and the Pacific; and 6 out of 26 in Latin America and the Caribbean. In Eastern Europe, the ratio declined in as many as 6 out of 9 countries. Western Europe and Other Developed Countries managed to more or less stand still: a decline was shown in 1 out of 23 countries.

Enrolment is only the first step in education. Gender-sensitive indicators are also needed for completion rates and on patterns of study, but they are not yet widely available. Closing the gender gap in education is necessary for achieving gender equality but it is far from sufficient. Moreover, despite the link between education and income, studies from all regions indicate that equal years of education do not translate into equality of job opportunities for women and men (see Box 7, p. 72). Males everywhere tend to get better jobs than women with the same years of education. One reason for this is the persistence of a gender gap in science and technology, while others pertain to on-going gender discrimination in employment.

Unequal Shares of Wage and Salaried Employment

There are no internationally agreed quantitative, time-bound targets for gender equality and women's empowerment in employment. Employment, like education, is multidimensional, and there are many relevant indicators — but for many of them data is available only for a limited number of countries or not at all. For instance, there is no indicator available in UN databases of women's and men's average real earnings (i.e., adjusted for price increases) or of the proportion of women and men who have employment that pays a living wage and offers social protection.

The UN Indicator Framework selected women's share of paid employment in industry and services as the indicator to track progress towards gender equality in employment. (Agriculture was excluded because data on wage and salaried work in agriculture are particularly unreliable, and most wage and salaried work tends to be outside agriculture.) It is important to note that this indicator does not,

United Nations/Milton Grant

Box 7: Gender Differences in Financial Returns to Education

In Jamaica, girls are better educated than boys. At the primary level, there is equality in enrolment, but at the secondary level, more girls are enrolled than boys (almost 75 per cent of Jamaican girls are enrolled in secondary school). On average, girls and young women obtain better examination results than boys and young men. But in the labour market, women experience higher levels of unemployment than men do, and are much more concentrated than men are in low-paying occupations: 80 per cent of women are reported as being at the lowest salary level, compared to 20 per cent of men (Jamaica Employees Federation 1995).

A similar picture emerges for the Philippines. About 56 per cent of university students are women, but a 1992 report from the Government Institute of Labour Studies reports that more college-educated women than college-educated men earn below the minimum wage. In the top three industries for average salaries, men make up the majority of the workforce. Beatrice Cabrera, head of the Guidance and Counseling Center of Far Eastern University, reports that "the companies that come in to recruit sometimes do have a preference for males or females. Women, for example, are wanted for clerks and executive secretaries, since they are (deemed) more patient than men" (Balgos 1998).

In Latin America, where girls have reached higher levels of education in many countries, research has shown that the belief that women's lower earnings result from their lower levels of education is a myth. On average, women in the labour market have a higher level of education than men. At the highest educational level (13+years of schooling), women's labour-force participation is almost the same as that of men, but their incomes are well below those of men. In no country do men and women with the same level of education receive identical wages (Arriagada 1998).

"The relative disadvantage in terms of hourly pay between adult women and men is equivalent to some four years formal education" (ECLAC1993).

and is not intended to show improvements or declines in women's standard of living, either on average or for particular groups. Rather, it shows whether women are being enabled to occupy a higher proportion of waged and salaried employment (rather than, for instance, employment on an unpaid basis in family enterprises). It signals the extent to which obstacles to women working in such jobs are crumbling.

The advantage of this indicator is that:

- it focuses on women's share of paid jobs in areas of expanding employment;
- because of the way the data are collected, it is more likely to reflect women's share of better paying formal employment than informal employment;
- it includes employment across the occupational spectrum, not just in "elite" jobs.

The indicator has several limitations, including:

- an increase in women's share of paid employment will not usually be matched by an equivalent increase in women's share of national income because women tend to be paid less than men;

- an increase in women's share of paid employment generally adds to women's total workload, taking into account women's unpaid care-giving work for family members as well as their paid work. Women gain in terms of cash, but lose in terms of time;
- women from less well-off families are often pressured to take poor-quality, low-paying jobs in industry and services to make up for falling family income, rather than through their own choice. This is particularly likely in situations of economic crisis and structural adjustment.

Table 3.2 presents women's share of paid employment, using the latest available ILO data. It is evident that little ILO data is available for this employment indicator for countries in Africa, about

UNDP/Sid Kane

80 per cent of which lack data, and countries in Central and Western Asia, about 74 per cent of which lack data. In addition, data is available for only 46 per cent of the countries of Asia and the Pacific. The gap between the availability of data in UN databases for the gender equality in education indicator and the gender equality in paid employment indicator is striking. There is, however, even less data available for other employment indicators.

There are only a few countries in the world where women's share of paid employment is around 50 per cent, and a handful in which it is somewhat higher than 50 per cent.

Chart 3.3 (p. 74) shows changes in female share of paid employment in industry and services. In most countries for which data is available the share has increased or stayed the same. It has fallen in the Ukraine, and in Lithuania and Estonia (see Box 8). The biggest increases (15 or more percentage points) were in Italy (23% to 38%), Portugal (30% to 46%), Slovenia (34% to 49%) and Sri Lanka (24% to 44%).

Women's entry into waged and salaried work in industry and services does not necessarily mean that they escape from subordination within their families.

Box 8: Women's Employment in Transition Economies

The proportion of adult women who are members of the labour force (the female participation rate or economic activity rate) was lower in 1997 than in 1985 in all transition countries. In some countries, men's participation rates fell too, but not by as much as women's rates. Women's employment fell by 40 per cent in Hungary, 31 per cent in Estonia, 33 per cent in Latvia, 24 per cent in Lithuania, 21 per cent in the Russian Federation, 16 per cent in Slovenia, 12 per cent in the Czech Republic and 13 per cent in Poland.

Women in the labour force lost jobs in the expanding and remunerative sectors of banking, insurance and real estate and became more concentrated in low-paid public services such as education and health. Women, despite high levels of education, are generally doing worse than men under increased competition in the labour market.

Source: Ruminksa-Zimny 1999.

Table 3.2: Female Share of Paid Employment in Industry and Services (latest data available)

Sub-Saharan Africa	Female share (%)
Botswana	38
Mauritius	37
Swaziland	33
Kenya	32
Ethiopia	28
Côte d'Ivoire	23
Zimbabwe	17
Burkina Faso	12
Malawi	11
Niger	9
Chad	5

Northern Africa	Female share (%)
Egypt	19

Central and Western Asia	Female share (%)
Israel	47
Cyprus	39
Jordan	23
Syria	11
Turkey	10
Bahrain	10

Asia and the Pacific	Female share (%)
Thailand	45
Sri Lanka	44
Singapore	44
Hong Kong, China SAR	42
Philippines	40
Korea, Republic	39
China	39
Indonesia	38
Malaysia	36
Fiji	31
India	15
Pakistan	8

Latin America and the Caribbean	Female share (%)
Jamaica	50
Bahamas	49
Honduras	47
Barbados	47
Colombia	46
Panama	44
Brazil	44
Paraguay	41
Ecuador	40
Argentina	40
Trinidad & Tobago	39
Costa Rica	38
Bolivia	37
Mexico	36
Chile	36
Venezuela	35
Peru	33
El Salvador	32

Eastern Europe	Female share (%)
Ukraine	54
Latvia	54
Lithuania	53
Hungary	51
Estonia	51
Slovakia	49
Croatia	48
Slovenia	47
Poland	47
Czech Rep.	46
Romania	43
Albania	41
Macedonia FYR	40

Western Europe and Other Developed Countries	Female share (%)
Iceland	52
Sweden	51
Norway	51
United Kingdom	50
Finland	50
United States	48
New Zealand	48
Denmark	48
Canada	48
Australia	47
Portugal	46
France	46
Ireland	45
Germany	44
Netherlands	43
Belgium	41
Austria	41
Switzerland	40
Japan	39
Greece	39
Italy	38
Spain	37
Luxembourg	36
Malta	29

Sources: ILO Website: http://laborsta.ilo.org and various ILO labour statistics yearbooks.

Chart 3.3: Change in Female Share of Paid Employment in Industry and Services (%), 1980-1997

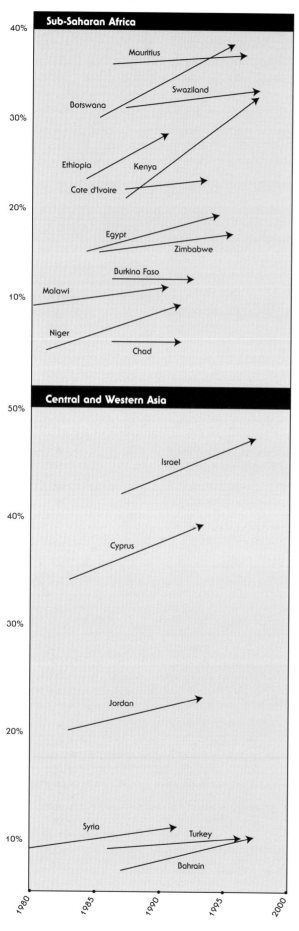

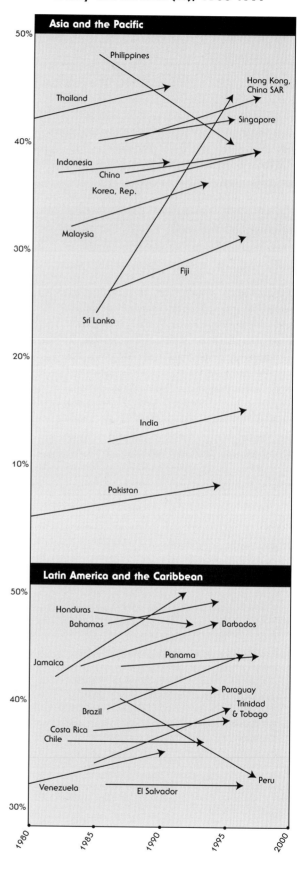

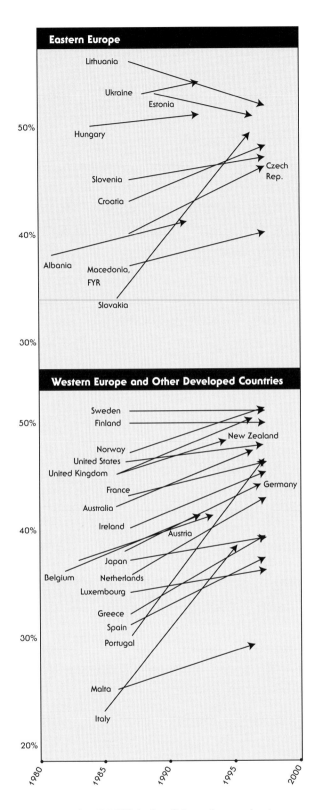

Sources: Based on ILO Website: http://laborsta.ilo.org and various ILO labour statistics yearbooks.

Moreover, they are often subject to new forms of subordination in the workplace (see Box 9). At the same time as women's share of paid employment in industry and services is rising, the rights associated with such employment are often falling.

The past two decades have witnessed the emergence of 'non–standard' forms of work in some sectors, which used to be characterized by regular wage employment. Among these, the most important numerically have been part-time employment and temporary work. They usually offer lower levels of social security coverage and of employment rights than regular jobs. Part-time and temporary work is also usually associated with lower wages and limited training opportunities or career prospects. Many forms of non-standard jobs... pose a real risk of marginalization in the labour market (UN 1999d).

Box 9: Limitations of Empowerment: Women's Entry into Paid Employment

Paid jobs do not necessarily free women from oppression in their families. Jasmine, age 13, lives in Bangladesh. She wrote to the UNICEF Web Forum Working Group on Girls:

"I have an older sister who was married off at the age of 15. She is pregnant and yet has to work in a garment factory from very early morning to very late at night because her husband refuses to work. She had to give 20,000 takas, plus some jewelry to her husband's family so that she could get married, but she is treated no better than a servant. She also has to do most of the housework, such as cooking and cleaning whenever she is not working."

Paid jobs do not necessarily give women control over their working conditions. Jill Carino describes how workers are treated in two factories in export processing zones in the Philippines:

"The management are very strict as to how the workers act in the workplace, for example, they are not allowed to talk to each other. If they do they are given a black mark in their record. That's why they are not given any masks, so that the supervisors can see if their lips are moving or not...

"In times of shipment, some people have to stay for up to 48 hours in the factory. They get one hour for eating and 1 hour for sleep in every 24 hours, However, when orders have stopped workers are laid off for 3 weeks to 1 month without salary."

And at a factory in Manila, where workers receive slightly above the minimum wage, $3.75 per day, management finds other ways to reduce costs. One is to deduct for taxes and social security without forwarding the money to the government, leaving workers without benefits at retirement.

Another is making the workers do other jobs outside their regular jobs: "Some workers [in a garment factory] are asked to report earlier by 30 minutes and leave 30 minutes later so that they can clean the workplace, because the company saves money by not hiring any workers to clean..."

Source: www.unicef.org/voy/meeting/gir/girhome.html; Women Working Worldwide 1998.

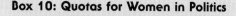

A critical issue for future progress of women is how the expansion of women's paid employment can be combined with the protection, promotion and fulfilment of women's human rights at work. One problem is the lack of indicators on the quality of employment, as distinct from the quantity of employment. The ILO's Key Indicators of the Labour Market do include indicators on extent of part-time work, hours of work and urban informal sector employment (based on a somewhat restricted definition of the informal sector). But there is no indicator for the extent to which workers enjoy social protection of their human rights at work. This is not an easy thing to measure. But without such a measure, the extent to which the increases in women's share of paid employment indicates progress of women will remain ambiguous.

Absence from Parliament

Greater equality in the numbers of women holding political office is important not only in its own right, but also because it may give women more of a voice in determining the laws and policies which regulate women's progress in other areas of life, such as the economy. A World Bank study on corruption and women in government concluded that higher rates of female participation in government are associated with lower levels of corruption, suggesting that women may be more concerned with the common good (Dollar et al. 1999). The target of women holding at least 30 per cent of political positions has been endorsed by both women's NGOs and governmental bodies, including the UN Economic and Social Council, and was reiterated in the Platform for Action. Global data on women's share of seats in national legislatures is updated regularly by the Inter-Parliamentary Union.

Table 3.3 shows women's share of seats in national parliaments in January 2000. This share is 30 per cent or above in only a few countries: Sweden, Denmark, Germany, Finland, Norway, Iceland, the Netherlands and South Africa. In most regions of the world, there is a wide range. In Sub-Saharan Africa, for instance, women hold 30 per cent of seats in South Africa, whereas their share is no more than 2 per cent in Ethiopia and Togo. There is a similar range in Asia and the Pacific and Latin America and the Caribbean. In Western Europe and Other Developed Countries the range is even wider – from Sweden, which is the only country in the world approaching parity of seats between women and men, to Greece, where women's share is only just over 6 per cent.

The wide variation within regions is in large part due to wide variations in electoral systems. Some countries have also established quotas for women's representation (see Box 10).

Inter-Parliamentary Union

Box 10: Quotas for Women in Politics

"Constitutionally entrenched quotas are the best way of ensuring that targets for increasing the representation of women are met."
— Commonwealth Secretariat (1998)

In an effort to increase the political representation of women several countries have introduced some form of quota system: legal or constitutional quotas, covering candidate lists for seats in national or local assemblies, or quotas adopted by political parties. As of March 2000, the former, typically from 20 to 30 per cent, had been adopted in at least 25 countries: Argentina, Belgium, Bolivia, Brazil, Chile, Dominican Republic, Costa Rica, Ecuador, Eritrea, Finland, Ghana, Guyana, India, Mexico, Morocco, Namibia, Nepal, Norway, Panama, Paraguay, Peru, Senegal, Sweden, Tanzania, Uganda and Venezuela. In France, a 1999 constitutional amendment instructs political parties to nominate equal numbers of men and women. And in the Philippines, an executive order encourages a minimum of 30 per cent representation of women in bagangay (municipal) assemblies.

In addition, one or more major political parties have adopted quotas for women candidates in at least 6 countries: Austria, Germany, Italy, Mozambique, South Africa and Turkey. The Labour Party in Australia introduced a "target" (as opposed to "quota") that 35 per cent of winnable seats in state and federal elections be allocated to women by 2002.

Comparing this list with Table 3.3 shows a clear correlation between countries with quotas and countries where women's representation is highest. But quotas are not popular everywhere. In Bangladesh, for example, women politicians reported that the system leads to nepotism and favouritism in the choice of women to run (Commonwealth Secretariat 1998). Favouritism was also widely believed to have characterized the selection of women candidates by the Communist Party in countries in Eastern Europe and the former Soviet Union, where legislatures themselves were seen as mere "rubber stamps" for the party. With the change in political system and the marginalization of the Communist Party, quotas disappeared – along with women's representation. Since then, there have been efforts to introduce quotas in some countries: Uzbekistan adopted a quota regarding the number of women in executive bodies in 1994. But quotas for women in electoral lists were rejected in Latvia, Poland and the Republic of Moldova. And rejection of quotas is not limited to countries with prior experience of quotas, as quota legislation was recently rejected in Switzerland (New York Times, 13 March 2000).

Sources: Commonwealth Secretariat 1998; ECLAC 1999b; UN 2000b.

Table 3.3: Women's Share of Seats in National Parliament, January 2000

Sub-Saharan Africa	Percentage of seats held by women
South Africa	30.0
Mozambique	25.2
Seychelles	23.5
Namibia	18.3
Uganda	17.9
Rwanda	17.1
United Rep. of Tanzania	16.4
Angola	15.5
Eritrea	14.7
Senegal	14.0
Zimbabwe	14.0
Mali	12.2
Congo	12.0
Lesotho	10.7
Burkina Faso	10.4
Zambia	10.1
Guinea-Bissau	10.0
Gabon	9.4
Ghana	9.0
Sierra Leone	8.8
Guinea	8.8
Botswana	8.5
Malawi	8.3
Madagascar	8.0
Côte d'Ivoire	8.0
Mauritius	7.6
Central African Rep.	7.3
Nigeria	7.3
Swaziland	6.3
Burundi	6.0
Benin	6.0
Cameroon	5.6
Sudan	5.3
Eq. Guinea	5.0
Kenya	3.6
Chad	2.4
Mauritania	2.2
Gambia	2.0
Comoros	2.0
Ethiopia	2.0
Niger	1.2
Togo	1.2
Djibouti	0.0

Northern Africa	
Tunisia	11.5
Algeria	3.8
Egypt	2.0
Morocco	0.6

Central and Western Asia	
Turkmenistan	26.0
Azerbaijan	12.0
Israel	11.7
Kazakhstan	11.2
Syria	10.7
Georgia	7.2
Uzbekistan	6.8

	Percentage of seats held by women
Iraq	6.4
Cyprus	5.4
Kyrgyzstan	4.7
Turkey	4.2
Armenia	3.1
Tajikistan	2.8
Jordan	2.5
Lebanon	2.3
Yemen	0.7
Kuwait	0.0
UAE	0.0

Asia and the Pacific	
Viet Nam	26.0
China	21.8
Lao PDR	21.2
Korea, DPR.	20.1
Philippines	12.9
Indonesia	11.4
Fiji	10.7
Malaysia	10.3
Bangladesh	9.1
India	8.9
Samoa	8.2
Cambodia	8.2
Mongolia	7.9
Thailand	6.6
Nepal	6.4
Maldives	6.3
Sri Lanka	4.9
Iran, Islamic Republic.	4.9
Singapore	4.3
Korea, Republic	3.7
Bhutan	2.0
Pakistan	2.0
Papua New Guinea	1.8
Vanuatu	0.0

Latin America and the Caribbean	
Cuba	27.6
Argentina	23.0
Barbados	20.4
Guyana	20.0
Bahamas	19.6
Trinidad & Tobago	19.4
Costa Rica	19.3
Mexico	17.9
Ecuador	17.4
El Salvador	16.7
Jamaica	16.0
Suriname	15.7
Dominican Rep.	14.5
Belize	13.5
Colombia	12.2
Uruguay	11.5
Venezuela	11.4
Peru	10.8
Bolivia	10.2
Nicaragua	9.7
Panama	9.7

	Percentage of seats held by women
Honduras	9.4
Chile	8.9
Paraguay	8.0
Guatemala	7.1
Brazil	5.9
Haiti	3.6

Eastern Europe	
Bosnia-Herzegovina	21.0
Estonia	17.8
Lithuania	17.5
Latvia	17.0
Czech Rep.	13.8
Belarus	13.2
Slovakia	12.7
Poland	12.6
Bulgaria	10.8
Moldova, Republic	8.9
Hungary	8.3
Ukraine	7.8
Slovenia	7.8
Macedonia, FYR	7.5
Croatia	7.1
Yugoslavia	6.1
Russian Fed.	5.6
Romania	5.6
Albania	5.2

Western Europe and Other Developed Countries	
Sweden	42.7
Denmark	37.4
Finland	37.0
Norway	36.4
Iceland	34.9
Germany	33.6
Netherlands	32.8
New Zealand	29.2
Austria	25.0
Belgium	24.8
Canada	23.1
Australia	22.4
Switzerland	22.3
Portugal	18.7
United Kingdom	18.4
Spain	18.0
Luxembourg	16.7
Ireland	13.7
United States	12.5
Italy	10.0
Malta	9.2
France	9.1
Japan	8.3
Greece	6.3

Source: Inter-Parliamentary Union
Website: http://www.ipu.org.

Doranne Jacobson

Progress in women's share of seats in the legislature is shown in Chart 3.4 (pp. 79-80). Fewer countries are included than in Table 3.3, owing to lack of recent data. The majority of countries show progress, but there are important regional differences. In Eastern Europe and Mongolia, for example, the elimination of quotas that accompanied the shift to democracy has resulted in dramatic falls in women's share of parliamentary seats. The most dramatic increase, by contrast, occurred in South Africa following the end of apartheid (1% to 30%). Increases of 10 to 15 percent occurred in countries in both the developed and developing world and were especially striking in countries that started at very low levels of participation, such as Uganda (1% to 17.9%), Ecuador (1% to 17.4%), Bahamas (4% to 19.6%) and Barbados (4% to 20.4%). However, progress could also be seen in countries where levels were higher to begin with, such as Austria (11% to 25%), New Zealand (14% to 29.2%), Iceland (21% to 34.9%) and Sweden (31% to 42.7%).

Comparisons between countries are complicated by several factors:

- legislatures in some countries may have little independent decision-making power, due to control exercised by political parties or by the executive arm of government;
- women representatives may come from a limited range of social backgrounds and pursue policies that benefit their own social group (including women) rather than policies designed to improve the lives of the majority of women;
- women representatives may be unable to change pre-existing policy agendas because officials lack an understanding of how these agendas operate to disadvantage women.

It is also true that just as more women are winning seats in national parliaments, the power to make decisions about economic policy has moved elsewhere. Not only has the balance of such power shifted between the state and the corporate sector, as discussed further in Chapter 5, but within governments themselves, decision-making power about macroeconomic policy has moved away from legislatures and has become concentrated in the financial ministries and the central banks (Sen 1999).

While it is not yet possible to present a global picture, substantial progress has been made in women's share of seats in local councils in at least some parts of the world. For instance in India, 33 per cent of the seats in local decision-making bodies are now reserved for women, following an amendment to the national constitution in 1992. And in Uganda, the 1995 constitution stipulated that a minimum of one-third of all seats in local councils must be filled by women.

The International Union of Local Authorities (IULA) reports that in general, the proportion of women elected representatives is probably higher at the local level than at the national level, but it emphasizes the lack of reliable information (IULA 1998). Committed to making equal the number of women and men in decision-making bodies at all levels and in all policy areas, IULA aims to construct a global database on women in local government, and has already distributed a questionnaire to its members (Website: www.iula.org).

"If local government is to meet the needs of both women and men, it must build on the experiences of both women and men, through an equal representation at all levels and in all fields of decision making..."

— International Union of Local Authorities, Harare, 1998

At the regional level, a multidimensional picture of women's participation in decision-making in Latin America and the Caribbean has been put together by ECLAC, covering not only government and political parties, but also trade unions, professional and employers organizations and women's social organizations (ECLAC 1999). If this survey is repeated at appropriate intervals, it will provide a good way of tracking progress over time.

The barriers to women occupying more decision-making positions are deep-seated, and often women are reluctant to put themselves forward for such positions. Many fear the hostility, sometimes organized, which they will almost certainly face, while others are reluctant to take on additional responsibilities owing to their obligations to take care of family and neighbours. Yet these barriers

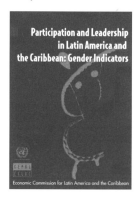

Participation and Leadership in Latin America and the Caribbean: Gender Indicators

Economic Commission for Latin America and the Caribbean

Chart 3.4: Change in Women's Share of Seats in National Parliament, 1987-2000

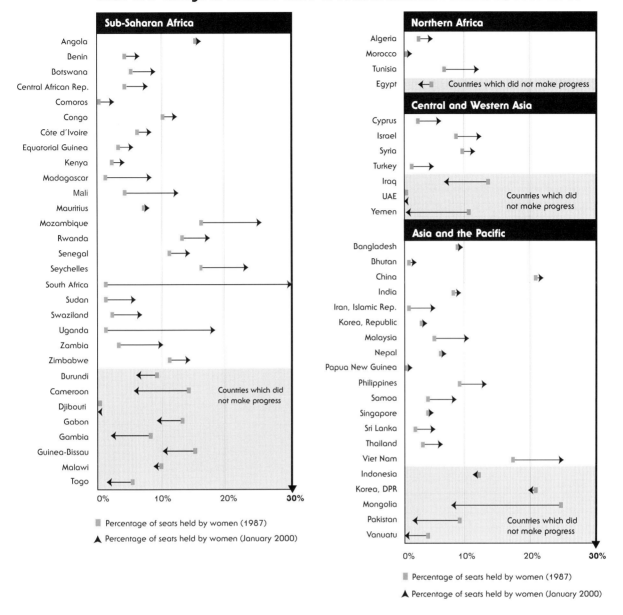

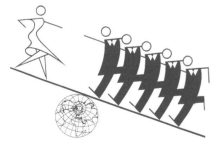

"The concept of democracy will only assume true and dynamic significance when political policies and national legislation are decided upon jointly by men and women with equitable regard for the interests and aptitudes of both halves of the population."

— Inter-Parliamentary Council, Resolution on "Women and Political Power," April 1992

Chart 3.4, continued

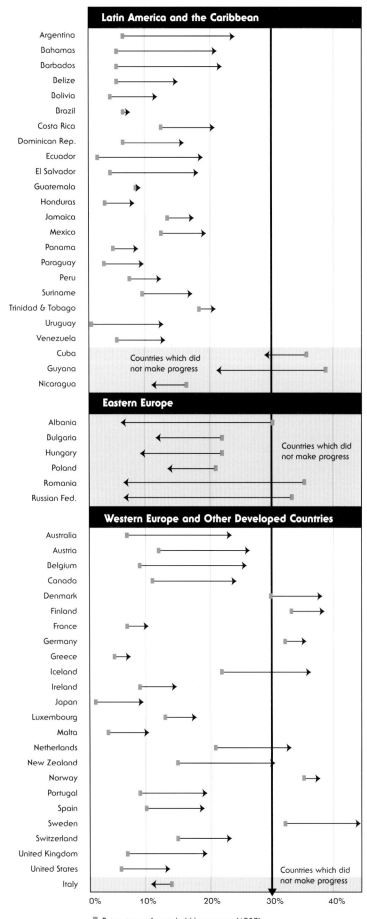

Percentage of seats held by women (1987)

▲ Percentage of seats held by women (January 2000)

Sources: Inter-Parliamentary Union Website: http://www.ipu.org; UN 1995a; UN 1990.

can be overcome with determined policies which open doors to women, provide women with support in both their public and private roles, and encourage men to take a greater share of caring responsibilities and to take pride in the public accomplishments of their wives and daughters (see Box 11).

Meeting Platform Targets for Gender Equality and Women's Empowerment

Applying the indicators to the agreed-upon targets for gender equality in education and parliament makes it possible to identify countries that have made progress in achieving the targets. Because of the underlying variability in the education enrolment data, it is wise to allow some leeway; and because of the fact that gender gaps can be eliminated at low, as well as at high levels of girls' enrolment, it is important to take absolute levels of girls' enrolment into account too. The judgement used here is that a country has met the target for gender equality in secondary education if the ratio of girls to boys' enrolment is between 95 and 105 and the level of girls' enrolment is 95 or higher.

In the case of women's share of seats in national legislatures, the underlying data are not subject to the same degree of error. So the judgement here is that a country has achieved the current target if 30 per cent or more of the seats are held by women. There is no target for women's share of paid employment, but it seems reasonable to consider a figure in the range of 45-55 per cent as indicating an equal share, given the variability of the data.

Table 3.4 lists those countries that have achieved the target for gender equality in education and the target for share of seats in national legislatures, together with a high share of women's paid employment in industry and services. It also includes countries that have come very close. This comparison shows that only four countries, all in Northern Europe, have accomplished all three goals. To date, one developing country, South Africa, and three additional European countries have also met both the target for gender equality in education and the target for share of political representatives. These achievements should be celebrated. But they should be taken as a signal not that nothing more needs to be done in these countries but that they are in a position to adopt more demanding targets.

Box 11: Awards to Supportive Men

Following the first free election in Nigeria after the downfall of the military regime, stories of hostility to women running for office or seeking senior government or party positions were rife. The new president, General Abasanjo, was credited with trying to promote women for appointed office, but had made little progress, owing to a pervasive patriarchal culture that views women as unqualified, regardless of their education or training. This is particularly true in the predominantly Muslim north, where representation of women is lower than elsewhere.

In an effort to promote new male role models, UNIFEM established an award to be given to men who supported their wives for political office:

The case of one award winner, Alhagi Salisu Soda, was most remarkable, as he is an illiterate who relentlessly pursues the empowerment of his wife at home, within the community and nation. Alhaji Salisu Soda, whom all participants hailed as the "Real Man," is an indigene of Kano state, born in 1941. He is a seasoned and honest businessman with little or no education. He met and married his wife, Hajiya Halima, in 1974. She has remained his one and only wife. The couple is happily married with four children. With his support and in defiance of the African culture that encourages denial of education for women, his wife decided to take a career in nursing which necessitated her being posted to various local governments. He encouraged her to return to school and further her education. The result was a Diploma in Public Administration. In his quest for academic excellence for his wife, he urged her to go back to school again to bag a degree. She has recently concluded her final examinations.

His encouragement was not limited to education but extended to participation in governance. He supported his wife in all her political endeavours. In 1979-80, he watched with pride, as Hajiya Halima Soda became the first married woman to be a card-carrying member of the People's Redemptive Party (PRP). She was later appointed Commissioner for Health, and currently is Commissioner for Women Affairs in Kano.

Alhaji Salisu Soda enabled his wife to become economically secure by introducing her into his business. Today, under his tutelage, she owns two companies, H.H. Soda Enterprises and G.U.S.F. Enterprises...UNIFEM salutes Alhaji Salisu Soda for his positive role modelling for the advancement of gender equality. He was not threatened by the fact that educating his wife might make her more "powerful."

Source: report to UNIFEM *Currents*, October 1999.

Table 3.4: Levels of Achievement in Gender Equality and Women's Empowerment

Country	Target: 30% women's seats in national legislatures	Target: 95-105% f/m ratio net secondary school enrolment	Female net enrolment ratio in secondary school	45-55% women's share of paid employment in industry and services
Sweden	42.7%	100	99.9	51.0%
Denmark	37.4%	101	95.4	48.0%
Finland	37.0%	102	96.2	50.0%
Norway	36.4%	101	98.0	51.0%
Iceland	34.9%	101	88.1	52.0%
Netherlands	31.5%	100	99.9	31.5%
Germany	33.6%	99	94.9	44.0%
South Africa	30.0%	104	96.9	41.0%

Reducing Obstacles to Gender Equality and Women's Empowerment

Increases in girls' enrolment in secondary school, in women's share of paid employment in industry and services, and of women's seats in parliament need to be situated in the context of changes in the level of per-capita income in different countries and the distribution of this income. Improvements in women's access to education, paid employment and political decision-making are hollow if the standard of living of women is not improving.

There is no one indicator that can adequately capture what is happening to women's standard of living. However, improvement is likely to depend upon the distribution of resources within and among countries, the national rate of growth of per-capita income and the level of national external debt. In particular, poor women are unlikely to benefit very much from a reduction in gender gaps, if the level of per-capita income in the country is falling, if income distribution in the country is worsening, and if the country is becoming more indebted.

Table 3.5 (pp. 83-84) presents a scoreboard that situates changes in the three UN indicators of gender equality and women's empowerment in the broader context of national economies. (It also shows the extent of information, and lack of it, in UN and other international databases, especially for Sub-Saharan Africa and Central and Western Asia.) The scoreboard shows improvement on all three gender equality indicators for 17 countries. Of these, only Jamaica also showed improvement in per-capita income and income equality indicators. Of the rest, 13 showed improvement in per-capita income but of these, 4 showed deterioration in income equality, 2 showed improvement, 2 showed no change and for 5 there was no income inequality data available from the World Institute for Economic Development.

"Scoreboards are particularly useful in... conveying more immediately an ongoing sense of the monitoring process. The concept of 'scoring', be it on a scoreboard, a score card or a record card, is readily grasped by most people and is thus more easily owned."

— International Women's Tribune Centre (2000)

The deterioration in economic conditions facing women in Sub-Saharan Africa is very evident. In 19 out of 48 countries, real per-capita income fell.

(The UN database had no information on changes in income inequality in most countries.) This was also true in Eastern Europe, where 9 out of 19 countries experienced a fall in real per-capita income and 15 experienced a rise in income inequality.

Increased indebtedness is also very striking: increases occurred in Sub-Saharan Africa (22 countries out of 48), Asia and the Pacific (10 countries out of 28) and Northern Africa (2 countries out of 5). Increased indebtedness seems to be associated with a deterioration in girls' enrolment in secondary school. An examination of countries with data available for both the education and the debt variables reveal that of the 16 in which girls' enrolment declined, 12 also experienced increased indebtedness. In Western Europe and Other Developed Countries there is no problem of external debt and per-capita real income on average increased. But in 12 out of 24 countries there was a deterioration in income equality.

Conclusions

Over the last two decades there has been progress in removing many obstacles to women's participation in education, in market-based production and in political decision-making. But in two regions, some obstacles have increased:

- to women's participation in secondary education in many countries in Sub-Saharan Africa;
- to women's participation in paid employment and political life in the countries of Eastern Europe and the former Soviet Union which have made the transition to market-based economies.

Moreover, where women have made inroads into secondary schooling and the market economy and into parliaments, they have found paradoxes:

- more women obtaining secondary educational qualifications but tending to receive a lower financial return for their qualifications than do men;
- more women entering into paid employment but at a time when the quality of jobs, in terms of social protection and rights to organize, are declining;
- more women taking legislative decisions but at a time when economic decision-making power is moving away from legislatures.

Further progress for the world's women requires a stronger commitment to place women's empowerment and gender justice at the heart of national and international development agendas.

Table 3.5: Progress of Women Scoreboard, mid 1980s - late 1990s

Country	Education	Employment	Parliament	Per capita income	Income equality	Debt reduction
Sub-Saharan Africa						
Angola	-	?	=	-	?	-
Benin	=	?	+	-	?	+
Botswana	+	+	+	+	?	+
Burkina Faso	+	=	?	+	?	-
Burundi	+	?	-	-	?	-
Cameroon	-	?	-	-	?	-
Cape Verde	+	?	+	?	+	?
Central African Rep.	-	?	+	-	?	-
Chad	+	=	?	-	?	-
Comoros	-	?	+	-	?	+
Congo	-	?	+	-	?	-
Cote d'Ivoire	-	=	+	-	?	-
Congo, DR	=	?	?	-	?	-
Djibouti	=	?	=	?	?	?
Equatorial Guinea	-	?	+	+	?	+
Eritrea	?	?	?	?	?	?
Ethiopia	+	+	?	+	-	-
Gabon	?	?	-	-	?	-
Gambia	+	?	-	-	?	+
Ghana	?	?	?	+	+	-
Guinea	-	?	?	+	?	?
Guinea-Bissau	+	?	-	+	?	-
Kenya	=	+	+	+	?	+
Lesotho	-	?	?	+	?	-
Liberia	?	?	?	?	?	?
Madagascar	?	?	+	-	?	-
Malawi	+	+	-	-	?	+
Mali	+	?	+	+	?	=
Mauritania	?	?	?	+	+	=
Mauritius	+	=	=	+	?	+
Mozambique	-	?	+	+	?	-
Namibia	+	?	?	+	?	=
Niger	+	+	?	-	?	=
Nigeria	?	?	?	+	-	-
Reunion	?	?	?	?	?	?
Rwanda	?	?	+	-	?	-
Senegal	+	?	+	=	?	+
Seychelles	?	?	+	+	?	+
Sierra Leone	?	?	?	-	?	?
Somalia	?	?	?	?	?	?
South Africa	+	?	+	-	+	?
Sudan	?	?	+	=	?	-
Swaziland	+	+	+	+	?	+
Togo	+	?	-	-	?	+
Uganda	?	?	+	+	-	-
Tanzania, UR	?	?	?	?	+	?
Zambia	=	?	+	-	-	+
Zimbabwe	+	+	+	=	?	-
Northern Africa						
Algeria	+	?	+	-	+	?
Egypt	+	+	-	+	+	+
Libya	+	?	?	-	?	-
Morocco	=	?	=	+	=	+
Tunisia	+	?	+	+	+	

Country	Education	Employment	Parliament	Per capita income	Income equality	Debt reduction
Central and Western Asia						
Armenia	?	?	?	-	-	?
Azerbaijan	?	?	?	-	-	?
Bahrain	-	+	?	+	?	-
Cyprus	?	+	+	?	?	?
Georgia	-	?	?	?	?	?
Iraq	-	?	-	-	?	?
Israel	?	+	+	+	=	?
Jordan	?	+	?	-	-	-
Kazakhstan	?	?	?	-	-	?
Kuwait	-	?	?	+	?	na
Kyrgyzstan	-	?	?	-	-	?
Lebanon	?	?	?	?	?	?
Oman	+	?	?	=	?	?
Qatar	-	?	?	?	?	?
Saudi Arabia	+	?	?	-	?	+
Syria	-	+	+	+	?	-
Tajikistan	?	?	?	-	?	?
Turkey	+	=	+	+	?	?
Turkmenistan	?	?	?	?	?	?
UAE	+	?	=	-	?	?
Uzbekistan	?	?	?	?	?	?
Yemen	?	?	-	?	?	?
Asia and the Pacific						
Afghanistan	?	?	?	?	?	?
Bangladesh	+	?	=	+	+	-
Bhutan	?	?	=	=	?	-
Brunei Darussalam	=	?	?	-	?	?
Cambodia	+	?	?	+	?	?
China	+	+	=	+	-	-
Fiji	+	+	?	+	?	+
Hong Kong, China SAR	=	+	?	+	-	na
India	+	+	=	+	=	-
Indonesia	+	=	=	+	-	-
Iran, Islamic Republic	+	?	+	-	?	-
Korea, Republic	+	+	=	+	?	+
Lao PDR	+	?	?	+	?	-
Malaysia	+	+	+	+	?	+
Maldives	?	?	?	+	?	+
Mongolia	-	?	-	?	?	?
Myanmar	+	?	?	?	?	?
Nepal	+	?	=	+	?	-
Pakistan	?	+	-	+	-	=
Papua New Guinea	?	?	+	+	?	+
Philippines	+	-	+	+	-	+
Samoa (Western)	?	?	+	=	?	+
Singapore	+	+	=	+	=	?
Sri Lanka	+	+	+	+	?	+
Thailand	+	+	+	+	+	-
Tonga	?	?	?	?	?	?
Vanuatu	+	?	-	-	?	-
Viet Nam	+	?	+	?	?	?

Table 3.5: Progress of Women Scoreboard

Country	Education	Employment	Parliament	Per capita income	Income equality	Debt reduction	Country	Education	Employment	Parliament	Per capita income	Income equality	Debt reduction
Latin America and the Caribbean							**Western Europe and Other Developed Countries**						
Argentina	+	?	+	+	-	+	Australia	+	+	+	+	-	na
Bahamas	=	+	+	-	+	?	Austria	+	+	+	+	=	na
Barbados	=	+	+	+	?	?	Belgium	=	+	+	+	+	na
Belize	=	?	+	+	?	=	Canada	=	?	+	+	+	na
Bolivia	-	?	+	+	+	+	Denmark	+	?	+	+	-	na
Brazil	+	+	=	+	-	+	Finland	=	=	+	+	-	na
Chile	+	=	?	+	=	+	France	=	+	+	+	-	na
Colombia	+	?	?	+	-	+	Germany	+	+	+	?	-	na
Costa Rica	+	=	+	+	-	+	Greece	+	+	+	+	=	na
Cuba	=	?	-	?	?	?	Iceland	+	?	+	+	?	na
Dominican Rep.	+	?	+	+	-	+	Ireland	=	+	+	+	-	na
Ecuador	-	?	+	=	?	-	Italy	+	+	-	+	?	na
El Salvador	+	=	+	+	?	+	Luxembourg	?	=	+	+	?	na
Guatemala	+	?	=	+	-	+	Japan	=	+	+	+	=	na
Guyana	=	?	-	+	?	+	Malta	=	+	+	+	?	?
Haiti	-	?	?	-	?	=	Netherlands	=	+	+	+	=	na
Honduras	-	=	+	=	=	-	New Zealand	+	+	+	+	=	na
Jamaica	+	+	+	+	+	+	Norway	+	+	+	+	-	na
Mexico	=	?	+	=	-	+	Portugal	+	+	+	+	=	na
Nicaragua	=	?	-	-	?	-	Spain	=	+	+	+	+	na
Panama	+	=	+	=	?	+	Sweden	+	=	+	+		na
Paraguay	+	=	+	=	-	+	Switzerland	+	?	+	=	?	na
Peru	+	-	+	+	+	+	United Kingdom	=	+	+	+		na
Suriname	?	?	+	?	?	-	United States	=	+	+	+		na
Trinidad & Tobago	=	+	+	-	?	-							
Uruguay	+	?	+	+	=	+							
Venezuela	+	+	+	=	-	+							
Eastern Europe													
Albania	?	+	-	-	?	?							
Belarus	?	?	?	-	+	?							
Bosnia-Herzegovina	?	?	?	?	?	?							
Bulgaria	-	?	-	-	-	-							
Croatia	-	+	?	?	-	?							
Czech Rep.	+	+	?	=	-	-							
Estonia	-	-	?	-	-	?							
Hungary	+	=	-	=	=	+							
Latvia	-	?	?	-	-	?							
Lithuania	?	-	?	-	-	?							
Macedonia FYR	?	+	?	?	-	?							
Poland	+	?	-	+	-	+							
Moldova, Rep.	?	?	?	?	-	?							
Romania	-	?	-	-	-	?							
Russian Fed.	-	?	-	-	-	?							
Slovakia	?	+	?	=	-	-							
Slovenia	?	+	?	?	-	?							
Ukraine	?	=	?	-	-	?							
Yugoslavia	?	?	?	?	=	?							

Reading the Scores:

Education: Change in female net enrolment at secondary level, 1985-1997

Employment: Change in women's share of paid employment in industry and services, early 1980s to mid 1990s

Parliament: Change in women's share of seats in national parliament, 1987-2000

Per capita income: Annual average change in real per capita GDP, 1985-1997

Income equality: Change in distribution of income as measured by the gini coefficient, 1980s to 1990s

Debt reduction: A reduction in the debt burden as measured by the ratio of external debt to GNP, 1985-1997

+   an increase or improvement (dark purple)
=   little or no change (light purple)
-    a decrease or deterioration (grey)
?   no data was available (black)
n.a not applicable; no external debt

For more details on indicators and sources, see Technical Annex

Chapter 4

Assessing the Progress of Women: A Broader Picture

Introduction

Assessing the progress of women in terms of the broader objectives of the Beijing Platform for Action requires a wider range of indicators than those designed for the agreed upon targets. A fuller assessment of women's economic progress can be made by looking at several income and employment indicators, including women's position in family enterprises and as business owners; in paid occupations with a higher degree of decision-making power; and in the labour market. This chapter presents these indicators, together with two cross-cutting issues: economic inequality among women and the feminization of income-poverty. In order to locate women's economic status in a broader social context, it also examines indicators of obstacles to women's empowerment, including violence against women, the increased incidence of HIV/AIDS among women and girls, and women's unequal share of responsibility for unpaid care work, in both family and community.

"Promote the further development of statistical methods to improve data that relate to women in economic, social, cultural and political development...."

— Platform for Action, 1995

In addition to indicators of specific dimensions of women's position, progress can be assessed by means of composite indicators, which aggregate several different dimensions into one index. The chapter considers the advantages and disadvantages of the two composite indicators introduced by the Human Development Report, namely, the Gender-Sensitive Development Index and the Gender Empowerment Measure. Finally, it takes up the issue of ways in which to improve information to enable an adequate assessment of progress of the world's women.

Women's Economic Status

Women are economically active in family enterprises, in their own small businesses and as employees. As discussed in Chapter 1, much of this work is informal, in the sense of being outside social protection, even for employees. Despite many improvements, available statistics still undercount informal employment in many countries, and reflect only the most visible dimensions of women's employment.

Women's Work in Family Enterprises and as Business Owners

Rural women are particularly likely to work in small family enterprises (farms and small manufacturing and service businesses) on an unpaid basis, without direct remuneration, or to be self-employed or running microenterprises that employ two or three other women ("own-account workers and employers" in the terminology of labour-force surveys). All else being equal, it is probably more advantageous for a woman to be an "own-account worker or an employer" than an "unpaid family worker," since the former puts cash into her own hands, whereas the latter does not. Benefits women receive from contributing unpaid labour to family businesses depend upon how their husbands, brothers or

---

Box 1: Where do the tea bonuses go?

In the mid-1990s, tea in Kenya was produced by smallholders and bought by the Kenya Tea Development Authority, which arranged for processing and exportation. Male farmers held the licenses to grow the tea and were paid for the amount of tea they delivered each month, and also received an annual bonus payment. Their wives and daughters harvested the tea and transported it to pick-up points from which trucks took the tea to the processing plants.

A study in Kericho District by a Kenyan researcher, Grace Ongile, found that the use of the bonuses was often a point of contention between women and men. She states that "it is publicly acknowledged that smallholder tea farmers spend part of the bonus payment from tea on personal leisure activities such as drinking," as illustrated in a cartoon in a Kenyan newspaper, *The Daily Nation* (a tea farmer spending his bonus money at the beer hall, where he is confronted by his wife).

While many women farmers did not express concerns about the way their husbands spent the tea bonus, others indicated considerable dissatisfaction.

Wife 1, age 42, with 10 young children: "The head of the family spends all the money recklessly leaving the family with nothing."

Wife 2, age 58, with 5 children: "The husband gives part of the bonus payment only to the elder wife and not myself."

In Central Province, another region of Kenya, some wives of tea farmers had earlier protested that their husbands spent the annual bonuses on beer, meat and other personal needs. They were successful in getting part of the bonus paid directly to them.

Source: Ongile 1998.

fathers distribute income generated by the family farm or enterprise. Women have often voiced dissatisfaction with this distribution (see Box 1). In a market-based world, workers who are not directly remunerated for work performed ("cash in hand") tend to be at a disadvantage. The proportion of women who work on this basis tends to be much higher than the proportion of men (see Table 4.1); and among men, it is more often young men who work on this basis. For them it does not mean a lifetime of economic dependence, since in due course they will be head of a family farm or business themselves.

One way to assess how far there has been a reduction in obstacles to the economic advancement of rural women is to examine whether the proportion of women working as unpaid family workers has been falling, and whether there has been a rise in women's share of positions as employers and in self-employment (see Charts 4.1 and 4.2, pp. 88-89).

Over time, the proportion of women who are unpaid family workers has been declining in many countries (in 36 out of 70 shown in Chart 4.1). But some countries appear to show a substantial increase (e.g., Bangladesh, Pakistan, Malawi). In some, this probably reflects efforts to improve labour-force surveys to include as unpaid family workers women who were previously classified as economically inactive housewives (this is probably the case in Bangladesh and Pakistan). In others (such as Malawi), it may reflect changes in the classification of the many farming women who are both "unpaid family workers" on their husband's fields and "own-account workers" on their own fields.

Running her own small business does give a woman decision-making power over what to do with her own time, unlike the lack of freedom experienced by women who work unpaid in family enterprises. But microenterprises are vulnerable to market fluctuations and changes in the economic environment, resulting from decisions of larger enterprises, governments and other economic institutions.

Women's share of work as an employer or as a self-employed person is high and rising in most of the countries in Sub-Saharan Africa, reflecting the preponderance of women in farming and small-scale

Table 4.1: Unpaid Male and Female Family Workers as Proportion of Male and Female Labour Force, 1990

Northern & Sub-Saharan Africa	Male %	Female %
Algeria	3	2
Benin	32	29
Botswana	18	15
Burundi	26	34
Central African Rep.	7	10
Côte d'Ivoire	23	48
Egypt	9	23
Lesotho	27	33
Malawi	61	93
Mali	44	82
Nigeria	9	15
Rwanda	27	79
Tunisia	5	18
Zambia	4	6

Central and Western Asia	Male %	Female %
Iraq	1	9
Israel	1	2
Kuwait	*	*
Syria	8	35
Turkey	13	64

Asia and the Pacific	Male %	Female %
Bangladesh	22	83
Brunei Darussalam	*	1
Fiji	16	16
Hong Kong, China SAR	*	1
Indonesia	9	34
Iran, Islamic Rep.	2	12
Korea, Rep.	2	23
Malaysia	3	14
Nepal	2	4
Pakistan	17	53
Philippines	9	18
Samoa (Western)	66	63
Singapore	1	2
Sri Lanka	6	14
Thailand	16	44
Tonga	23	20

Latin America & the Caribbean	Male %	Female %
Bahamas	*	1
Bolivia	4	11
Brazil	8	12
Chile	2	4
Costa Rica	3	4
Ecuador	4	10
El Salvador	9	7
Guatemala	15	10
Haiti	11	10
Mexico	10	17
Panama	4	2
Paraguay	2	4
Peru	3	7
Suriname	2	2
Trinidad & Tobago	1	3
Uruguay	1	3
Venezuela	1	1

Eastern Europe	Male %	Female %
Hungary	1	3
Poland	5	18

Western Europe and Other Developed Countries	Male %	Female %
Australia	1	1
Belgium	1	7
Canada	*	1
Denmark	*	3
Finland	1	*
Greece	4	22
Ireland	1	2
Italy	2	6
Japan	2	12
Luxembourg	*	4
Netherlands	*	2
New Zealand	1	2
Norway	1	1
Portugal	1	2
Spain	2	6
Sweden	*	*
United States	*	*

* less than 1 per cent
Source : Wistat, version 4.

UNIFEM/Simone Buechler

"A man cannot stay at home all the time. He has to go out to the town to get news on what is happening within the town. My wife has to ask me for permission even when she is going to visit a friend. I can only give permission if she has finished all the work for the day."

— Kenya tea farmer, 1995 (Ongile 1998)

Chart 4.1: Change in Female Unpaid Family Workers as % of Female Labour Force, 1980s-1990s

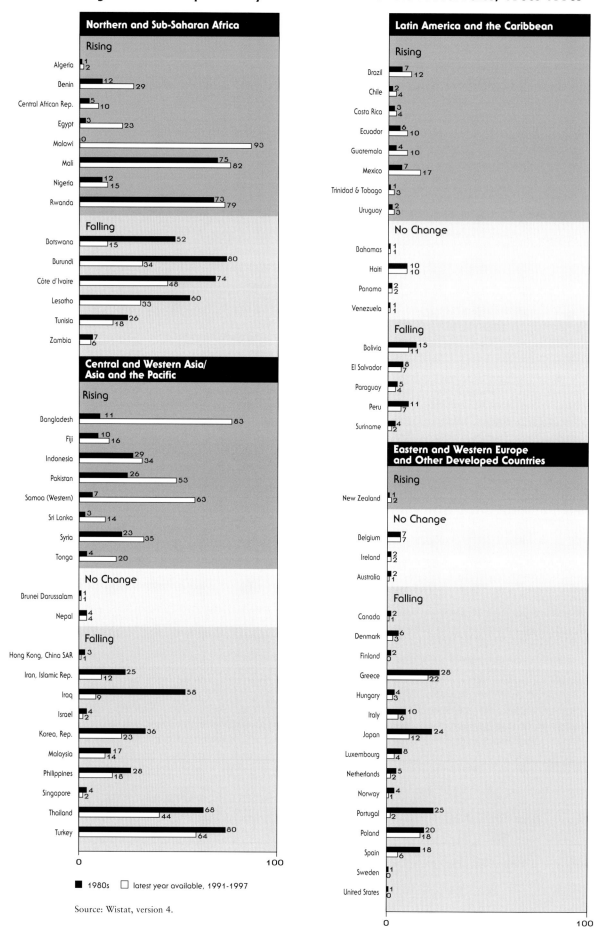

Source: Wistat, version 4.

Chart 4.2: Employers and Own-Account Workers: Change in Female Share (%), 1980s-1990s

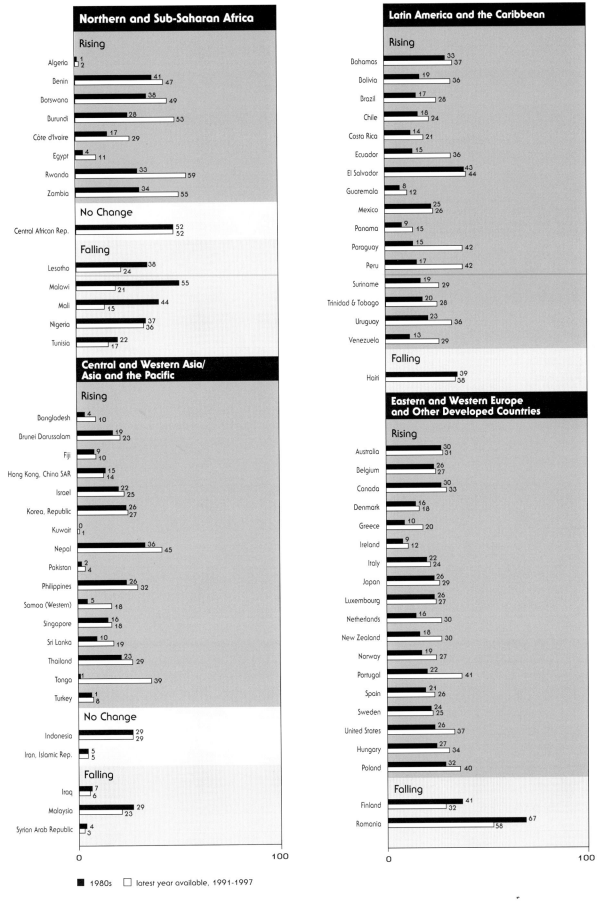

Source: Wistat, version 4.

services, such as trading. Their share is low and shows no tendency to rise in Northern Africa and Central and Western Asia. In the rest of the world the pattern is very variable, but levels are generally below those of Sub-Saharan Africa. UNIFEM is supporting women's enterprise development in many countries in developing activities that range from traditional embroidery to mining to e-commerce.

A more accurate assessment of progress with regard to women's paid employment would take into account information on how remunerative women's businesses are, and how much economic power the women who run them have (see Box 2). Unfortunately, no international database contains information on business ownership, differentiating businesses by scale of both assets and employment (from self-employed to thousands of employees), and giving the sex of their owners. And no international database provides sex-disaggregated data on business start-up rates and survival rates.

United Nations/Milton Grant

Gender Equality in Decision-making Occupations

It is easier to track progress in women's share of seats in national parliaments than it is in other public decision-making positions. Women's share of managerial, administrative, and professional and technical occupations is often used as a proxy for women's share of decision-making positions in the economy. However, this indicator will tend to overestimate women's decision-making power because these occupations cover a range of levels of responsibility, and women tend to be concentrated in the lower levels of responsibility within each of these occupational groups. Moreover, women's share of professional and technical occupations is pushed up by the fact that some professions, such as teaching and nursing, are highly feminized, though even here, higher level decision-making jobs are occupied mainly by men. Also, clerical work is sometimes grouped with managerial and administrative work, which also inflates women's share. This report considers the share of managerial and administrative occupations alone.

Chart 4.3 shows changes women's share of these occupations. In 51 of 59 countries, women's share has risen, reaching 30 per cent or more in 16. This is higher than the number of countries (8) in which women have 30 per cent or more of seats in national parliaments. Lacking is any indicator of how women are using their increased occupancy of managerial and administrative positions to transform workplaces. (See Box 3, p. 92, on women in the UN system.)

UNIFEM

Box 2: Ugandan Women Speak About Their Businesses

"I started with a few goods because I had little money. I used to pick a few cabbages, but now I buy a whole bag. I buy a whole box of tomatoes. But you have to start small, save slowly, slowly. ...This season is dead, lost. Things are in pieces. Rains spoiled the harvest. So when you sell, the price is high, beyond what a consumer can afford... We continue to repay [our loan] even though we have no money remaining. Work has become more difficult and less rewarding."

— Margaret Namuga (46), widowed with three children, sells vegetables

"I eat and drink from my business. I built a house so that I no longer rent. I bought my plot from cassava [earnings]. I have been able to educate my children. That is very important – an even better achievement than building a house. "

—Betty Nakiganda (48), widowed with eight children, sells cassava

"Through my business I have achieved a lot: I managed to construct a house, buy things for it, buy a vehicle and open two more shops like this one. I believe that ...there is nothing men can do that we cannot do. "

—Teddy Birungi (36), married with five children, wholesales beer, soda and whiskey

"I started what they were calling *magendo* (informal trade) in those days, that is, buying sweets and selling them, making a little profit to add to my salary. Later I baked buns and that was more rewarding. ...I started looking for a shop. I got a small place in Kisura, but I lived in Nakaserto so it took me a long time to commute. I had to run the shop after office hours. At 5 p.m. I would pick [up] my children, take them home, give them tea, run through their homework then rush to the shop. Kisura was hard."

—Alice Karugaba (50s), separated with four children, owns two furniture and soft-goods stores

Source: Snyder 2000.

Chart 4.3: Change in Female Share of Administrative and Managerial Positions, mid 1980s - mid 1990s

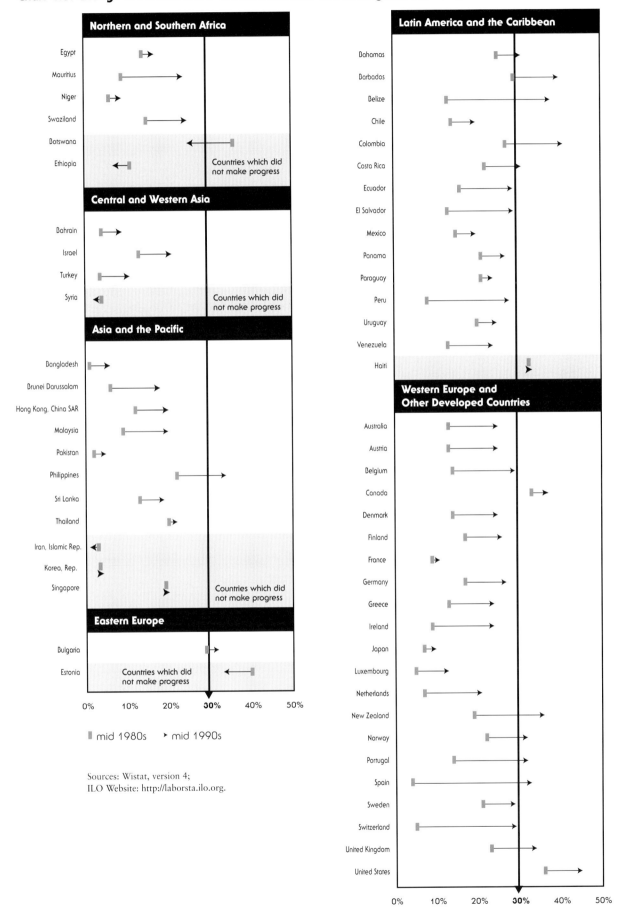

Sources: Wistat, version 4;
ILO Website: http://laborsta.ilo.org.

Box 3: Women in the UN System

The 24 organizations, programmes and funds that comprise the UN system have three types of posts:

- **geographical posts** are subject to geographical quotas, based on a weighted formula that considers a country's membership, population and level of assessment for contributions. These posts offer greater opportunities for career advancement via a grading structure that contains more posts at the decision-making level;

- **non-geographical posts** have no geographical quotas and are primarily in areas such as translation and interpretation which have comparatively low career ceilings;

- **project posts** are connected to a specific project, often in developing countries. These are generally of limited duration, ranging from six months to five years.

The General Assembly requested the UN system to achieve gender parity (50/50) in posts by 2000. Between 1991 and 1996, women's share of posts increased:

- 22.0 to 27.2 per cent in geographical posts;
- 30.4 to 33.9 per cent in non-geographical posts;
- 12.9 to 24.1 per cent in project posts.

If increases remain at this rate, gender parity will not be achieved in geographic posts until 2018; in non-geographic posts until 2013.

Women remain concentrated in lower-level positions. About 60 per cent of women work in support functions, in administration, language and library-related fields. This has not substantially changed since 1984. Women hold only 20 per cent of the geographical posts at senior management level (P5 and above). There has been only a one percentage increase in the number of women at this higher level over the period 1991-1996. At this rate, reaching gender parity will take 44 years.

Source: International Civil Service Commission 1998.

The Gender Gap in Wages

Women's share of paid employment in industry and services has been increasing in most countries. But has women's share of wages in this employment also been increasing? A comprehensive answer is difficult, because international databases have information for only a very limited range of countries. The Wistat database provides information on female wages as a proportion of male wages for some countries (for non-agricultural activities and for manufacturing). This is presented in Table 4.2, together with information from ECLAC (1998) for female income from employment as a percentage of male income from employment in urban households in selected Latin American countries, and information from UNICEF (1999) on female monthly wages as a percentage of male monthly wages in countries in transition to market economies. Because of differences in coverage and reliability of the surveys on which the underlying data is based, the table has to be used with caution (see Annex: Technical Notes). Countries are presented in alphabetical order by region, as the data are not sufficiently comparable to permit a ranking of countries. The table shows that women's average wages are less than men's in all 63 countries for which data is internationally available.

The gender gap in wages in the industrial and services sector ranges from 53 per cent to 97 per cent, with a median of 78 per cent. In manufacturing the range is 54 per cent to 99 per cent, with a median of 75 per cent. The gender wage gap in the United States is close to the median. In 1998, women's wages in the United States were 76.3 per cent of men's wages on a weekly basis, (US Department of Labor 1999).

It is even more difficult to assess change over time, as international databases for industrial and service-sector activities have data for only 29 countries. In the majority of these, the ratio of female to male wages has risen since 1980, in some cases substantially; while in all but one of the cases where it has fallen, the fall is small (see Chart 4.4, p. 94). Even less data is available in international databases to assess progress in the gender wage gap in manufacturing. Chart 4.5 (p. 94) indicates that out of 22 countries, female wages have risen as a percentage of male wages in 20 countries, and have fallen, although only slightly, in 2.

The experience of countries of Eastern Europe and Central and Western Asia that are in transition to the market is shown in Chart 4.6 (p. 94). Only one country, Bulgaria, shows a big rise (5 percentage points) in the gender pay gap between 1990 and 1997. The gap has been relatively stable in Slovenia and Russia and has narrowed considerably in the Czech Republic, Slovakia, Poland and Hungary. The pay gap does not, of course, capture other dimensions of women's labour-market experience in countries in transition, including a decline in female employment and job security. Evidence of gender bias has been reported in recruitment practices of some employers in Hungary, Poland, the Czech Republic and Slovakia, despite employment laws that are supposed to guarantee equal treatment (UNICEF 1999).

Charts 4.4-4.6 suggest some progress in the limited group of countries for which data is available in reducing the gender gap in wage earnings. Data on the wage gap are likely to reflect mainly the earnings of full-time formal sector employees, since the enterprise surveys that generate the data tend to omit part-time, home-based seasonal and temporary employees and do not cover very small enterprises. Thus they do not cover a great deal of informal employment. In the European Union, there is a larger gender wage gap (on an hourly basis) for part-time employees than for full-time employees (Rubery et al. 1998). Studies undertaken by Women in Informal Employment Globalizing and Organizing (WIEGO) suggest that the gender gap in earnings in developing countries is larger in informal than in formal employment.

A narrowing of the gender gap in earnings does not necessarily mean an increase in women's living standards. The gap can narrow while real earnings of both women and men fall, if men's real earnings fall faster than those of women.

There is an urgent need for more and better data on the gender wage gap. The new ILO report on Key Indicators of the Labour Market (KILM) contains 18 indicators, and those for employment and unemployment are generally disaggregated by sex (ILO 1999). But the indicators for wages focus on the issue of labour costs and international competitiveness rather than equality in labour markets. It is important to extend KILM so that it can be used to monitor the gender gap in wages, preferably on a separate basis for full-time and part-time employment. Ideally, indicators for the gender gap should be complemented by indicators for the average real wages of men and women, so that it is possible to see if the gender gap narrows as a result of equalizing up or equalizing down.

Economic Inequality Among Women

As the scoreboard at the end of Chapter 3 shows, income inequality is growing in many countries. This suggests that inequality is likely to be growing among women, with highly educated women enjoying rising incomes and good conditions of employment while women with less educational qualifications have stagnant or falling incomes. Although there is no international database with comprehensive information on inequality among women, several pieces of evidence support the idea.

UNHCR/T. Bølstad

Table 4.2: Female Wages as % of Male Wages, circa 1997

	Industry & Services	Manufacturing
Northern & Sub-Saharan Africa		
Egypt	97	74
Eritrea	58	n.d
Swaziland	n.d	71
Central and Western Asia		
Azerbaijan	53	n.d
Cyprus	62	60
Jordan	87	62
Kazakhstan	72	n.d
Kyrgyzstan	72	n.d
Turkey	n.d	99
Uzbekistan	81	n.d
Asia and the Pacific		
Malaysia	n.d	58
Myanmar	n.d	96
Korea, Rep.	62	56
Singapore	76	60
Sri Lanka	90	85
Thailand	72	68
Latin America & the Caribbean		
Argentina	87	n.d
Bolivia	75	n.d
Brazil	76	54
Chile	73	n.d
Colombia	95	n.d
Costa Rica	85	86
Dominican Rep.	88	n.d
Ecuador	88	n.d
El Salvador	89	95
Guatemala	85	n.d
Honduras	78	n.d
Mexico	78	71
Nicaragua	67	n.d
Panama	83	n.d
Paraguay	74	77
Uruguay	83	n.d
Venezuela	79	n.d

	Industry & Services	Manufacturing
Eastern Europe		
Bulgaria	69	n.d
Czech Rep.	81	n.d
Estonia	73	n.d
Hungary	77	70
Latvia	80	89
Lithuania	71	81
Poland	79	n.d
Romania	76	n.d
Russia	70	n.d
Slovakia	78	n.d
Slovenia	86	n.d
Ukraine	72	n.d
Western Europe and Developed Countries		
Australia	90	85
Austria	n.d	66
Belgium	80	80
Denmark	n.d	85
Finland	n.d	79
France	81	79
Germany	n.d	74
Greece	n.d	81
Iceland	71	n.d
Ireland	n.d	75
Luxemburg	70	63
Netherlands	77	n.d
New Zealand	81	78
Norway	n.d	87
Portugal	67	69
Sweden	n.d	90
Switzerland	67	69
United Kingdom	80	72

n.d. = no data
Sources: Wistat, version 4; ECLAC 1998, table 39; UNICEF 1999, table 2.2.

Chart 4.4: Change in Female Wages as % of Male Wages in Industry and Services, c.1980-c.1997

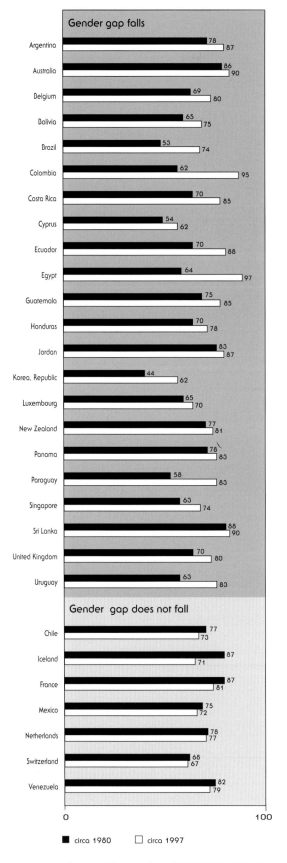

Sources: Wistat, version 4; ECLAC 1998, Table 39; ILO Website:http://laborsta.ilo.org.

Chart 4.5: Change in Female Wages as % of Male Wages in Manufacturing, c.1980-c.1997

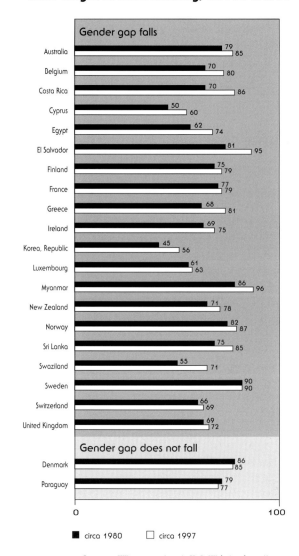

Sources: Wistat, version 4; ILO Website: http://laborsta.ilo.org.

Chart 4.6: Female Monthly Wages as % of Male Wages in Transition Countries, c.1987-c.1992

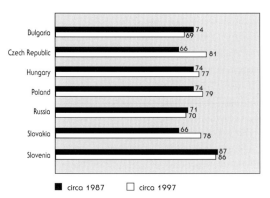

Source: UNICEF 1999, table 2.2.

An analysis of the dispersion of earnings among women in nine countries in Latin America in 1990 and 1997, for example, shows that inequality among women increased in all but two countries, Brazil and Honduras, in both of which inequality was already high (Gálvez 1999).

New evidence for the UK indicates that it is married women with no skills or medium-level skills who experience the greatest economic penalty from the gender gap in wages and from becoming a parent (UK Cabinet Office 2000). The life-time earnings gap for low-skilled and medium-skilled married childless women (as compared to similar men) is 37 per cent of their life-time earnings. For high-skilled, married women without children it is only 12 per cent of life-time earnings. UK women who have children spend some time out of the labour market, and forego some earnings as a result. For a low-skilled woman with two children the loss is largest: £285,000. For a medium-skilled woman, the loss drops to £140,000 and for a high-skilled woman it is only about £19,000 — since women with this level of skills spend much less time out of the labour market.

The Feminization of Poverty

The Beijing Platform for Action refers to the "feminization of poverty" and asks national and international statistical organizations to collect gender-disaggregated data on poverty. The Platform does not define "feminization of poverty," but as Nilüfer Çağatay (1998) points out, the concept is used as "shorthand" for a variety of ideas, including one or more of the following:

- women have a higher *incidence* of income-poverty compared to men;
- women's income-poverty is more *severe* than men's income-poverty;
- over time, the incidence of income-poverty among women is *increasing* compared to that among men.

Income-poverty refers to the lack of sufficient income to support an adequate standard of living. Its incidence is the proportion of the population whose income or consumption level falls below a nationally or internationally agreed poverty line. The severity of income-poverty may be measured by adjusting the incidence of income-poverty for the difference between the poverty line and the average income of the population living under the poverty line (poverty-gap ratio). If this average income is just below the poverty line, then poverty is not as severe as it is if this average income is far below the poverty line. Individuals are considered poor if the per-capita real income/consumption of the household to which they belong is below the poverty line.

Unfortunately, indicators of income-poverty incidence and severity are not usually calculated and presented in a gender-sensitive way. The figures indicate what proportion of the population is in poverty (in the sense of having inadequate incomes), but not how many are men and how many are women. Without a gender-sensitive income-poverty indicator there is no way of estimating the extent of feminization of poverty — leading to the use of global "guesstimates" such as the much-repeated claim that 70 per cent of the world's poor are women. No one can identify the empirical evidence on which this claim is based, and demographic analysis has shown that it is not credible (Marcoux 1998).

Comparisons are often made between the incidence of income- or consumption-poverty among female-headed households and that among male-headed households. But definitions of female headship vary widely, as do reasons for female headship, and empirical investigations reveal no general association between poverty and female headship, though they are associated in some countries (Çağatay 1998; Quisumbing et al. 1995). The widespread consensus is that comparing female and male-headed households is not an appropriate way to measure the degree to which poverty is feminized (Fukuda-Parr 1999; Razavi 1999).

An alternative is to focus on dimensions of poverty besides household income. Box 4 presents a poverty pyramid in which personal consumption

Box 4: Poverty Pyramid

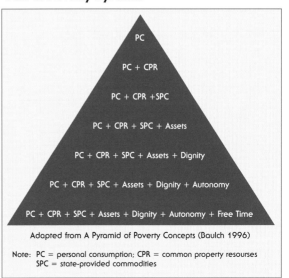

Adapted from A Pyramid of Poverty Concepts (Baulch 1996)

Note: PC = personal consumption; CPR = common property resources
SPC = state-provided commodities

Table 4.3: Adult Population in Poverty, Russian Federation

Gender/age group	% of population below subsistence level			% of respective demographic group		
	1992	1994	1997	1992	1994	1997
Women (age 31+)	32.6	29.1	29.8	71.2	40.4	37.5
Men (age 31+)	21.4	21.8	20.7	59.6	31.7	27.5

Source: Based on UNDP 1998c, table 2.10.

Table 4.4: Gender Poverty Ratio in Selected Countries, 1980s

Sub-Saharan Africa

Country	Women per 100 men in the poorest quintile[1]
Botswana (1993)	192
Côte d'Ivoire (1986-88)	123
Ethiopia (1989-90)	127
Ghana (urban) (1987-88)	141
Ghana (rural) (1987-88)	140
Madagascar (1992)	109
Niger (1989-90)	113
Rwanda (1985-86)	132

Asia & the Pacific

Country	Women per 100 men in the poorest quintile[1]
Bangladesh (1992-93)	130
Indonesia (1988-89)	124
Nepal (1991-92)	93
Pakistan (1986-89)	106
Philippines (Bukidnon) (1984-85)	93

[1] Based on adult equivalents

Latin America & the Caribbean

Country	Women per 100 men in the poorest quintile[1]
Guatemala(1988)	95
Honduras (1988-89)	105

Western Europe & Other Developed Countries

Country	Women per man[1] below the poverty line[2]
Australia (1985-1986)	1.34
Canada (1987)	1.28
Germany (FR) (1984)	1.29
Italy (1986)	1.02
Netherlands (1987)	1.02
Sweden (1987)	0.90
United Kingdom (1986)	1.19
United States (1985)	1.41

[1] aged 18-57

[2] defined as living in a household whose disposable income (after taxes and transfers) is less than 50% of the median disposable income for that country, adjusted for differences in family size.

Sources: UN 1995a, chart 5.21; Caspar et al. 1994.

(PC) is only one element. Other elements are the enjoyment of common property resources (CPR) such as forests and rivers; state-provided commodities (SPC) such as health care and education; and assets such as land and equipment. Besides these tangible dimensions, poverty also includes lack of dignity and autonomy and free time.

Much policy attention is still focused on the conventional measures of income-poverty, so it is important to consider how measures of income-poverty could be made more gender-sensitive. New ways of analysing and presenting existing data could be used to track the feminization of income-poverty. The raw data from household surveys always includes the numbers of males and females in each household and their ages. Thus, it is in principle possible to calculate the proportion of the people in households below the poverty line who are women and the proportion who are men. Table 4.3 presents the example of the Russian Federation, where household surveys over three years found that in each year, adult women comprised a larger share of the population in poverty than did adult men, and poor adult women comprised a larger share of all adult women than poor adult men did of all adult men, suggesting that poverty is indeed feminized.

A particularly useful gender-sensitive indicator is the gender-poverty ratio, that is, the number of women per 100 men (or per man) in the population below the poverty line, or poorest fifth of the population (see UN 1995a). Estimates presented in Table 4.4 indicate that there is feminization of poverty in 12 out of 15 developing countries for which data is available and in 5 out of 8 developed countries for which data is available. This is a measure that deserves to be more widely used, since the statistics to construct it are collected routinely by household surveys in many countries.

Social Obstacles to Women's Empowerment

Many obstacles remain to women enjoying a better return for their participation in the market economy and more scope for shaping the institutions and policies of the societies in which they live. Some of the most important barriers result from the way in which family life and the life of the community are organized in all societies, from the most "traditional" to the most "modern." Three of the most important of these are interrelated: violence against women, the burden of HIV/AIDS and the unequal sharing of unpaid caring work. There are big gaps in information required to track the extent to which each of these obstacles is getting stronger or weaker. But in all three cases, new efforts are underway that should make it easier to track progress in reducing them.

Violence Against Women

The United Nations Declaration on the Elimination of Violence Against Women, adopted by the UN General Assembly in 1993, defines violence against women as "any act of gender-based violence that results in, or is likely to result in, physical, sexual or mental harm or suffering to women, including threats of such acts, coercion or arbitrary deprivation of liberty, whether occurring in public or in private life."

The Declaration states that violence against women encompasses, among other things, "physical, sexual and psychological violence occurring in the family and in the general community, including battering, sexual abuse of female children, dowry-related violence, marital rape, female genital mutilation and other traditional practices harmful to women, non-spousal violence and violence related to exploitation, sexual harassment, and intimidation at work, in educational institutions and elsewhere, trafficking in women, forced prostitution, and violence perpetrated or condoned by the state" (UN 1993a). All of these forms of violence are associated with power inequalities: between women and men, between children and their care-givers, as well as with growing economic inequalities both within and between countries.

It is not easy to measure the precise extent of violence against women, as it requires inquiring into sensitive areas of women's lives about which women may be very reluctant to speak. However, there are a number of studies of one widespread kind of violence against women: domestic violence committed by a husband or boyfriend. The results of the most comprehensive of these studies are presented in Table 4.5. The different methods used in different studies make it impossible to draw definite conclusions about where the problem is most severe. But the figures show that the violation of women's human rights is widespread and substantial, affecting between about 10 per cent to over 50 per cent of adult women in all regions of the world. Since domestic violence tends to be underreported, the true incidence is probably higher.

These stark figures underline the fact that although the home and community are places where women provide care for others, they are also where millions of women experience coercion and abuse. The challenge is to institutionalize the measurement of violence against women, so that data is collected by national statistical offices, on a comparable basis, in a wider range of countries. This would enable progress in reducing violence against women to be tracked over time. The World Health Organization (WHO) is currently undertaking a multi-country study on women's health and domestic violence against women which seeks,

Table 4.5: Prevalence of Violence Against Women by an Intimate Partner

	Year	Adult women assaulted by intimate partner (%)
Northern and Sub-Saharan Africa		
Egypt	1995-1996	34.4
Ethiopia	1995	45.0
Kenya	1984-1987	42.0[1]
Nigeria	1993 P	31.4
South Africa	1998	13.0
Uganda	1995-1996	40.0
Zimbabwe	1996	17.0
Central and Western Asia		
Turkey	1998	57.9
Asia and the Pacific		
Bangladesh	1993	42.0[1]
Cambodia	1996 P	16.0
India	1999	40.0
Korea, Rep.	1989	38.0
Philippines	1993	5.1
Thailand	1994	20.0[1]
Latin America and the Caribbean		
Barbados	1990	30.0
Bolivia	1998	17.0[2]
Chile	1993 P	26.0[1]
Colombia	1995	19.0[1]
Mexico	1996	27.0
Nicaragua	1997	30.2[2]
Paraguay	1995-1996	9.5
Peru	1997 P	30.9[2]
Uruguay	1997	10.0[2]
Eastern Europe		
Moldova, Rep.	1997	14
Western Europe and Other Developed Countries		
Australia	1996	8.0[1]
Canada	1993	29.0
Netherlands	1989	20.8
New Zealand	1994	35.0
Norway	1989 P	18.0
Switzerland	1994-1996	12.6
United Kingdom	1993 P	30.0
United States	1998	22.1

[1] In current relationship
[2] In past 12 months
P indicates year of publication rather than year data was gathered

Sources: WHO database; Wistat, version 4; Johns Hopkins Population Information Program, www.jhuccp.org/pr/111edsum.stm.

among other things, to obtain reliable estimates of the prevalence and frequency of violence against women in both urban and rural locations. Participating countries include Brazil, Peru, Namibia, Thailand and Japan. UNIFEM intends to support further work on developing indicators relevant to the measurement of efforts and achievements in ending violence against women.

Many cultures have beliefs, norms and social institutions that legitimize and so perpetuate violence against women. Acts that would be punished if directed at an employee, a neighbour or an acquaintance often go unchallenged when directed by men at women, especially within the family. UNIFEM is working to help create a world free of violence against women, by supporting innovative programmes by women's organizations and governments around the world (see Box 5).

Impact Visuals/Cedric Nunn

Women and HIV/AIDS

HIV/AIDS is the fourth most common cause of death worldwide (WHO 1999). Women experience a double burden as a result of the spread of HIV/AIDS: a burden of suffering and a burden of caring for those who are suffering. The latest regional figures from UNAIDS show that 55 per cent of those living with HIV/AIDS in Sub-Saharan Africa are women. In other regions women are in a minority among those living with HIV/AIDS – but they bear most of the burden of caring for men and children who are infected. Coercive relations with sexual partners is a major way in which women become infected with HIV/AIDS. Infection rates among pregnant women are also rising. Approximately 90 per cent of the 1 million children under age 15 living with HIV worldwide have acquired the disease from their mothers during pregnancy, at birth and through breast-feeding.

Table 4.6 shows the prevalence of HIV/AIDS by country, in 1997. More data is available for the regions where the epidemic is more long-standing,

Box 5: End Violence Against Women

"Imagine a world free from gender violence where homes are not shattered; where shame and silence are cast aside for new, joyful melodies; where women and men develop the capacity and the courage to live to their full potential." –Noeleen Heyzer, March 1999

In 1998, the 50th Anniversary of the Universal Declaration of Human Rights, UNIFEM drew together several initiatives to focus the world's attention on ending violence against women. First, it coordinated existing regional campaigns to end violence against women in Africa, Asia and the Pacific, and Latin America and the Caribbean. These campaigns generated a public outpouring on an issue that had long been silenced, receiving widespread media attention and impelling political and religious leaders to come out publicly against religious and cultural practices harmful to women and girls.

On 8 March 1999, UNIFEM sponsored a global interagency videoconference, "A World Free of Violence Against Women," which linked together the UN General Assembly in New York with audiences in New Delhi, Mexico City, Nairobi, and the European Parliament in Strasbourg, France. More than 2000 people filled the General Assembly and the other four sites, and viewing audiences from all over the world hooked up to the videoconference via satellite, the Internet and videoconference technologies. Government leaders joined with the courageous survivors of gender-based violence in focusing a global spotlight on what Secretary-General Kofi Annan called "the most shameful human rights violation."

In preparation for the videoconference, UNIFEM initiated an on-line discussion group, <end-violence>, to enable individuals and groups worldwide to talk to each other about their work to end the incidence and impact of violence against women and girls. Focusing on what works and what does not, the discussion group has taken on a life of its own; more than 1,300 participants have continued to exchange e-mail information, generating ideas and strategies to share with women in different parts of the world.

"This is the positive, human side of globalization...A woman from Papua New Guinea asks about working with male batterers, and an activist from Moscow answers her questions."
— *Toronto Star,* 6 February 1999

UNIFEM manages a Trust Fund in Support of Actions to Eliminate Violence Against Women. As of August 2000, the fund had mobilized $5.1 million, supporting 88 organizations in 54 countries.

Break the silence . . .

. . . say no to violence against women and girls

Table 4.6: Prevalence of HIV/AIDS (at the end of 1997)

Sub-Saharan Africa

	Women with HIV/AIDS/ adults with HIV/AIDS (%)	Adults with HIV/AIDS/ adult population (%)
Angola	52	2.12
Benin	50	2.06
Botswana	49	25.10
Burkina Faso	49	7.17
Burundi	50	8.30
Cameroon	48	4.89
Central African Rep.	50	10.77
Chad	51	2.72
Congo	49	7.78
Côte d'Ivoire	49	10.06
Congo, DR	50	4.35
Djibouti	50	10.30
Equatorial Guinea	48	1.21
Eritrea	n.d	3.17
Ethiopia	48	9.31
Gabon	50	4.25
Gambia	48	2.24
Ghana	50	2.38
Guinea	50	2.09
Guinea-Bissau	52	2.25
Kenya	49	11.64
Lesotho	50	8.35
Liberia	50	3.65
Madagascar	50	0.12
Malawi	49	14.92
Mali	50	1.67
Mauritania	49	0.52
Mauritius	n.d	0.08
Mozambique	48	14.17
Namibia	50	19.94
Niger	51	1.45
Nigeria	50	4.12
Reunion	n.d	0.04
Rwanda	49	12.75
Senegal	50	1.77
Sierra Leone	50	3.17
Somalia	n.d	0.25
South Africa	50	12.91
Sudan	n.d	0.99
Swaziland	51	18.50
Togo	51	8.52
Uganda	49	9.51
Tanzania	49	9.42
Zambia	51	19.07
Zimbabwe	51	25.84

Northern Africa

	Women with HIV/AIDS/ adults with HIV/AIDS (%)	Adults with HIV/AIDS/ adult population (%)
Algeria	n.d	0.07
Egypt	10	0.03
Libyan	n.d	0.05
Morocco	n.d	0.03
Tunisia	n.d	0.04

Central and Western Asia

	Women with HIV/AIDS/ adults with HIV/AIDS (%)	Adults with HIV/AIDS/ adult population (%)
Armenia	n.d	0.01
Azerbaijan	n.d	0.00
Bahrain	n.d	0.15
Cyprus	n.d	0.26
Georgia	n.d	0.00
Iraq	n.d	0.00
Israel	n.d	0.07
Jordan	n.d	0.02
Kazakhstan	n.d	0.03
Kuwait	n.d	0.12
Kyrgyzstan	n.d	0.00
Lebanon	n.d	0.09
Oman	n.d	0.11
Qatar	n.d	0.09
Saudi Arabia	n.d	0.01
Syria	n.d	0.01
Tajikistan	n.d	0.00
Turkey	n.d	0.01
Turkmenistan	n.d	0.01
UAE	n.d	0.18
Uzbekistan	n.d	0.00
Yemen	n.d	0.01

Asia and the Pacific

	Women with HIV/AIDS/ adults with HIV/AIDS (%)	Adults with HIV/AIDS/ adult population (%)
Afghanistan	n.d	0.00
Bangladesh	15	0.03
Bhutan	n.d	0.00
Brunei Darussalam	n.d	0.17
Cambodia	50	2.40
China	12	0.06
Hong Kong, China	39	0.08
India	24	0.82
Indonesia	25	0.05
Iran	n.d	0.00
Korea, PDR	n.d	0.00
Korea, Rep.	13	0.01
Lao PDR	52	0.04
Malaysia	20	0.62
Maldives	n.d	0.05
Mongolia	n.d	0.01
Myanmar	21	1.79
Nepal	40	0.24
Pakistan	19	0.09
Philippines	30	0.06
Singapore	20	0.15
Sri Lanka	30	0.07
Thailand	38	2.23
Viet Nam	20	0.22

Latin America and the Caribbean

	Women with HIV/AIDS/ adults with HIV/AIDS (%)	Adults with HIV/AIDS/ adult population (%)
Argentina	18	0.69
Bahamas	34	3.77
Barbados	33	2.89
Belize	25	1.89
Bolivia	14	0.07
Brazil	23	0.63
Chile	18	0.20
Colombia	15	0.36
Costa Rica	26	0.55
Cuba	32	0.02
Dominican Rep.	33	1.89
Ecuador	14	0.28
El Salvador	24	0.58
Guatemala	25	0.52
Guyana	33	2.13
Haiti	34	5.17
Honduras	24	1.46
Jamaica	31	0.99
Mexico	12	0.35
Nicaragua	24	0.19
Panama	25	0.61
Paraguay	18	0.13
Peru	15	0.56
Suriname	33	1.17
Trinidad & Tobago	33	0.94
Uruguay	17	0.33
Venezuela	15	0.69

Eastern Europe

	Women with HIV/AIDS/ adults with HIV/AIDS (%)	Adults with HIV/AIDS/ adult population (%)
Albania	n.d	0.01
Belarus	n.d	0.17
Bosnia-Herzegovina	n.d	0.04
Bulgaria	n.d	0.01
Croatia	n.d	0.01
Czech Rep.	n.d	0.04
Estonia	n.d	0.01
Hungary	n.d	0.04
Latvia	n.d	0.01
Lithuania	n.d	0.01
Macedonia, FYR	n.d	0.01
Poland	n.d	0.06
Moldova, Republic	n.d	0.11
Romania	n.d	0.01
Russian Federation	n.d	0.05
Slovakia	n.d	0.00
Slovenia	n.d	0.01
Ukraine	n.d	0.43
Yugoslavia	n.d	0.10

Western Europe and Other Developed Countries

	Women with HIV/AIDS/ adults with HIV/AIDS (%)	Adults with HIV/AIDS/ adult population (%)
Australia	5	0.14
Austria	19	0.18
Belgium	36	0.14
Canada	13	0.33
Denmark	25	0.12
Finland	20	0.02
France	n.d	0.37
Germany	19	0.08
Greece	n.d	0.14
Iceland	n.d	0.14
Ireland	n.d	0.09
Italy	30	0.31
Japan	6	0.01
Luxembourg	0	0.14
Malta	n.d	0.11
Netherlands	n.d	0.17
New Zealand	15	0.07
Norway	n.d	0.06
Portugal	19	0.69
Spain	21	0.57
Sweden	24	0.07
Switzerland	34	0.32
United Kingdom	n.d	0.09
United States	20	0.76

"0.00" means that the estimated rate is less than 0.005%
"0" means that the estimated number was less than 100.
n.d. = no data
Source: Wistat, version 4.

Box 6: Addressing the Challenge of HIV/AIDS

UNIFEM is partnering with UNAIDS and UNFPA to devise new strategies to increase awareness of the gender dimensions of AIDS. The joint initiative, "Gender Focused Responses to Address the Challenges of HIV/AIDS," concentrates on strengthening the capacity of women's groups to address HIV/AIDS as a gender issue; increasing the knowledge base of UNIFEM and its partners about the concerns of women living with HIV/AIDS, and forging new partnerships between government, civil society, and the private sector to leverage support for women living with HIV/AIDS.

Workshops in three regions enabled participants to learn from each other about the concerns of women with HIV/AIDS in different parts of the world and the strategies to address them. Following the workshops, three core groups are focusing on human rights advocacy, information gathering and capacity building.

The human rights advocacy group encourages journalists to write stories about women living with HIV/AIDS, seeking to build an archive of articles recording the violation of human rights of people living with HIV/AIDS. Lydia Cacho, a journalist with the Mexican news service CIMAC, attended a workshop in Senegal in October 1999. Since her return, she has written numerous newspaper articles on gender and HIV/AIDS in Africa and organized her own workshops on gender-focused journalism. She says: "After working for three years on gender and HIV/AIDS, I was burnt out and tired. I was re-charged after participating and [the workshop] stirred my desires to work on the issues."

The information group has focused on community-based research on the gender dimensions of HIV/AIDS. Among their findings:

• in India, knowledge about the protective aspects of condom use became available to women only once they had become infected;
• in Senegal, women's lack of knowledge about sexuality and the transmission of disease is greater among housewives than among sex workers;
• in Zimbabwe, home-based care-givers seek information on how to cope with the disease rather than how to prevent it.

The capacity-building group is drawing from two ongoing initiatives in the field to develop a resource guide to empower women to negotiate safe sexual practices:

• a project on STD and HIV/AIDS prevention in Calcutta, which has successfully reduced the HIV/AIDS prevalence rate among sex workers through greater use of condoms, improved access to health care facilities and organizing into a union;
• a project to promote the female condom in Senegal in response to a woman-initiated demand for a means to protect themselves against HIV/AIDS.

and its prevalence is higher: Sub-Saharan Africa, Asia and the Pacific, Latin America and the Caribbean, and Western Europe and Other Developed Countries. Data was not available for 1997 for the regions where the epidemic is of low maturity: Northern Africa, Western and Central Asia, and Eastern Europe. Areas of low maturity cannot afford complacency, however, since once the proportion of the adult population living with HIV/AIDS is above 1 per cent, the disease spreads very rapidly. In Asia, incidence has doubled since 1994. The steepest curve in rising infection rates in 1999 was in the newly independent states of the former Soviet Union, according to UNAIDS.

The epidemic is at its worst in Sub-Saharan Africa, where in 1999 more people died from HIV/AIDS than as a result of armed conflict. Statistics do not really reveal the agony:

> *Permit me to begin with a statement recently made by a woman living with HIV/AIDS in Africa. This woman who for eight months weathered bouts of diarrhea, fought herpes zoster, lived with a persistent cough, vomited most of what she ate and bore drenching night sweats and ulcers, cried out with firmness and commitment, "Let us stop pretending about the problem. The problem is real. I am a living example. There are thousands suffering out there. The disease is spreading like wildfire every day and night. So why all this pretense? The sooner we face reality as individuals and as a society the better for all of us."*

—Madhu Bala Nath, New York, February 2000

Many agencies, including UNIFEM, are supporting programmes that respond to the gender dimensions of the epidemic, focusing on women's lack of knowledge of or control over their own bodies and the terms on which sexual activities take place (see Box 6). Strong prevention programmes can reduce the spread of the disease. For example, in Uganda and Thailand "the incidence of new infections, particularly in young populations, has declined by about one-third in response to intensive information and protection campaigns" (UNFPA 1999:10).

However, pressure to cut public expenditure makes it harder to finance programmes to prevent and to treat HIV/AIDS. And some measures taken to increase health service efficiency make it more difficult for women with HIV/AIDS to get access to drugs and treatments to palliate the disease. Community-based research by UNIFEM and other partners in Mexico found that although official policy provides free access to expensive anti-retroviral drugs for people living with AIDS, access is through market-based health insurance schemes that cover only people in formal sector employment. This leaves out the majority of women, who are in informal employment.

The insurance scheme of last resort is the extended family, but under the onslaught of HIV/AIDS this is showing signs of vulnerability. In Sub-Saharan Africa, women widowed by HIV/AIDS cannot always count on the support of kin. In Asia, more and more women living with HIV/AIDS are living as single deserted women.

Unequal Share of Unpaid Care Work

In this report "no name" work is given a name: unpaid care work. Chapter 1 discussed how such work is defined and how it relates to unpaid work in family businesses and to paid work (whether inside or outside the home). Here the focus is on measurement through time-use surveys, which can reveal how much time men and women spend on unpaid care labour, and how this compares with the time spent on market-oriented work. Indicators of time spent in unpaid care labour are not yet included in the Wistat or any other global database. Currently national time-use studies are available for a limited number of countries, but many more countries are in the process of designing and implementing such surveys (see Box 7).

> "Vietnamese women spend a lot of time on 'no name' work such as housework to take care of the family, care of the elderly and the handicapped and child care."
>
> — Lucita Lazo (1999)

Most available studies show that women spend much more time on unpaid care labour than do men, and this imbalance persists even when women have full-time paid jobs or full-time responsibilities for producing food for their families.

Information on time use in Western Europe and Other Developed Countries and Eastern Europe, in the late 1980s and early 1990s shows that women as a whole typically provide around 70 per cent of the time spent on unpaid care work within the family while men provide around 30 per cent (UN 1995a, table 4.8). The same pattern seems to prevail in several developing countries for which information is currently available (see Box 8, p. 102). The obligation to care for others puts care-givers at a disadvantage in the market economy. In developed countries with ageing populations, more and more of that care is for elderly people. One small US study found that people caring for elderly relatives sacrifice substantial wages and benefits by foregoing promotions, training and transfers and taking

Box 7: Progress in Measuring Unpaid Care Work

Since 1995, at least 24 developing countries have designed or undertaken national time-use surveys or have included time-use modules in household surveys, including:

- Africa: Benin, Chad, Mali, Morocco, Nigeria, South Africa;
- Latin America and the Caribbean: Cuba, Dominican Republic, Ecuador, Guatemala, Mexico, Nicaragua;
- Asia: China, Indonesia, Laos, India, Nepal, Oman, Palestine, Philippines, Republic of Korea, Thailand, Viet Nam.

The Statistical Office of the European Commission, Eurostat, is coordinating a Europe-wide time-use survey involving 18 countries in Eastern and Western Europe. Among other developed countries, Japan conducts national time-use studies every five years; Australia conducted surveys in 1992 and 1997; Canada included three questions on unpaid work in the 1996 national census and has conducted time-use surveys at regular intervals since the early 1980s; and the United States is undertaking preliminary studies for a time-use survey.

Many more developing countries, including Pakistan, Sri Lanka, Malaysia and Bangladesh, are interested in conducting time-use surveys. Support for the efforts of developing countries is being provided by the UN Statistical Division, the United Nations Development Programme Project to Promote Gender Equality in the Asia Pacific Region and the International Development Research Centre, Canada.

Sources: Guerrero 2000; UN 2000c; Lazo 1999.

UNICEF/Carolyn Watson

Box 8: Time Spent in Unpaid Care Work

Mexico

In 1995, women spent on average 28.4 hours a week on unpaid work in the home, and 32.7 hours per week on employment outside the home. Men spent 11.9 hours a week on unpaid work in the home and 39.9 hours a week on employment outside the home. In addition, 90.5 per cent of economically active women also carried out unpaid work in the home, compared to only 62.4 per cent of economically active men.

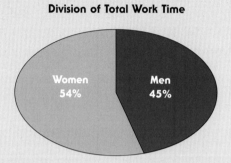

Division of Total Work Time

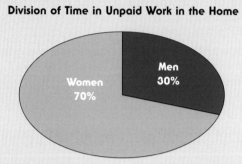

Division of Time in Unpaid Work in the Home

Bangladesh

Paid employment of women in the manufacturing sector grew rapidly in Bangladesh in the 1980s, with the expansion of the garment industry. But women manufacturing workers still had responsibility for most of the unpaid care work within families.

Average Weekly Hours of Work of Urban Manufacturing Workers, 1990-1991

	Male		Female	
	Formal Sector Workers	Informal Sector Workers	Formal Sector Workers	Informal Sector Workers
Manufacturing Work	53	23	56	21
Unpaid Care Work	13	14	31	24
Total	66	37	87	44

The total working hours of women were longer than those of men in both the formal and informal sectors. Those working the longest hours were women in the formal sector.

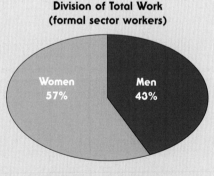

Division of Total Work
(formal sector workers)

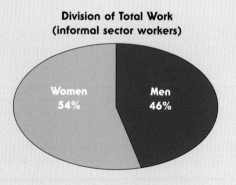

Division of Total Work
(informal sector workers)

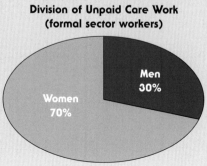

Division of Unpaid Care Work
(formal sector workers)

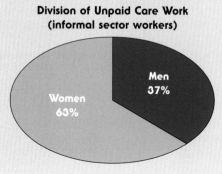

Division of Unpaid Care Work
(informal sector workers)

Sources: Mexico: UNIFEM/CONMUJER 1999:65; Bangladesh: Zohir 1998.

extended time away from their paid work. It v
estimated that individuals in the study on aver:
lost more than half a million dollars in lost wa;
social security and pension benefits over t'
lifetimes (*New York Times*, 27 November 199'

"Time is the one unit of exchange we all
have in equal amounts, the one investmen
we all have to make, the one resource we
cannot reproduce."

— Marilyn Waring (1999)

Composite Indicators

In addition to looking at indicators of specific
dimensions of women's lives and the obstacles to
women's empowerment, it is possible to construct
composite indicators that attempt to aggregate
several indicators into a single index. The best-
known composite indicators are the Human
Development Index (HDI), the Gender Sensitive
Development Index (GDI) and the Gender
Empowerment Measure (GEM), used in UNDP's
Human Development Reports (see Box 9). These
all draw attention to the fact that economic growth
does not automatically translate into progress for
people, and make clear that human development
does not always translate into gender equality.

The GDI and GEM were introduced in 1995, and
the 1999 Human Development Report published GDI
for 143 countries and GEM for 102 countries. It is
important to note that neither the GDI nor the GEM is
a direct measure of gender inequality, because they
include pointers both to the relative capabilities and relative exercise of economic and political power of
women and men, and to the absolute capabilities and
powers of women and men. This is in many ways a
strength – progress for women is not a matter just of
narrowing the gap between women and men, but also
of an improvement in the level of the quality of life
enjoyed by women and their communities and the level
of resources over which they have command. An exclu-
sive focus on gender gaps can divert attention from dete-
riorations in the general standard of living enjoyed by
both men and women, which may outweigh any
progress made in narrowing gender gaps. However,
when a single index aims to reflect both relative and
absolute dimensions of progress, it leads to complica-
tions in the construction and interpretation of the index.

The GDI was introduced to adjust the HDI for
gender disparities so that a given level of achievement
on the HDI indicators counts for less if it is based on
different achievements for men and women. If there
were no differences between men and women in life

standard
the HDI.
than men,
ted on the
ndex and a
e expectan-
capita. The
ch indicator
ige, with the
ountries with
which the GDI
is less than u.. he size of the
gender gap for each componen... d the penalty
factor applied to the gap.

*An identical gender gap in income shares (e.g.
women earning 20% and men 80% of earned
income) will yield more than four times the
gender penalty in a rich country such as
Saudi Arabia than in a poor country such as
Bangladesh. In most countries, the earned
income gap accounts for more than 90
per cent of the gender penalty* (Bardhan and
Klasen 1999: 987).

Box 9: Composite Indices: HDI, GDI and GEM

HDI

The Human Development Index (HDI) measures the
average achievement of a country in basic human
capabilities. The HDI indicates whether people lead a
long and healthy life, are educated and knowledgeable
and enjoy a decent standard of living. The HDI examines
the average condition of all people in a country;
distributional inequalities for various groups of society
have to be calculated separately.

GDI

The Gender-Related Development Index (GDI) measures
achievement in the same basic capabilities as the
HDI does, but takes note of inequality in achievement
between women and men. The methodology used
imposes a penalty for inequality, such that the GDI falls
when the achievement levels of both women and men
in a country go down or when the disparity between
their achievements increases. The greater the gender
disparity in basic capabilities, the lower a country's GDI
compared with its HDI. The GDI is simply the HDI dis-
counted, or adjusted downwards, for gender inequality.

GEM

The Gender Empowerment Measure (GEM) examines
whether women and men are able to actively
participate in economic and political life and take part
in decision-making. While the GDI focuses on expansion
of basic human capabilities, the GEM is concerned with
the use of those capabilities to take advantage of the
opportunities of life.

Source: UNDP 1995.

Unfortunately, the measurement of the earned income gap is the most unreliable component of the GDI. It cannot be measured directly, so it is estimated on the basis of data on female non-agricultural wages as a percentage of male non-agricultural wages, and female and male shares of the economically active population. But it is subject to the same problems of data availability discussed earlier. For the majority of countries covered by the GDI, data on the gender wage gap is not available from the ILO. So the HDR assumes that the ratio is 75 per cent, and the female and male shares in earned income are estimated on this basis. Moreover, although male and female shares of the labour force are available for most countries, the female share tends to be underestimated, especially in poor agricultural countries where women's participation in the agricultural labour force is generally undercounted.

The Gender Empowerment Measure attempts to assess the comparative political and economic power of men and women, taking into account not only their relative power over the national "pie" but also the size of the pie itself. "Richer countries should rank higher on GEM on the basis of income alone. If they do not, this indicates the need for more progress in achieving gender equality" (UNDP 1995: 86).

This concern makes the measure more complicated than if the objective were simply to measure the relative power of men and women over the national pie, but this complexity addresses an important issue. Women may increase their power to make decisions about how to produce and consume the national pie – but if the national pie is itself very small, then women's increased power relative to men in their country does not give them much more power over real resources.

The GEM is a measure that aims to set the relative economic and political power of men and women in any particular country in the context of the scale of that country's resources, as measured by its GDP per capita. If women in a rich country and in a poor country have equal relative shares of economic and political power in relation to men in that country, the GEM will show the women in the rich country having greater power than the women in the poor country. This seems appropriate for a measure that is applied internationally. It sets women's empowerment in an international development context and relates gender equality to inequality between countries. But it means that a higher GEM cannot be interpreted in a straightforward way as an indication of the extent to which the country with the higher GEM has policies better able to provide gender equality, because the higher GEM also reflects the fact that the country is itself richer.

A simplified explanation of the way in which the GEM is constructed is shown in Box 10.

Because the GEM takes into account purchasing power as well as the exercise of economic and political decision-making power, it is not appropriate simply to add up the different shares and divide by the number of components to get a composite index. That would be the equivalent of adding apples and pears. Thus the GEM follows the pattern of the HDI and the GDI: Step 1, the identification of components and indicators, is followed by Step 2, the construction of an index for each component, before Step 3, when the scores on each index are summed and divided by the number of components (implying an equal weight for each component index).

Like all composite indices, the GEM is open to criticism on the choice of components to include. Moreover, empowerment is a complicated idea and a single global quantitative index will be unable to capture many important dimensions of empowerment. The GEM is an average measure at the national level, designed for global comparisons. It is not designed to measure empowerment of particular groups of women in particular localities but to capture average differences between countries. It is particularly useful for cross-country analysis, such as that of the relation between women's empowerment and public expenditure.

Chart 4.7 shows that there is some tendency for a higher score on the Gender Empowerment Measure to be associated with a higher level of non-military government expenditure as a percentage of GNP. This may be because in societies in which women have more of the kind of power measured by the GEM, they press for more public services and income transfers from better off to poorer people; or because in societies where there is more provision of public services and income transfers from better off to poorer people, women are able to acquire more of the kind of power measured by the GEM. It is probably a mixture of the two. It would be interesting to explore this relationship comparing, say, with different measures of women's empowerment and more detailed measures of public provision, the amount of time women have to spend on getting fuel and water and preparing food with public expenditure on energy, water and transport services to households. But the data required to do this are not readily available.

Box 10: The Gender Empowerment Measure (GEM)

Step 1	Types of Power	Indicator
	Economic Power: Purchasing power	Women's share of real GDP (PPS $)
	Decision-making power	Women's share of administrative and management positions, and of professional and technical positions.
	Political Power: Parliamentary decision-making	Women's share of seats in parliament
Step 2	**Indices of Gender Gaps in Power**	
	Economic Power: Purchasing power	Gap between female and male proportional income-shares, weighted so as to penalize gender inequality and weighted by the level of real GDP per capita.
	Decision-making power	Gap between female and male proportional shares of administrative & management positions, weighted to penalize gender inequality. Gap between female & male proportional shares of professional & technical positions weighted to penalize gender inequality.
	Combined Decision-making Power Index	Simple average of administrative and management index and professional and technical index
	Political Power: Parliamentary decision-making	Gap between female and male proportional shares of seats in parliament, weighted so as to penalize inequality
Step 3	**Composite Index** GEM	Add together the three indices calculated in Step 2 and divide by 3.

"Quantified data are a crucial lever for any analysis of change".

— Devaki Jain and Samia Ahmad (1999)

Chart 4.7: GEM and Public Expenditure

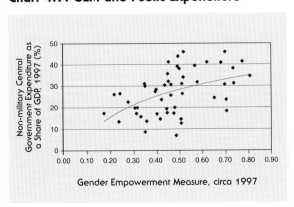

Gender Empowerment Measure, circa 1997

Source: Calculated from data in the Human Development Report CD-ROM.

Women in India have adapted the idea behind the GEM to the circumstances in their country, constructing for each state three different composite indexes of women's empowerment, based on indicators of women's relative representation at different levels of the political system, relative exercise of the right to vote, relative literacy rate, relative life expectancy and relative income share (Jain and Ahmad 1999; Mehta 1996).

Improving Information on the Progress of Women

UNIFEM supports a number of initiatives to improve statistical information about women's lives, including the production of a set of statistical profiles of women and men in the countries in the Asia Pacific region and in Mexico, Colombia and Ecuador. It supports ongoing programmes to improve gender statistics and indicators in South and South East Asian and Pacific countries; Arab countries, Central America and the Spanish-speaking Caribbean, and East Africa.

Two particularly noteworthy programmes are the creation of a computerized system of sex-disaggregated social and economic indicators for Mexico (SISESIM) and the "engendering" of the Indian Census 2001. SISESIM is a system of indicators for women's policy design, implementation and evaluation that covers education, health, work (market-oriented and unpaid care), political participation and housing. It includes disaggregations by age, level of education and place of residence, as well as by sex. The system was developed through a series of interactive workshops between producers and users of statistics. One outcome was an agreement to collect information on the ownership or tenancy of housing by sex in the National Time Use Survey. Before this, no national survey in Mexico included this information.

The "engendering" of the Indian Census comprises a series of activities to ensure that women's work is more visible in the world's largest regular census. The Indian Census of 1981 indicated that only 13 per cent of women were economically active – but other research showed that about 89 per cent of Indian women participated in informal employment in unregistered enterprises. The way the census was conducted clearly did not capture the full extent of women's economic activity. UNIFEM built an alliance between key Indian officials and research institutes to press for changes in the conduct of the census, which resulted in a wide range of changes in 1991. Among other things, the questionnaire was modified to explicitly include casual or seasonal unpaid work in family farms and enterprises. Enumerators were encouraged to think about the wide variety of work that women do in family farms and enterprises and trained to ask detailed questions about such work. A public information campaign, including a theme song by a popular singer, portrayed the various roles of women workers in rural and urban settings. In addition, a series of workshops helped senior government officials to understand the ways in which the new census data could be used in their ministries. Building upon this experience, UNIFEM is supporting further improvements in the conduct of the 2001 census, including further training for enumerators and wider public information efforts.

UNIFEM is also a partner in Women Informal Employment Globalizing and Organizing (WIEGO), an international network that is working to improve statistics on women's informal sector employment in accord with priorities developed by grass-roots organizations. These include the inclusion of street vendors and home-based workers in surveys and the compilation of statistics on contribution of the informal sector to GNP, disaggregated by sex.

At the national level, technical assistance is being provided to Central Statistical Offices of Kenya and India. At the international level, WIEGO is represented in the Expert Group on Informal Statistics, the International Conference of Labour Statisticians and a variety of other UN expert groups and has influenced the content of the new ILO manual on informal sector surveys. As improved statistics become available, they are used in policy advocacy by HomeNet, SEWA (India), SEWU (South Africa) and the International Alliance of Street Vendors. These organizations find that statistics that give women greater visibility also give them greater voice.

Priorities for New Information

Different ways of assessing women's progress are feasible and appropriate at local, national, regional and global levels. This report has drawn upon UN databases to assess global progress in meeting objectives agreed at UN conferences. A great deal of the information that would be useful in such an assessment is not available in those databases. The Beijing conference stressed the importance of more information on women's unpaid work for their families and communities – and many more countries are now in the process of collecting this through time-use surveys. Priorities for further sex-disaggregated data include:

- gender poverty ratios to track the feminization of poverty;
- business ownership by sex of owner and size of business;
- job quality, by proportion of women and men in paid employment with jobs that have social protection rights attached to them;
- income inequality among women;
- incidence of violence against women.

"Figures can really help change things."

— Renana Jhabwala, SEWA, Ottawa, 1999

Information on the status of women will not by itself improve their lives. Strategies must be agreed for using all available data to hold governments, corporations and international bodies accountable for the impact of their policies on women.

Chapter 5

Accountability for the Progress of Women: Women Demanding Action

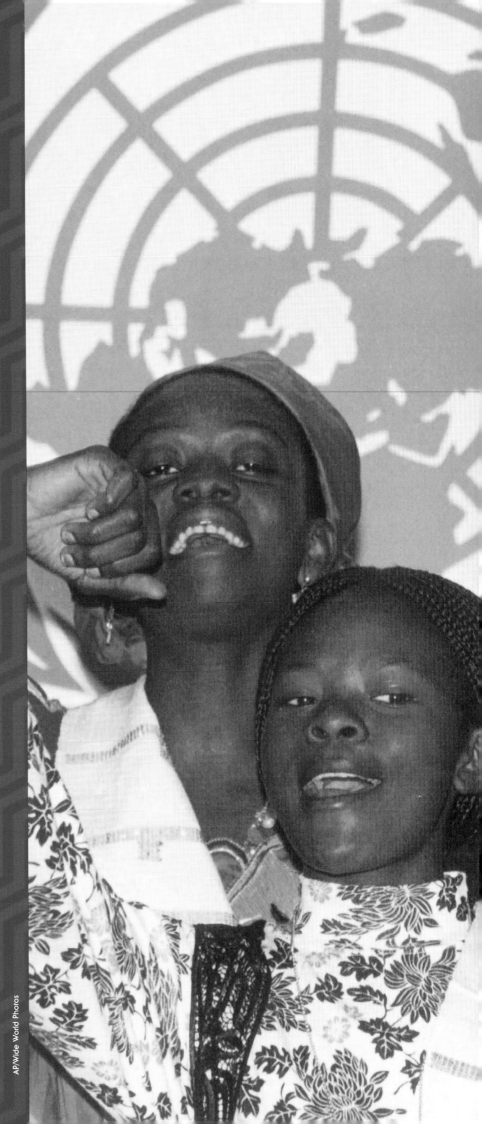

Introduction

Assessing the progress of women against agreed-upon targets reveals how much change there has been – but also how much still remains to be done. The next step is to identify the institutions and individuals that can deliver on commitments and find ways to hold them accountable for doing so. The major actors are governments and business corporations at the national level, and multilateral agencies, international financial institutions and global and regional trade institutions, notably the World Trade Organization, at the global level. This chapter will discuss how women can become more effective in holding governments to account for the way they raise and spend money, and corporations to account for the ways they make money.

"...the surge of new approaches for measuring progress [is] matched by a growing interest in forging tools for accountability that are constructive, participatory and promote ownership of the process by women and the institutions involved at the community and country level."

— International Women's Tribune Centre (2000)

As discussed in Chapter 1, people's livelihoods everywhere are being reshaped by globalization, an international process of market extension and liberalization that brings about new opportunities and new uncertainties. More women than ever are participating in the market economy, but they do so on terms that are often precarious. Globalization is an uneven process, which is concentrating economic power in fewer countries and fewer corporations and constricting the power of governments to deliver on policies that sustain human development and promote gender equality.

As noted in Chapter 2, states have made national and international policy commitments to advance the status of women. However, with globalization, non-state institutions now increasingly affect the ability of governments to promote or hinder women's progress. Organizations of civil society, labour unions, chambers of commerce and business corporations, as well as multilateral agencies and international economic institutions, are part of a decision-making universe that reflects a shift from govern*ment* to gover*nance*. Governance entails a system of partnerships among governmental, para-governmental and non-governmental organizations in which the state is not sovereign but seen as a first among equals (Jessop 1997:575).

There is a vigorous debate about the extent to which modern nation-states have in fact been "hollowed out" and lost their power, and the extent to

Anne Marie Goetz

Box 1: Right-to-Information Campaign in India

The efforts of a small organization in rural Rajastan, struggling for the rights of poor people, particularly women, to a minimum wage, have triggered a nationwide right-to-information campaign. Since 1994, the Mazdoor Kisan Shakti Sangathan (Workers' and Farmers' Power Association, or MKSS) has highlighted the importance of access to information in securing poor people's livelihoods. In a series of public hearings, or social audits, they demand that government officials explain how money was spent on local development projects. Hearings begin with a puppet show, portraying the diversion of development funds by village leaders, politicians, and government officials. They focus on public works, especially famine and drought-relief projects, which employ mainly women. MKSS activists, including large numbers of women, compare official records of work done with what was actually done. They investigate where the funds actually went and who had approved the spending. These events draw hundreds of villagers, as well as lawyers and journalists from as far away as Delhi. As documents are presented, workers see their names registered against amounts far in excess of what they had received, alongside those said to have received drought-relief payments who had in fact died years before. They frequently confront officials, demanding return of money pilfered from programmes for the poor.

These hearings are part of MKSS's broad campaign for people's rights to view official documents and obtain certified photocopies. In 1995, pressed by one of the movement's best-known leaders, Ms. Aruna Roy, the state's chief minister declared that citizens had the right to receive accounts of local development projects. Bureaucrats resisted, finally agreeing to let people inspect documents in local offices. This provoked further protests and an MKSS strike, supported by a sympathetic press, trade unions, and some prominent public service officers.

The right-to-information movement links information to accountability by highlighting the misuse of development funds and the failure to enforce labour and environmental standards. The struggle has expanded to a nationwide movement for the right to access official information, related not only to development spending, but to all official decision-making.

Source: Bhatia and Dreze 1998; Jenkins and Goetz 1999; Roy 1997.

which state power is simply being redeployed in new ways to facilitate the operation of international markets and investments (Jessop 1997:573). Either way, it is clear that the shift to wider governance structures means that no single agent within this cluster can on its own deliver progress for women. Accountability now has many dimensions, and demanding it is a multipronged process. Nevertheless, governments remain a vital focus of this process, as they are frequently the enforcers of policies derived from global governance structures.

The shift from government to governance presents both problems and opportunities for women's advancement. For instance, the increasing concentration of government economic decision-making in ministries of finance and central banks subordinates social policies to market-based indicators and criteria. But the new emphasis on "partnerships" and decentralization opens up new avenues for women to demand accountability, often at the local level (see Box 1).

How Can Women Demand Accountability?

Accountability can mean different things to different women and can be exercised in a variety of ways. Women's multiple roles as citizens, producers, and providers of family and community care offer a range of positions from which they can demand accountability for progress in the empowerment of women.

- As citizens and voters women can hold politicians and elected officials accountable at the polls and through the voice of public opinion.
- As elected representatives, women can hold governments accountable through parliamentary reviews of existing laws and policies and as advocates for the greater representation of women in politics.
- As government officials and staff in national women's departments or offices, women can hold other government departments to account. For example, in Turkey the Directorate General on the Status and Problems of Women has worked successfully with NGOs and the international human rights infrastructure to hold the government to account for its human rights policies. Expanded dialogue with women's groups has encouraged greater governmental accountability in terms of opening up the consultative process for Turkey's Sixth Five-Year Plan (Kardam and Ertürk 1999).
- As members of NGOs acting as "watchdogs" women can hold governments and corporations to account by publicizing reports and organizing hearings and demonstrations. For example, as part of the Beijing +5 review process, a US-based NGO, Equality Now, worked with international women's groups to produce a report identifying specific laws

Reuters/Gleb Garanich/Archive Photos

in 45 countries that contradict the spirit and text of the Platform for Action as well as other UN conventions. As a result of this report, a substantial number of countries are in the process of reviewing or changing these laws (Equality Now 1999).

A pre-condition for greater accountability is the ability of women to be active political subjects rather than the objects of public policies. Beyond that, effective accountability requires autonomy, transparency, meaningful participation and effective monitoring. There are several pre-requisites, including:

- the existence of free and independent associations separate from the state. This requires a state commitment to women's equality and an atmosphere of openness about women's issues in the society at large. It also may require state support and guaranteed media access for groups otherwise marginalized from power;
- the right of citizens to information and participation, along with official tolerance of criticism of the state and room for compromise among social partners, and the ability to engage in "public action," the combined action of states, pressure groups and political activists in the public domain;
- the resources to enable women to monitor governments, international financial institutions and corporations in order to verify information about operations and procedures. Such resources need to be available on terms that do not compromise the autonomy of women's groups.

Holding Governments Accountable for Conference Commitments

The UN conferences of the 1990s have played a vital role in putting the issue of gender equality on the global agenda. In order to have a significant impact at the national level, however, implementation and follow-up are essential. All of the UN conferences of the 1990s include a five-year process of review and appraisal, by which governments are asked to report on the implementation process, including achievements as well as obstacles. The review is coordinated by the relevant UN agency and in most cases culminates in a special session of

Box 2: Beijing +5: Are Governments Matching Commitments to Budgetary Allocations?

Matching Platform commitments to actual spending can be used as a benchmark of government accountability. However, evaluating the allocation of resources to implement the Platform is very difficult, given enormous differences in wealth and resources between countries and great variations in how governments interpret spending on implementation. Estimates of resource allocation are found in the Review and Appraisal document for Beijing +5 (UN2000b), which analyses government reports on implementation of the Platform and in a review of national plans done by the Women's Environment and Development Organization (WEDO 1998).

The Review and Appraisal document identifies three trends in terms of resource allocation strategies:

- countries which did not report specific allocations of budget resources to meet Platform goals;
- countries reporting targeted resources to specific programmes designed to improve the status of women;
- countries reporting that gender was mainstreamed through the budget process, incorporating gender into all budget areas.

The document notes the absence of any discussion of the comparative impact on women and men of budget items not targeted to women, which represent some 95 per cent of all expenditures in most countries. It also notes that most developing countries relied on resources from UN agencies and other international development agencies to implement the Platform, making cutbacks in funding for gender-specific programmes on the part of these donors significant.

WEDO estimated in 1998 that 31 per cent of reporting countries indicated an increase in the budget for women's programmes since Beijing. An almost equal number reported their budget has remained the same and 9 per cent reported a decrease. Overall, the budget for women's programmes is a small percentage of the national budget. WEDO notes that compounding the tendency to assign a low priority to "women's issues" are fiscal austerity measures undertaken as part of IMF and World Bank-imposed restructuring programmes. Gender mainstreaming of departments and ministries is reported by a number of governments but this is particularly difficult to evaluate. It appears that many governments have earmarked funds for spending on Category 1 (see diagrams in Box 6, pp. 116-18) but few have extended their plans to cover Categories 2 and 3.

Sources: UN 2000b; WEDO 1998.

the UN General Assembly. In June 2000, the General Assembly is holding such sessions for both the Beijing and the Copenhagen conferences: Beijing +5 and Copenhagen +5.

Beijing +5: Women 2000

In 1995, ten years after the completion of the UN Decade for Women, a review of the Nairobi Forward Looking Strategies to the Year 2000 found the pace of implementation to be so slow that it risked derailing the entire policy (IWTC 2000). As a result, the Beijing Platform of Action paid particular attention to implementation and follow-up. It recommended that governments prepare national plans of action by 1996, outlining implementation strategies in consultation with major institutions and civil society organizations. The UN Economic and Social Council (ECOSOC) requested governments to submit national action plans to the UN Division for the Advancement of Women for review by the Commission on the Status of Women beginning in March 1997. UNIFEM has been supporting a number of women's departments or offices within government (known as national machineries) in the preparation and implementation of these plans.

By January 2000, a total of 116 Member and Observer States had submitted national action plans. Many of these were prepared in cooperation with NGOs and relevant actors in civil society, whose contributions were important in encouraging governments to draw up specific actions to advance the status of women in one or more critical area. The majority of these focused on four critical areas: education and training, women in power and decision-making, women and health, and violence against women (UN 2000b; UN 1999f). However, only a few of the plans established comprehensive, time-bound targets and indicators for monitoring such progress. And most made no reference to sources of financing for the actions agreed to (UN 2000b:161).

Following the preparation of national plans, governments were invited to assess achievements in and obstacles to implementation of the Platform in response to a detailed questionnaire from the UN Secretary-General. By December 1999, a total of 133 Member and Observer States had responded. Most reported achievements in at least some of the critical areas. But again, the majority stated that a shortage of resources was a major obstacle to progress in all areas, citing constraints ranging from IMF-imposed structural adjustment programmes and the impact of globalization to the ravages of natural disasters and armed conflicts (see Box 2). While not included in the government reports, it was clear that a global shift in spending priorities, from the public to the private sector, was

also an issue. Indeed, in all regions of the world, except South Asia, the trend for public expenditure to rise as a proportion of national income ended in the mid 1980s (World Bank 1997).

In their reports to the Secretary-General, governments were asked to include an account of NGO activities in each of the critical areas. In many cases, NGOs were major participants in the gathering of information and preparation of the reports. In addition, NGOs were also invited to submit shadow reports, which in most cases offered a different perspective, both on achievements and the reasons limiting them.

As part of the Beijing +5 process, a series of preparatory meetings was held in each of the regions, leading up to the final preparatory meeting at the CSW's 44th Session in March 2000. UNIFEM played an active role in supporting NGOs to participate in these meetings, where they lobbied to strengthen government commitments in the document to be agreed upon in June. Together with the UN Non-Governmental Liaison Service, UNIFEM produced a detailed guide for NGO participation: "Gender on the Agenda: A Guide to Participating in Beijing +5."

Copenhagen +5

As part of the five-year review process of the Social Summit, the Secretary-General issued a report on the implementation of the Programme of Action, based on reports from 74 countries as well as information from other UN sources. This stressed the need to reconcile social and economic policy, noting particularly the high social and economic costs of growing income disparities. It noted the failure of countries to increase funds allocated for social development and concluded that while some progress was achieved in terms of gender-sensitive programmes and institutional frameworks, these were most often inadequately funded.

Despite the importance of gender differences within each of the Copenhagen Programme of Action commitments, gender is a focus only in Commitment 5: to promote further initiatives to enhance equality and equity between women and men. During the Copenhagen +5 process, however, women's groups succeeded in getting an agreement on gender mainstreaming in all levels of policy-making and planning and a renewed commitment to ensure that gender is mainstreamed within all further initiatives related to each of the ten commitments.

In general, the review process has concentrated less on targets and indicators, which tend to focus attention on shortcomings in resource-poor countries, and more on the extent to which governments

in developed countries have taken steps to implement commitments to make more resources available to poor countries. It was noted that in 1998, for example, official development assistance (ODA) was only 0.23 per cent of donor countries' GNP, far below the 0.7 per cent OECD benchmark (see Chapter 2).

In addition, developing countries have endeavoured to get donor countries to accept some responsibility for policies that perpetuate resource shortages: namely, the high costs of debt repayment, structural adjustment programmes, deleterious international trade agreements and reductions in development assistance. They recommended that creditor nations should regard 2000 as a landmark year to commit themselves to a five-year time frame for debt cancellation for developing countries.

The International Council on Social Welfare (ICSW), a global coalition of civil society organizations in over 80 countries, organized regional and global forums to review implementation of Summit commitments and identify priority areas for action. The priorities for donor countries include:

- agreement on a timetable for achieving the 0.7 per cent ODA target by 2010;
- agreement that by 2005 at least half of their ODA will be directed to countries with which they have entered into a 20-20 agreement, relating to the proportion of ODA and recipient country budgets to be devoted to expenditure on basic social services;
- agreement on a "limited liability code" establishing limits on liability for debts incurred after its introduction.

Holding Governments Accountable for Budgets

Given the tendency of commitments to women to flounder for lack of resources, NGOs have sought ways to focus attention on the issue of resources, and the political and economic priorities that determine their allocation. One such strategy is to analyse national budgets from women's perspectives, allowing women to "follow the money" to see if government rhetoric is followed in practice. Implementation of international conference commitments, national policy statements, and obligations under human rights treaties can be linked to government spending and revenue raising decisions.

"If you want to see which way a country is headed, look at the country's budget and how it allocates resources for women and children."

— Pregs Govender, South African MP

Since the Beijing Platform for Action specifically calls for gender-sensitive budgets (see Box 3), gender-sensitive budget analysis can be used to check whether adequate resources are budgeted to implement a country's plan of action and how fiscal policies are affecting women, as compared to men. One problem in implementation is that there is often a gap between the process of policy development and that of budget appropriations. A gender-sensitive budget analysis can bring the two processes together, helping government to implement policy effectively. A case in point is the allocation of resources to the Commission on Gender Equality in South Africa. The Commission's budget falls within that of the Department of Justice. However, analysis by the Women's Budget Initiative revealed that the 1997/98 budget allocation to the Commission in its first year of operation was not even sufficient to cover the remuneration of commissioners, and provided nothing to pay executive staff and office costs. It was also far less than that allocated to the Human Rights Commission and the Youth Commission. The Parliamentary Joint Committee on the Improvement of the Quality of Life and Status of Women highlighted this fact, and the government subsequently increased the Commission's budget allocation substantially.

Doranne Jacobson

More generally, gender-sensitive budget analysis is a mechanism to address three key objectives:

- raising awareness within governments about the impact of budgets (and the policies and programmes which they support) on women;
- informing women about the gender implications of government expenditures and revenues;
- increasing effectiveness of government resource allocations to promote gender equality and human development.

Government Budgets Are Not Gender Neutral
National budgets may appear to be gender-neutral policy instruments. They deal with financial aggregates—expenditures and revenues, surpluses or deficits – rather than with people. Yet policy-makers should not assume that government expenditures and revenues will impact equally on men and women. Rather, since men and women generally occupy different social and economic positions, budgets typically affect them very differently. Ignoring the gendered impact of policy is not gender neutrality but *gender blindness*.

The socially determined roles, responsibilities and capabilities of men and women are usually structured so that women are in an unequal position with less economic, social and political power, frequently resulting in unequal access to resources. Gender differences and inequalities mean that a gender-blind budget will have different impacts on men and women, boys and girls. For example, most countries' education budgets are gender-neutral in design, but because in many countries more boys than girls actually attend school, boys derive more benefit from educational expenditure than do girls (see Box 4).

One of the barriers to making budgets more accountable to women is that the conceptual frameworks and statistics used to prepare national budgets are themselves gender-blind. For example:

- women's contribution to the market economy is underestimated because of incomplete statistics concerning women's paid employment;
- the unpaid care economy, in which women do most of the work of maintaining the labour force and the social framework of the community, is not counted at all;
- the interaction between the paid and unpaid economy is not taken into account.

Box 4: Benefit Incidence of Public Spending on Health and Education in Ghana

By bringing together estimates of the cost of providing a public service and information on the use of public services by men and women and boys and girls, one can see how public spending is distributed by sex. In Ghana, in 1992, because girls' enrolment in secondary school was less than that of boys, girls received only 40 per cent of total public expenditure on secondary education. On a per-capita basis, this worked out at 3561 cedis per girl of secondary school age, and 5702 cedis per boy of secondary school age.

The gender gap in health expenditure was in the opposite direction. Women and girls received 56 per cent of total public spending on health. On a per-capita basis, this worked out to 3576 cedis per male and 3959 cedis per female.

Source: Demery et al. 1995.

Gender-Sensitive Budgets Enhance Human Development

There is growing awareness that gender inequality is costly not only to women, but also to children, and to many men. It exacts costs in lower productivity, lower development of people's capacities, less leisure and lower levels of well-being. Gender inequality in the labour market may promote rapid but unequal growth based on a persistent gender gap in earnings. However, if women were better trained and prepared, countries might lose some relative advantage in terms of cheap labour, but they could gain a productivity advantage. This would lead to a combination of more output, greater development of people's capacities, more leisure and higher levels of well-being, based on gender-equitable development strategies.

- Research on agricultural productivity in Africa shows that reducing gender inequality could significantly increase agricultural yields. For example, giving women farmers in Kenya the same level of agricultural inputs and education as men farmers could increase yields obtained by women farmers by more than 20 per cent (Saito and Spurling 1992).

- Research on economic growth and education shows that failing to invest in girls' education lowers gross national product (GNP). All else being equal, countries in which the ratio of female-to-male enrolment in primary or secondary education is less than 0.75 can expect levels of GNP that are roughly 25 per cent lower than countries in which there is less gender disparity in education (Hill and King 1995).

- Research on gender inequality in the labour market shows that eliminating gender discrimination in occupation and pay could increase not only women's income, but also national income. For instance, if gender inequality in the labour market in Latin America were to be eliminated, not only could women's wages rise by about 50 per cent, but national output also could rise by 5 per cent (Tzannatos 1991).

Gender-Sensitive Budget Initiatives

Gender-sensitive budget initiatives are taking place in a growing number of countries. What is covered, who participates and how the results are reported vary in different countries. A few such initiatives cover only expenditures directed specifically at women, although most cover untargeted spending categories. Some initiatives are local, others national. Some are located within government, others are launched by groups outside of the official government machinery. Elected representatives can play roles in both. In addition, the Commonwealth has developed a gender budget initiative in partnership with ministries responsible for women's affairs and ministries of finance in a number of member countries. UNIFEM has been active in supporting gender-sensitive budget initiatives, sponsoring a series of workshops and offering technical support for training at the national and local levels (see Box 5).

In early 2000, gender-sensitive budget initiatives were underway in 20 countries in four regions. These included: Australia, Barbados, Botswana, Fiji, Kenya, Malawi, Mauritius, Mozambique, Namibia, Philippines, South Africa, Sri Lanka, St. Kitts, Switzerland, Tanzania, Uganda, UK, United States, Zambia and Zimbabwe.

"The strategy is to work together with actors in the government machinery, while keeping a distance so that they do not hijack our agenda and our course of action."

— Gemma Akilimali, Tanzanian Gender Network Programme (SIDA 1998)

George Nyamukubva

Box 5: UNIFEM Support for Gender Budget Initiatives

Following a presentation by MP Pregs Govender on the Women's Budget Initiative in South Africa at UNIFEM's 20th Anniversary Colloquium in 1996, UNIFEM was asked to help build capacity in the SADC region. A first workshop, "Engendering Budgets: The Southern African Experience," was held in November 1998 in Harare, Zimbabwe, at which experiences and initiatives in engendering budgets were presented by participants from South Africa, Zimbabwe, Zambia, Mozambique, Malawi and Tanzania. NGOs, parliamentarians, government finance and planning officials as well as academic researchers participated from the five countries.

A follow-up workshop was held in Harare in November 1999 to discuss progress on the implementation of action plans developed during the first workshop, share experiences in engendering budgets, provide tools on gender budget analysis and develop national action plans for engendering budgets. Participants examined the advantages and limitations of gender budgets conducted inside government compared to those done outside government, stressing the problems of stakeholder access in the former versus problems of implementation in the latter. Several participants stated that apart from social sectors, there are very few women in government ministries, and none are involved in the budget process at the top. Members of parliament said they need support from government in pursuing gender budget initiatives, especially from finance and planning officials.

"Money talks. Men listen to money talk. These truisms are at the heart of the enthusiasm with which the idea of the women's budget has been embraced by gender activists. When we talk budget, we finally have a sense that we are getting to the heart of the matter...and that men will sit up and listen." — Colleen Lowe-Morna, former CEO, Commission on Gender Equality, South Africa.

In partnership with Indian Ocean Island States, UNIFEM sponsored a similar workshop in March 2000. This was followed in April with a conference to take stock of gender-sensitive budget initiatives, organized by UNIFEM, the Commonwealth Secretariat and the International Development Research Centre (IDRC, Canada). And as part of its support for gender analysis of national budgets, UNIFEM presented a position paper to ECLAC in November 1999, which was taken to the ECLAC Council of Ministers in February 2000.

A challenge for the future is to bring together gender equality, poverty and environment perspectives on the budget. A June 1999 workshop on Pro-Poor, Gender- and Environment-Sensitive Budgets organized by UNDP and UNIFEM convened an international group of practitioners and experts from governments, trade unions, civil society organizations, development agencies, donors and academia to compare participatory budget initiatives both inside and outside of government and review their technical and political dimensions. A Web page was set up as the basis of an international knowledge network (see www.undp.org/poverty/initiatives/budgets.htm).

Source: Budlender 1999; UNIFEM 1999a.

The Pioneer: Women's Budget Statements in Australia

The first gender-sensitive approach to budgets was launched in Australia in 1984, when the federal government provided an assessment of the budget's impact on women. During the 1980s and 1990s similar assessments were introduced at various times by state and territory governments, and the federal government provided an annual assessment until 1996.

The women's budget statements went beyond expenditure targeted to women to look at the gender consequences of the entire range of government spending. Women's budget statements raised awareness in the bureaucracy about the budget's impact on women and generated a wealth of information on how government departments were spending money. Women's units within government were able to use this information for advocacy and policy interventions. The comprehensive assessment of all government spending also brought women into the economic debates of the day in a new way. Women were able to intervene in policy debates outside of the conventional social sectors since impact assessments revealed that a wide range of fiscal policies (for instance, tax and wages policy) could have very different effects on women and men.

In 1996, following a change of government, the initiative was abandoned at the federal level, although governments in the state of Tasmania and in the Northern Territory continue to undertake gender-sensitive budget analyses. Rhonda Sharp, who has been closely involved in women's budget initiatives in Australia, suggests that greater attention to partnership with women's organizations would have bolstered the institutional position of the Women's Budget Initiative. She suggests that economic restructuring also played an important role in undermining the support for a national-level women's budget in Australia. As pressure to reduce public expenditure increasingly came to dominate the political agenda, gender equality advocates lost their political prominence (Sharp and Broomhill 1998).

"The budget is presented on budget day and Parliament must either accept it as is, or reject it completely. Rejection is not really a feasible option in that by the time budgets are presented, the departments and agencies must almost immediately begin spending. In practice, in the debates on the budget votes most parliamentarians say very little about the budget".

— Debbie Budlender,
South African Women's Budget Initiative, 1998

The South African Women's Budget Initiative (WBI)
Women in South Africa were inspired by the Australian women's budget statements to analyse the budget of their own government. In 1996, a group of NGOs in conjunction with the Parliamentary Joint Committee on the Improvement of the Quality of Life and Status of Women launched the Women's Budget Initiative (WBI). Each year, the initiative analysed various sectors of government spending and revenue. By the end of 1999, four volumes had been produced, covering all areas of government spending as well as taxation and macroeconomic policy. The Women's Budget Initiative also strives to make its work more accessible to women at the community level (see Box 7, p. 120).

As the South African Women's Budget Initiative progressed, its contributors acquired a deeper understanding of the advantages and disadvantages of a gender budget initiative done outside government, rather than within, as in the Australian case. Volume 3 of its expenditure analysis, completed in 1998, explained that one of the primary aims of the initiative is to empower members of parliament to raise gender issues in relation to budgets. But along with deficiencies in gender analysis and information, parliamentarians confront a more structural problem: they cannot amend budgets.

This point highlights a limitation of gender-sensitive budget initiatives that are not undertaken within the government ministry or department responsible for drawing up yearly budget proposals, typically the Ministry of Finance.

The Commonwealth Gender Budget Initiative
The Commonwealth Gender Budget Initiative (GBI), agreed upon at the 1996 meeting of

Commonwealth Ministers Responsible for Women's Affairs, was designed precisely to engage with ministries of finance. South Africa was the first country to join this initiative, thanks to the prior advocacy of parliamentarians involved in the WBI.

Other countries involved in the Commonwealth scheme include Sri Lanka, Barbados, St. Kitts and Nevis and Fiji. Sri Lanka and South Africa successfully completed the pilot stage during the period January - November 1998. In Sri Lanka, where the project was managed by the National Planning Division of the Ministry of Finance, gender-sensitive sectoral analyses were launched in several areas, including agriculture, industry, health, education, social services and public sector employment. The result has been the identification of areas where gender-based inefficiencies and inequalities exist as well as efforts to improve capacity for gender-disaggregated data collection. Barbados has launched case studies focusing on gender-specific expenditures, expenditure on government employees (especially training) and mainstream expenditures. Training of staff and officials is also underway in Fiji and St. Kitts and Nevis as the first stage of gender-sensitive budget initiatives in those countries.

The goal of the Commonwealth Gender Budget Initiative is to ensure that gender-sensitive analysis is part of overall budget formulation and evaluation and it brings together government actors who might not otherwise work with each other. It may overcome one of the structural limitations of the Australian exercise, namely, the relative isolation of gender-equality advocates and initiatives from key economic ministries and officials.

Box 6: Gender Analysis of National Budgets: Tools for Promoting Accountability

Gender analysis of a budget cannot be reduced to a technical "fix," merely reformulating budget classification and coding systems. It requires officials and ministers to think about government activities in a new way. It requires dialogue as well as statistical analysis. A number of tools for carrying out gender budget analysis have been developed by researchers and activists associated with the initiatives in Australia, South Africa and the Commonwealth Budget Initiative (Commonwealth Secretariat 1999; Budlender and Sharp 1998).

A good starting point is to divide the expenditure of each government department into three categories: expenditure specifically targeted at women or men; equal opportunity initiatives in the public sector; and gender impact of mainstream budget expenditure (see Diagram A). The last category represents the vast majority of any national budget, and can be analysed using tools 1, 3 and 5. Similarly, government revenue can be divided into three categories (see Diagram B). Tool 4 is useful in analysing revenue while tools 6 and 7 look at the budget as a whole.

Tool 1: Gender-Aware Policy Appraisal. Applying a gender-aware policy appraisal means looking at the policies and programmes funded by the budget from a gender perspective by asking: "In what ways are the policies and their associated resource allocations likely to reduce or increase gender inequalities?"

Example: The South African government's land reform programme is proceeding at an increasing pace, with corresponding increases in expenditure for everything from owner compensation to microfinance programmes. However, women's access to land as well as to the financial resources necessary for its development is impeded by legal restrictions on women's land ownership and rights to conclude contracts. Women who do have access to land tend to have access to smaller plots with poor irrigation, and women-headed households typically have no wage or salary earners. As a result, women are far less able to benefit from the reform process and related expenditures. When the Department of Land Affairs received this gender-aware appraisal of land reform it started to integrate gender concerns into its monitoring and evaluation system and has begun providing gender training for staff (see Budlender and Sharp 1998:39).

Tool 2: Beneficiary Assessments. Beneficiary assessment is a means by which the voice of the citizen can be heard. In these exercises, the actual or potential beneficiaries of public services are asked to assess how far public spending is meeting their needs as they perceive them. This can be done through opinion polls, attitude surveys, group discussion or interviews. Questions can focus on overall priorities for public spending or upon the details of the operation of public services.

Diagram A: Public Expenditure Categories

Category 1

Specifically targeted expenditures by government departments and authorities to women or men in the community intended to meet their particular needs.

For example, women's health programmes, domestic violence counselling for men, programmes for women with young children.

Category 2

Equal employment opportunity expenditure by government agencies on their employees.

For example, training for lower level clerks (where women may predominate), paid parental leave, child-care facilities for children of employees.

Category 3

General or mainstream budget expenditures by government agencies which make goods or services available to the whole community, but which are assessed for their gender impact.

For example, who are the users of primary health care? Who are the learners in government-provided literacy classes? Who receives agricultural support services?

Total Expenditure

Source: Sharp 1995.

Diagram B: Government Revenue Categories

Taxation

For example, direct (income) tax, indirect taxes (e.g., VAT, customs and excise) and tax "expenditures" (e.g., tax incentives and rebates)

Donor Funds

Loans and grants

Other Revenue

For example, user pays fees, asset sales and borrowings

Total Revenue

Source: Budlender and Sharp 1998.

Example: In the United States, alarm over a national debt "crisis" reached a peak in the mid 1990s, creating pressure to cut government expenditures in order to reduce the deficit. In 1996, the Women's International League for Peace and Freedom initiated a Women's Budget Project, asking women to answer a series of questions about the choices they would make in allocating national budget resources. Pointing out that few women benefit from military spending programmes because they are severely under-represented both in the armed forces and in military contractor jobs, the project calculated the costs of various defence-related programmes and compared them to potential social welfare expenditures. It then asked: Which would you choose? Fund the F-22 fighter plane programme for the current year ($2.1 billion) OR pay for the annual health care expenses for 1.3 million American women? Fund Seawolf attack submarines for the current year ($1.7 billion) OR provide low-income

home energy assistance for 5.6 million households? The project estimated the savings from proposed cuts in military spending and outlined the ways in which such savings could be invested to benefit women, including employment and training programmes, campaigns against gender-based violence, and services for the elderly, the majority of whom are women.

Tool 3: Public Expenditure Incidence Analysis. Incidence analysis of public expenditure is a useful tool for helping to assess the gender distribution of public spending. It can give a sense of how gender-inclusive such expenditures actually are by comparing the distribution of the benefits of public spending among women and men, girls and boys. Similarly it can suggest the gender impact of supposedly gender-neutral budget cuts.

Example: Sri Lanka's food ration and stamps programme provides an example. Changes to the food ration and subsidy programme in the 1980s revealed that despite rapid economic growth, the real value of stamps eroded in the first half of the decade and there was a decline in the real incomes of the poor. A gender-disaggregated analysis concluded that within poor households, girls and women took the brunt of the increasing food deficit, citing higher levels of malnutrition among pre-school and school girls and declining birth weights of babies born to low income mothers (see Budlender and Sharp 1998:47).

Tool 4: Revenue Incidence Analysis. The manner in which governments raise revenues and the level of revenues raised in relation to the need and demand for public expenditures can have different effects on women and men. Revenue incidence analysis can be used to calculate how much in taxes or user charges is paid by different categories of individuals or households. Total budgeted revenue can be divided into three categories, including direct and indirect taxes, loans and grants, and other revenues, such as user charges on government services and intergovernmental income transfers (see Diagram B). One of the problems in doing this analysis is that equal sharing of income within households is often assumed.

Example: In Canada, the National Association of Women and the Law (NAWL), in a submission to the House of Commons Standing Committee on Finance, noted that the current system of tax benefits for private retirement savings needs to be reformed to remove or reduce existing gender bias. Tax subsidization of retirements savings is gender biased because women have fewer opportunities to be employed in full-time jobs with pension benefits, experience more frequent labour force interruptions due to care-giving responsibilities, and earn less than men on average. As a result, women accrue lower benefits under government-sponsored retirement schemes and are less likely to participate in employer-sponsored registered pension plans (NAWL 1998).

Tool 5: Sex-Disaggregated Analysis of the Impact of the Budget on Time Use. Changes in government resource allocation have impacts on the way in which time is spent in households. In particular, cuts in some forms of public expenditure are likely to increase the amount of time that women have to spend in unpaid care work for their families and communities in order to make up for lost public services. Thus whenever cuts are proposed, the question should be asked: Is this likely to increase the time that men and women spend on unpaid care provision?

Example: Between 1983 and 1985, real per-capita expenditure on health fell by 16 per cent in Zambia. People had to travel greater distances and wait for longer periods of time to get treatment and drugs. Zambian women interviewed for a study by Alison Evans and Kate Young reported having to spend more time caring for sick family members, including time spent with them in hospital providing meals and helping to nurse them (Evans and Young 1988).

Tool 6: Gender-Aware Medium-Term Economic Policy Framework. The ultimate aim of gender analysis of national budgets is to incorporate gender variables into the models on which medium-term public expenditure planning are based. This might be done by disaggregating by sex variables that refer to people (e.g., labour supply) or by including new variables to represent the unpaid care economy (see Çağatay et al. 1995).

Example: A gender-aware medium-term economic framework has not yet been adopted by any government. In South Africa, however, the government invited members of the Women's Budget Project to address a workshop on the development of a new Medium Term Expenditure Framework (MTEF) in 1996. The idea was to plan expenditure on a three-year rolling basis rather than on the present year-by-year basis. The Women's Budget Initiative commented that while this did not mean that the MTEF would necessarily be gender sensitive, it did signal a willingness by the Ministry of Finance to engage with gender-equality issues. In fact, the National Expenditure Survey produced by the Ministry of Finance in 1999 did incorporate more gender analysis.

Tool 7: Gender-Aware Budget Statement. Any government can issue a gender-aware budget statement utilizing one or more of the above tools to analyse its programmes and budgets and summarize their implications with a number of key indicators. It requires a high degree of co-ordination throughout the public sector and is essentially an accountability report by government regarding its commitment to gender equity.

Example: The Third Women's Budget produced by the South African Women's Budget Initiative draws upon suggestions made by Diane Elson for the Commonwealth Budget Initiative to identify which indicators might be used in the South African context to prepare a gender-aware budget statement. A number of indicators are suggested as starting points for a continuous process of monitoring resource allocations and linking these to government commitments and policies. These include:

- the share of expenditure targeted to gender equality – equivalent to Category 1 in Diagram A – for example, Ministry of Welfare's Flagship Programme;
- gender (and in this case, racial) balance in public-sector employment, which looks at the number of women and men in different levels and different jobs;
- the share of expenditure devoted to women's priority public services, which in South Africa might include services such as water provision;
- the share of expenditure devoted to the Office of the Status of Women, the gender units within each agency and the Commission for Gender Equality;
- the share of expenditure devoted to women's priority income transfers, which would include the Ministry of Welfare's child-support grants that provide monthly payments to care-givers of young children in poor households;
- gender balance in business support, such as the subsidies provided by the Department of Trade and Industry and the Department of Agriculture;
- gender balance in public sector contracts, including contracts to build houses for those obtaining Department of Housing subsidies, or for public works;
- gender balance in membership of committees and other decision-making bodies and forums, for example in water and other community-level committees, ideally also specifying whether women and men are remunerated for their contribution;
- gender balance in training, for example in public works and other programmes for the unemployed.

Darrane Jacobson

Outside Government Initiatives: A Critical Voice in Policy Debates

Women in several other countries, both North and South, have launched gender-sensitive budget initiatives outside government. Such initiatives, launched by civil society forces — sometimes in cooperation with parliamentarians — are aimed at making fiscal policy more responsive to the needs of women by drawing public attention to the budget process and its impact.

"The preparation of government budgets is generally considered to be a job for technical experts, not for ordinary Canadians. Governments of all ideological stripes have found it politically convenient to perpetuate this myth: the less people know the less they can challenge the prevailing political orthodoxy as expressed in budgets...."

— John Loxley, co-coordinator,
Alternative Federal Budget (Choices 1998)

In the UK, the Women's Budget Group (WBG) has been active since 1989, issuing press releases on every budget and working to put questions on gender and budgets on the policy agenda. Focusing on changes in the tax and social security system that have threatened to transfer cash from the hands of women to the hands of men, the WBG pointed to evidence that shows the benefits to children of keeping cash in the hands of mothers, as well as the benefits to women themselves. Since the election of the Labour government in 1997, the WBG has been actively consulted by the government.

In Switzerland, gender budget activities are organized by trade unions and NGOs. A series of studies initiated in 1994 examined the effect of austerity measures on the employment of women and men, the unpaid work of women and the incidence of benefits. More recently, an analysis of expenditures that have an impact on unpaid care work estimated that in the canton of Bern, about 20 per cent of expenditure supports unpaid care work. However, this has decreased in relation to other budget expenditures, indicating a contraction of resources going to support such unpaid work.

Uganda too has an outside arrangement, the result of a collaboration between the Parliamentary Women's Caucus and the Forum for Women in Democracy, an NGO. The Women's Caucus is the most organized lobby within parliament and has won important legislative changes, such as reserving 30 per cent of seats on local councils for women. In 1997, the Women's Caucus embarked on a three-year gender budget initiative to examine the impact of recent structural adjustment packages. In Tanzania, the Tanzania Gender Networking Programme, is responsible for coordinating the gender budget initiative (see Box 7, p. 120). Other initiatives underway in Africa include those in Namibia, Mozambique and Zimbabwe.

George Nyamukubva

Gender Budget Initiatives: Strengths, Weaknesses and Future Challenges

Gender-sensitive budgets offer a way for women to hold governments to account for their international and national commitments to the advancement of women by linking such commitments to budget allocations. Activists and researchers have stressed that policy-makers cannot assume that government expenditures and taxation measures impact equally on men and women, given the generally different social and economic positions of men and women. So all good policy-making requires a gender-sensitive analysis of fiscal policies.

The Commonwealth Gender Budget Initiative provides several useful lessons for undertaking gender budget initiatives within government:

- demonstrating the concrete and practical nature of a gender-sensitive budget is important for drawing governments into the process;
- gender-sensitive budget analysis within government is best placed in the ministry of finance as the key stakeholder within government; yet, ministries of finance also provide the greatest resistance to such initiatives, given the relatively few women who work in them and the reliance of finance ministries on conventional, gender-blind economic analysis;
- the technical knowledge for conducting a gender-sensitive analysis is often lacking in all government ministries and departments;
- securing political support at the top creates an important enabling environment;
- partnering with civil society organizations is vital to monitoring and accountability.

Box 7: Making Budgets Matter for People: Three Popular Education Initiatives

South Africa

Efforts are currently underway to make the Women's Budget Initiative material available to citizens who do not have access to the four volumes of analysis. *Money Matters: Women and the Government Budget* was produced in 1998. Targeted to a second-language English speaker with ten years of education, the book is intended also as a lobbying tool, concentrating on government policies and expenditures that can give women greater economic independence and provide the catalyst for real change. It looks at the policies and budget allocations of eight government departments: labour, public works, trade and industry, land affairs and agriculture, education, health, welfare, safety and security, and shows how gender-sensitive policies and budgets can improve the lives and opportunities of the most disadvantaged: poor, black women.

MP Pregs Govender, Chairperson of the Parliamentary Committee on the Quality of Life and Status of Women, states in her introduction: "Women often respond to the words 'economics,' 'macroeconomics,' 'budgets,' and so on with feelings of fear and inadequacy. We associate these with 'experts' who do not look like us. They do not have to balance caring for children, the elderly or the sick, doing domestic chores and working in fields and factories or offices. Yet it is women who are expected to stretch their time to catch the fall-out from decisions made by economists, for example, macroeconomic choices resulting in cuts to health, welfare and so on."

Canada

A similar, broad-based effort aimed at giving ordinary people the knowledge and ability to hold governments to account and demand a more just economy, was launched in Canada in 1998. *Show Us the Money! The Politics and Process of Alternative Budgets*, is a "how-to" manual that unpacks government budgets and suggests an alternative, participatory process and outcome. Building on the Alternative Federal Budget (AFB) initiative that was launched in 1995 by a coalition of trade unions, social movement activists and researchers, the manual gives some background on budgeting as well as alternative views of the economy. In the words of John Loxley, one of the founders of the AFB: "The central message of this book is that budgets are, above all, political documents and that people should not be afraid of them. Democratizing the budget process is important if we are to effectively resist the platform of the neo-conservatives and replace it with a public policy more in tune with the needs of ordinary Canadians."

Tanzania

"A gender budget is one which demonstrates sensitivity to the different needs and privileges, rights and obligations which men and women have in the society...The first pre-requisite, therefore, to the budgeting exercise entails a gender analysis of the population."

The Tanzania Gender Networking Programme (TGNP), an NGO committed to women's empowerment, spent nearly three years tracing the process of national planning and resource allocation, noting how it impacts on women and men, youth and the elderly. As part of its Gender Budget Initiative, in 1999 TGNP produced a booklet, *Budgeting with a Gender Focus*, which popularizes its findings in four sectors: the ministries of finance, education, and health plus the Planning Commission. The booklet shows the power that all of these sectors have through the distribution of national resources and calls attention to significant gender gaps, especially in health and education.

Box 8: Gender Budgeting in the UN System

Following the Beijing Women's Conference, the UN General Assembly requested that efforts be made within the UN system to ensure that medium-term plans and programme budgets visibly mainstream a gender perspective. As part of the Beijing +5 process, a UN Task Force on Gender Mainstreaming in Budgets was set up in 1999 by the Office of the Special Adviser on Gender Issues to develop concrete tools for UN departments, agencies and commissions to assess their budgets from a gender-sensitive perspective. The Task Force reviewed efforts to mainstream gender equality in budgets within the UN system, as well as in a range of other institutions, including some large NGOs and private sector organizations. Among its findings:

- there is no clear consensus on what gender mainstreaming means in budgets;
- there is often no clear method of tracking resources allocated and linking allocations to results;
- the rationale for visibly mainstreaming gender needs to be clear.

Among UN organizations, the Task Force found that even when gender equality is written into the agency's central objectives and planning documents, it often drops out of budgets, which are seen as purely technical. Part of the exercise of the Task Force review is to get work that is being done to mainstream gender classified and coded as such so that it can be tracked and counted. As one CIDA (Canada) official observed: "What gets counted, gets done."

Building on these findings, the Task Force worked with five UN organizations to develop concrete strategies and methodologies for gender mainstreaming in the programme budget process: UNFPA in New York; the Department of Political Affairs in the Secretariat in New York; WHO in Geneva; ESCAP Regional Commission in Bangkok; and the Office of the High Commissioner for Human Rights in Geneva. The results, to be presented at for the Beijing +5 Session in June 2000, are intended to provide models that are applicable to different types of agencies within the UN system.

South Africa currently has both an outside-government initiative, the Women's Budget Initiative, and an inside-government initiative, the Pilot Project of the Commonwealth Gender Budget Initiative. The most visible change resulting from this combination of outside-government and inside-government initiatives has been that government sector reviews now incorporate a gender perspective. One result in terms of policy has been an improved targeting of expenditures within each sector. For instance, in 1997 the National Public Works Programme did an evaluation of its Community Based Public Works Programme, which has a budget of about R 250 million out of a total R 350 million allocated to National Public Works. Of those employed on the projects, 41 per cent were women and 12 per cent were youths. While the figure for women is lower that the female proportion of the population in the rural areas in which the projects operate, it is almost certainly higher than would have been the case without explicit targeting. Unfortunately, the evaluation showed that women were often assigned the more menial jobs, that their average wages were lower, that they were employed for shorter periods than men, and that they were less likely than men to receive training (37 per cent of the men received training, compared to 32 per cent of the women). The evaluation results have formed the basis of the Department's current plans to finetune the programme and further improve targeted budget allocations (Budlender and Sharp 1998: 67).

Debbie Budlender, the editor of the four volumes of analysis produced by the South African Women's Budget Project, warns against expecting quick results. She stresses the importance of what she calls "standing on two legs"– one inside and the other outside of government. Governments cannot be expected to provide cutting-edge critiques of themselves and advocates often do not have access to key officials or information that those inside government might have. She also points out that gender budget analysis is learned through practical engagement, through making a start and continually adapting tools to the local environment.

Holding Corporations to Account

One of the pressures for reducing public expenditure comes from the ability of transnational corporations to lobby for lower taxes. Gobalization has resulted in an enormous increase in the power of transnational corporations, which have wrested greater freedom from state regulations through trade liberalization and the privatization policies of the International Monetary Fund and the World Bank. As a result, accountability of corporate management has been shifting steadily towards shareholders and away from stakeholders (including workers, the community and, to some degree, governments). This shift is most pronounced in Anglo-Saxon countries such as the United States, the UK and Canada as well as Australia and New Zealand. By comparison, shareholders in Europe and Japan are not so dominant.

"Multinational corporations accounted for an estimated $9.5 trillion in sales in 1997. Their value added was 7% of world GDP in 1997, up from 5% in the mid 1980s. "Multinational corporations now dwarf some governments in economic power"

— Human Development Report, 1999

In the 1990s, these changes have been met by increasing calls for social responsibility and accountability of the major corporations, not only to their own shareholders but also to a wider public. In the 1970s, there were attempts to institute mandatory international codes of conduct to regulate the social and environmental conditions under which products are produced and marketed, through an international agency such as the UN Conference on Trade and Development (UNCTAD). This effort did not succeed, and the implementation of codes of conduct has been left to corporations themselves — prodded by trade unions and other organizations of civil society. Women have been active — as consumers, as workers and trade union members as well as shareholders — in campaigns designed to hold corporations to account. These include codes of conduct that set minimum working conditions, social labels that specify the social conditions under which a product is produced and initiatives directed at ethical consumption and investment.

To date, all corporate codes of conduct remain voluntary. However, transnational corporations are coming under increased scrutiny, especially regarding labour practices. Their freedom from state regulations has led to a mobilization of civil society actors worldwide, skilled at using the Internet to publicize company abuses around the world. An anti-sweatshop movement has effectively reached almost every corner of the globe, pressuring transnationals to cut back on the use of child labour, limit the number of hours required on the job and restrict their use of dangerous chemicals. The message is that businesses must operate in ways that promote the realization of human rights.

Codes of Conduct: NGO Initiatives

Women have helped organize student sit-ins at schools and universities, picketed in front of stores and participated in letter-writing campaigns. They have also engaged in:

- advocating for corporate codes of conduct and effective implementation strategies;

- campaigns for social labelling, for products produced under "fair labour" conditions;
- advancing intergovernmental and governmental initiatives to create standards;
- demanding social accounting and social auditing for company internal monitoring.

One example of a worker-driven initiative led by women is the code of ethics for employers operating in free trade zones in Nicaragua, called "Employment Yes, But with Dignity." Workers in the zone, primarily women, were locked behind chain link fencing all day, obliged to reach out through the links to vendors lined up outside to purchase their food. With extensive media coverage, workers gathered some 30,000 signatures on a petition with which they successfully lobbied the national parliament for regulations on corporations operating in the zone.

"Of course we know that the code will not solve our problems. It is just a mechanism to help us. The underlying problems of poverty and unemployment are what make workers accept poor conditions and bad wages."

— Sandra Ramos, Maria Elena Cuadra Women's Movement, 1998

The code of ethics, which will be monitored by women workers in conjunction with the Central American Network in Solidarity with Women Workers in the Maquilas, requires companies to:

- eliminate discrimination on the basis of sex, race, religion, age, disability or political orientation;
- guarantee job security and safeguard pregnant or post-natal women from dismissal;
- engage in no physical or psychological or verbal abuse;
- ensure that workplaces guarantee health, hygiene and well-being, including regular health check-ups and worker training to prevent job-related accidents and illness;

Fair Wear

You pay
$150

outworker
paid $0.00

- pay the legal wage and social security contributions;
- respect working hours and overtime pay according to law;
- allow workers to organize and negotiate collective agreements;
- employ no workers under the age of 14.

Elsewhere women's NGOs have been working in concert with trade unions to evaluate and propose corporate standards on working conditions. In 1997-1998, for example, Women Working Worldwide (WWW), a UK-based civil society organization, organized a series of consultations with women's groups in South Asia and the Philippines, designed to get feedback on the value of company codes of conduct from women workers' organizations and women workers themselves. A number of regional organizations collaborated with WWW in conducting research and facilitating discussions with workers. They discovered that workers felt that codes could strengthen their bargaining ability provided that they are only one strategy among many, and never replace the right to organize and bargain collectively.

In some cases, NGOs and unions have joined corporations in working out codes of conduct. An example is the Ethical Trade Initiative (ETI) in the UK, launched with government support in 1998 to negotiate what is known as a "roundtable model code" in the food and garment retail industries. The first companies involved have been retailers who are at the front-line of consumer complaints and wish to avoid bad publicity. In 1998, the ETI negotiated a Base Code that incorporates the ILO Declaration on Fundamental Principles and Rights at Work and other international standards as well as the notion of a "living wage," in accord with local standards of living. The ETI is now turning its attention to how to monitor and verify the Base Code, developing benchmarks, criteria for judging

the competency of monitors, and ways to further dialogue between stakeholders and capacity-building in the South. Three pilot monitoring projects are underway, including wine production in South Africa, horticulture in Zimbabwe and clothing production in China.

Codes of Conduct: Company Initiatives

Elsewhere companies have instituted their own voluntary codes of conduct. Comprehensive codes of conduct generally apply to company headquarters and subsidiaries as well as other companies in the supply chain (sub-contractors). For instance, garment production for a large retailer can be scattered around the globe, with design taking place at company headquarters in the North and cutting, sewing and assembly being done in factories and homes of the South. Codes typically go beyond anti-corruption and shareholder relationships to include a wide range of regulations such as those governing forced labour, child labour and health and safety and environmental standards. The International Labour Organization (ILO) currently lists over 215 multinationals that have some form of voluntary code of conduct, including Levi Strauss (jeans), Dow Chemical, Walt Disney, Ford Motor Company, General Electric, Johnson & Johnson (pharmaceuticals), sportswear giants Reebok and Nike and retail chains Wal-Mart and Sears Roebuck (see Box 9, p. 124).

Because they are voluntary, these codes can be as inclusive or as vague as the corporation desires and are not legally enforceable. Consumer and human rights advocates point to several other problems, including:

- failure to refer to ILO standards related to child labour, discrimination or the rights of workers to form their own trade unions and bargain collectively;
- highly variable definitions of living wages or health and safety standards;
- failure to specify implementation methods.

All of these were true in the case of the code of conduct introduced by the football stitching industry in Pakistan, rendering it basically empty. Then a group of women, concerned about the exploitation of young children in particular, brought together government and NGOs to find a way to end the use of child labour in the stitching of soccer balls in Sialkot, Pakistan. The three-pronged Partners Agreement includes the ILO, UNICEF, the Save the Children Fund, the Punjab Department of Education, along with various football industry associations and the World Federation of Sporting Goods Industries.

Richard Rollins

Box 9: Reebok's Human Rights Initiatives

Reebok is a sports footwear and apparel company that produces in many parts of the world, including the Americas, Asia, Europe, and a limited amount in the Middle East and South Africa. In 1992, Reebok systematized its factory-monitoring practices by adopting a formal, worldwide code of conduct concerning the treatment of workers. Under the Reebok Human Rights Production Standards, factories that manufacture Reebok products must:

- implement reasonable working hours and overtime;
- provide fair compensation;
- respect the right to freedom of association;
- offer a safe and healthy work environment.

The code mandates:
- NO discrimination against workers;
- NO forced or compulsory labour;
- NO child labour.

The code further states that every factory will publicize and enforce a non-retaliation policy that permits factory workers to speak with Reebok staff without fear of retaliation by factory management.

In October 1999, Reebok released a report on two Indonesian factories producing Reebok footwear, based on a study conducted by Insan Hitawasana Sejahtera (IHS), an independent research and consulting firm based in Jakarta, Indonesia. The report, entitled Peduli Hak ("Caring for Rights") profiles conditions at two of the largest factories, PT Dong Joe Indonesia (DJI) and PT Tong Yang Indonesia (TYI), outlining problems and steps taken to correct them. It includes findings that are critical of factory management's communication with workers, gender equity and health and safety procedures.

Reebok is the first company in the industry to make public an in-depth, third-party critique of labour conditions in factories making its footwear. Reebok is also a co-founder of "Business for Social Responsibility" and together with the US-based Lawyers Committee for Human Rights established Witness — a programme that equips frontline human rights activists with hand-held video cameras to document human rights abuses. The company sponsors an annual Reebok Human Rights Award and awards grants to human rights NGOs worldwide.

Source: www.reebok.com/humanrights.

One problem with company codes of conduct is that they are rarely subject to independent monitoring, especially at the thousands of sub-contracting factories where most of the work is actually carried out. For example, The Gap, a US sportswear retailer, adopted a comprehensive code of conduct in the early 1990s. But although this was supposed to cover factories run by their suppliers, conditions at these factories remained appalling. In 1996, following widely publicized exposure of labour practices at one such supplier, the Mandarin factory in El Salvador, The Gap agreed to accept independent monitoring by local human rights groups. However, The Gap has 1,000 contractors in 50 countries, and the Mandarin factory in El Salvador is the only one that has agreed to independent monitoring.

"This was the first time that workers from both groups had heard about codes of conduct. They also said that their managers and supervisors do not know about codes. Not one clause of the code was implemented. There was no union, no living wage, no minimum working hours. There was also child labour, particularly in the Sialkot sportswear factories."

— Simy Gulzar, Working Women Organization, Lahore

Enforcing Corporate Responsibility

How codes of conduct are enforced lies at the heart of the issue of corporate citizenship, inspiring campaigns to force parent companies to take responsibility for conditions wherever goods are produced. For instance, public attention was focused on conditions in a Honduran factory that produced clothing for Wal-Mart because a line of

Sam Milford

sportswear bore the name of a prominent US television personality, Kathie Lee Gifford. Gifford initially declined to speak out against the sweatshop conditions reported at the factory. However, the public outcry generated by this and other incidents encouraged her to join the White House Apparel Industry Partnership, comprising companies such as Nike, Reebok and Liz Claiborne along with unions, human rights groups, religious organizations and consumer advocates. Initiated with great fanfare in 1996, the partnership was charged with creating an industry-wide code of conduct and monitoring system. However, it floundered over the terms of independent monitoring, the right to form a union and companies' refusal to include a living wage provision. Most union and NGO representatives pulled out, and the companies and remaining NGOs formed the Fair Labor Association (FLA) in 1998. In an effort to improve its credibility, the FLA secured the participation of over 100 universities that license the companies to make apparel. At the same time, union and human rights groups joined student organizations to form a more rigorous monitoring group, the Workers Rights Consortium, which to date has been joined by some 50 universities.

At the international level, several specific product codes of conduct have had some success in inducing companies to be more socially responsible. One of the best known is the longstanding international women's campaign regarding the marketing of babymilk, or infant formula (see Box 10). Governments can combine both international and national codes in regulations governing the production and marketing of certain products. In India, for example, the government has passed legislation on the marketing of babymilk in line with the World Health Organization (WHO) Code, which specifies the way in which labels and advertisements must be worded so as to avoid improper use. The legislation allows companies and their executives who violate these guidelines to be prosecuted, subject to prison terms of up to three years.

Another strategy for demanding corporate responsibility is litigation. However, it is very difficult for workers in one country to take legal action against a multinational corporation that has its headquarters in another country. Transnational corporations argue that they are subject only to the laws in each country, and judges usually support this claim. Recently, trade unions and human rights groups have won some important legal rulings where courts in a company's home country have accepted that the company is legally responsible for employment conditions in its operations overseas. In 1997, for example, a judge in the UK awarded a group of workers in South Africa approximately $1.5 million for injury caused by mercury poisoning at a plant owned by the UK-based Thor Chemical Holdings (ICEM 1997). More recently,

Box 10: The Babymilk Campaign

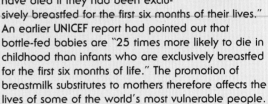

UNICEF/Carolyn Watson

"Welcome to Nigeria where babies are healthy and happy," read a billboard near the Lagos airport, sponsored by a transnational infant formula, or babymilk, manufacturer. However, according to UNICEF's 1995 report, *The State of the World's Children*: "In 1990, more than one million infants died who would not have died if they had been exclusively breastfed for the first six months of their lives." An earlier UNICEF report had pointed out that bottle-fed babies are "25 times more likely to die in childhood than infants who are exclusively breastfed for the first six months of life." The promotion of breastmilk substitutes to mothers therefore affects the lives of some of the world's most vulnerable people.

The Swiss-based Nestlé is the world's second largest food company and largest producer of infant formula. In the 1980s, churches and NGOs in the United States began a consumer boycott of Nestlé products which soon spread to Canada, Europe and New Zealand. The World Health Organisation and UNICEF issued a code of conduct for the marketing of breastmilk substitutes. This was approved by governments at the World Health Assembly in May 1981 by a vote of 118 to one, with only the United States voting against it. In May 1994, in an attempt to tighten up loopholes in the Code, the World Health Assembly adopted unanimously a resolution to strengthen breastfeeding worldwide.

Transnational corporations appear to be interpreting the code in a way that does not interfere greatly with their promotion strategies. In April 1998, the Interagency Group on Breastfeeding Monitoring (IBFAN), which by then comprised more than 150 groups in over 90 countries, published a new report, *Breaking the Rules*. Based on the monitoring of company practices in 39 countries, this alleged that manufacturers are still giving samples to mothers and breaking and stretching the rules. As a result, lawyers from the United States, the UK, India, Bangladesh, the Philippines, Norway and Sweden formed a research group to investigate legal action against the milk companies. The group plans to work with authorities in developing countries to coordinate possible litigation initiatives.

Some 69 developing countries now collect regular data on breastfeeding, more than double the 1993 figure. A total of 16 countries have achieved full compliance with the code and another 111 countries have taken legally enforceable action on some aspects. This means that over half of the world's population now live in countries that have broadly implemented the code as law.

Sources: Madeley 1999; Burns et al.1999.

Box 11: The Labour Behind the Label Campaign

The Labour Behind the Label network involves development cooperation organizations, local support groups, trade unions and ethical retailers who are working to improve labour conditions in the international garment industry. Using consumer pressure on retailers, the Labour Behind the Label campaign is encouraging retailers to:

- adopt codes of conduct respecting the ILO core conventions and guaranteeing good working conditions, a living wage and the right to join independent trade unions;
- accept independent verification of how codes are put into practice;
- make information available to consumers to facilitate better informed choices.

One member of this network, the Clean Clothes Campaign, a Dutch-based NGO with links to networks in five other countries, was set up in 1989 to support women workers in garment-producing units in developing countries and in Europe. The CCC drew up a Fair Trade Charter for Garments which is a code of conduct for retailers selling clothing in the Netherlands. Companies who sign the Charter guarantee that the clothes they sell have been produced according to ILO standards and not by child labour. Following a media campaign by Oxfam, the Dutch retail chain C&A announced in 1996 that it would change its buying operation to end sweatshop labour by some of its suppliers.

Source: Women Working Worldwide; Madeley 1999.

three class-action suits were filed against US retailers for mistreatment of workers in factories run by non-US suppliers operating on US soil, specifically on the Pacific island of Saipan. Brought by the garment workers union (UNITE) and three NGOs (Sweatshop Watch, Global Exchange and the Asian Law Caucus), these charged that companies had knowingly contracted with factories that violate US labour laws (IUR 1999). In late 1999, nine retailers agreed to a $3 million settlement that not only guarantees regular wages and basic working conditions but also funds an independent monitoring body to enforce standards (Block 2000).

However, as all of these hard-fought campaigns by worker and consumer groups make clear, legislation and agreements about codes of conduct will remain fragmented and piecemeal unless they can stimulate more concerted action by governments and international development agencies. A number of groups working on corporate accountability, including Labour Behind the Label, Women Working Worldwide and the International Confederation of Free Trade Unions, have agreed to use the ILO's Tripartite Declaration of Principles

concerning Multinational Enterprises and Social Policy as a basis of a corporate code of conduct. These principles specify that codes of conduct be simple and easy to use, and must:

- include all core ILO labour standards and state company responsibility in agreements with contractors, subcontractors and suppliers;
- establish a labour contract;
- ensure high-quality independent monitoring;
- involve workers and unions in implementation and monitoring;
- hold the company responsible for the cost of monitoring;
- include reproductive rights protection and sexual harassment clauses.

"Multinational corporations are too important and too dominant a part of the global economy for voluntary codes to be enough."

— Human Development Report, 1999

Consumer Action: Alternative Trade Organizations

Another approach to corporate responsibility depends not on state regulation but on the market itself. Beginning in the 1970s, a number of alternative trade organizations (ATOs) emerged in Europe and North America, building on earlier precedents such as the cooperative movement in 19th-century Europe and a variety of Northern based movements in solidarity with people in revolutionary societies. During the 1980s and 1990s, alternative or fair trade organizations concentrated on strengthening the position of small producers of goods such as coffee, cocoa and honey in the South by appealing to the so-called ethical consumer market in the North (see Box 12). But unlike the solidarity trade movement, the fair trade movement seeks to influence more mainstream trade, through the impact of consumer choice rather than the intervention of the state (Murray 1998).

The 1990s saw the growth of national fair trade mark organizations, which issue "Fair Trade Marks" which set out set out ethical standards for overseas suppliers of products. Like the longstanding Union Labels, awarded by labour unions in different countries to demarcate items produced by unionized firms, Fair Trade Marks are part of a wider movement known as "social labelling," or the promotion of products on the basis of their claims to be environmentally or socially responsible.

Social labels are the opposite of warning labels, messages on products that indicate that they are "green" – that is, environmentally friendly — or that they are produced under "fair labour conditions." Like codes of conduct, labels are voluntary responses to market demands. But unlike codes of conduct, they are only relevant in the highly developed consumer markets of the North, where people have many similar products to choose from. As such, they have little or no impact on the environmental and labour standards of producers who lack a high consumer profile in the North.

Social labelling campaigns are designed to encourage companies selling toys, clothes and food to adopt codes of conduct with regard to labour practices and environmental standards. The case of Rugmark is often cited as an example of how consumer power can be used to raise awareness of how goods are produced and to encourage changes in the entire chain of production. Rugmark is a label awarded to domestic carpet producers in India who do not exploit child labour. It is a fairly unusual initiative in that it focuses not on global corporations but on producers in the Indian subcontinent and mobilizes consumer action in the importing countries.

"Today I bought a Kodak camera... I learned that Kodak has undertaken a $13 million initiative to implement pay equity in its work force. I believe in supporting companies that behave ethically toward their workers."

— Judy Mann, Washington Post, October 20, 1999.

Social Accounting and Social Auditing

Corporate accountability requires standard setting and implementation, which includes independent monitoring and verification. This latter concern has given rise to "social accountants" and "social auditors" who are hired by companies to carry out inspections and advise and train employees in socially responsible practices.

Social accounting refers to a company carrying out internal monitoring, evaluation and reporting on its operations against a set of benchmarks. It combines international standards with new forms of accountancy around social, ethical, and environmental factors alongside the standard financial ones. Social auditing means a company brings in an outside firm to verify whether its social accounts are complete and accurate. One of the best known is Ernst & Young, which advises Nike, among others.

With both practices, there is concern about to whom social auditors are accountable and what standards they apply (e.g., ILO standards versus private benchmarks). In an effort to get beyond this, the Council for Economic Priorities in the United States launched SA 8000, or Social Accountability 8000, designed to be "a comprehensive, global, verifiable standard for auditing and certifying compliance with corporate responsibility." Based on core ILO conventions, the UN Universal Declaration of Human Rights and the UN Declaration on the Rights of the Child, the standard is intended to be applied to both developing and developed countries.

The SA 8000 Advisory Board consists of representatives from Reebok, Toys 'R' Us, Sainsbury's, the Body Shop and Otto Versand. An audit is carried out by a private company accredited to the Council on Economic Priorities Accreditation Agency to see whether a company meets the SA 8000 standard. It is then granted a certificate that shows good practice to consumers and

Box 12: Twin Trading and CaféDirect

Twin Trading is a London-based alternative trading organization, established in 1985, which now buys coffee from 14 organizations of small farmers in seven countries. The coffee is processed and marketed as CaféDirect, a brand now available in most UK supermarkets as both fresh-ground and freeze-dried instant coffee. The brand was launched in 1991 and sales grew rapidly. In 1997 it had 3-4 per cent of the UK market for fresh-ground coffee.

Twin Trading provides a minimum guaranteed price for coffee farmers, and a premium above the world price, when this goes higher than the minimum price. It provides pre-payment to farmers, and develops a long-run close working relationship with them to enable them to improve the quality and reliability of their deliveries. The farmers can take advantage of their increased know-how to sell to a wider range of traders – Twin Trading provides up-to-date market information to them and enables them to visit London to see how their crop is marketed and consumed.

"A few years ago, before initiatives like CaféDirect... it seemed like farmers were only good for walking long distances with coffee on their backs... I think that the comerciantes [local traders] just couldn't ever imagine that one day we would be working directly with people from the outside... They certainly never thought we would be in the trade ourselves."
— Eleanor Arbildo, Northwest Peru

Source: Hide 1997.

policy-makers. Some weaknesses at present are that none of the supporting evidence concerning the audits is made public and the certificate only applies to one site rather than to all of the subcontractors in the production chain.

Ethical Investment and Shareholder Action

Ethical investment initiatives involve screening organizational investment portfolios according to ethical and social considerations. Women in church organizations, trade unions and NGOs, as well as public sector agencies, have joined and at times initiated campaigns to prohibit investment in companies that discriminate on racial, gender or religious grounds, and to promote investment in socially responsible companies (see Box 13).

Women have also been active in shareholder action campaigns in which they buy shares, attend shareholder meetings and question directors on their environmental and social record. In the United States, the Union of Needletrades, Industrial and Textile Employees (UNITE) has waged shareholder campaigns against companies such as The Gap, Nike and Disney, combined with public demonstrations and media outreach.

Conclusion

The accountability of government and corporate institutions to all citizens is a cornerstone of democratic society. Effective accountability to women requires:

- a political commitment to women's equality and an atmosphere of openness about women's issues in the society at large;
- free and independent women's associations to counterbalance the influence of dominant "malestream" forces with ready access to decision-making structures and the media;
- greater participation of women within national parliaments and ministries of finance, as well as the boards of transnational corporations;
- access to the media by organizations working to challenge gender-blind policies of globalization and restructuring;
- resources to monitor state and non-state actors as well as to train and develop the research capabilities of women in order to facilitate independent assessments.

First, *governments* should take steps to link commitments made at Beijing to their national budget allocations. These need to go beyond allocations to women's programmes to include an assessment of all budget items for their gender-specific impacts and outcomes.

Box 13: Women-Friendly Ethical Equities Fund

The UNIFEM National Committee in Singapore has created an ethical equities fund, the first in South East Asia, which will invest in publicly-listed companies that support UNIFEM objectives. Individual savings will be channelled to women-friendly companies, while dividends and income from the fund will in turn be used to benefit UNIFEM's work in South East Asia. In addition to demonstrated investment potential, listed companies must demonstrate a commitment to the empowerment of women. This is defined as:

- significant female representation at the board level
- women-friendly hiring and promotion programmes
- pro-maternity and adoption benefits
- comparable pay for comparable work
- on-site or subsidized child-care programmes
- mentoring programmes for women staff
- manufacture/market products and services of benefit to women.

Companies that consistently subvert the empowerment of women by, for instance, relying on below-minimum wage female workers or subcontracting to economies which abuse female and child labour, could be excluded from the proposed fund. An Advisory Committee comprised of UNIFEM representatives and women investment professionals would audit the investment criteria and choices every six months.

Source: UNIFEM National Committee Singapore, 1998.

Second, *transnational corporations* must be held to more stringent codes of conduct, subject to independent monitoring. Codes should include: the application of all core ILO labour standards, action programmes to combat sexual harassment, and reproductive rights protection clauses. The right to own and operate a business has to be defined and utilized in ways that promote rather than violate the human rights of employees, customers, and local communities.

Finally, progress for the world's women demands that women become active agents in the policy-making process. No longer content to be the objects of policy, women across the globe are demanding an equal role in the formulation of policies that will shape their future, as discussed in Chapter 6.

Chapter 6

**Future Progress
for Women:
Reshaping
Globalization**

WEDO

Introduction

This report has situated the progress of the world's women in the context of existing globalization, a process whereby owners of capital are enabled to move their capital (whether in the form of money or goods) around the globe more easily and quickly than ever before. This process has been facilitated by the spread of new information and communication technologies and the removal of state controls on trade and investment. Over the last two decades, the process of globalization has given greater impetus to women's participation in the market economy. However, it has contributed to widening inequality within and among countries, and has been punctuated by economic and social collapse in parts of Sub-Saharan Africa and countries in transition (in Eastern Europe and the former Soviet Union) and by financial crises in Asia and Latin America.

"Globalization is clearly an unfinished business, a work in progress that can be shaped and steered by human interventions and values of equality, poverty reduction and social justice."

— Noeleen Heyzer, statement at Sesssion on Decent Work in the Global Economy, UNCTAD, February 2000

As discussed in Chapter 2, the Beijing Platform for Action and the Copenhagen Programme of Action addressed some of the problems of globalization, with a particular emphasis on structural adjustment programmes that require governments to liberalize markets for goods, services and capital. However, the solutions proposed for women in these documents were largely microeconomic, with a particular focus on enabling poor women to obtain access to credit.

The analysis presented in Chapters 3 and 4 shows that while some progress has been made towards empowerment of women, there has also been regress in some countries. Moreover, it is highly likely that the gains accompanying globalization have been concentrated in the hands of better-off women with higher levels of education and with greater ownership of resources and access to capital. If a wider range of women are to gain, globalization must be reshaped so that it is people-centred instead of profit-centred and made more accountable to women.

Chapter 5 discussed strategies that women are employing to hold governments accountable for achieving greater gender equality in the ways they spend public money and to hold business corporations accountable for greater gender equality in the ways they use and reward workers to make money. Chapter 6 examines progress towards reshaping globalization, highlighting ways that women are organizing to enter, challenge and change the operation of markets, the use of new technology and the formulation of economic policy at national and international levels.

As Devaki Jain, Indian feminist economist and one of the founders of DAWN, points out (1999), many of the people and organizations who have been promoting globalization are now taking a more nuanced approach. They refer more often to problems of inequality, poverty and social exclusion and to the need to subject the globalization process to some regulation, often expressed in terms of "global governance." They acknowledge the importance of the nation-state as a site for organizing the transformation of economic and social processes. As a result, Jain argues, there are new opportunities for women to intervene and renegotiate globalization in order to enable information and communication technology to be used in equitable ways and markets to be used to serve human ends.

Entering and Transforming Financial Markets

Microcredit programmes have become one of the key strategies for addressing women's poverty. Microcredit programmes come in several varieties: targeted towards poor people or women only; individual or group based; credit-only or credit and other services; and government or non-governmental organization sponsored. Some programmes focus on savings as well as loans and are more properly called "microfinance." Examples of every combination may be found in practice somewhere in the world.

The Microcredit Summit in 1997 set a target of 100 million of the world's poorest families, especially the women of those families, to be receiving credit for self-employment, and other financial and business services by the year 2005. This summit brought together a series of councils representing advocacy organizations, banks and commercial financial institutions, corporations, domestic government agencies, donor agencies, educational institutions, philanthropic foundations, heads of states, international financial institutions, non-governmental organizations, parliamentarians, practitioners, religious institutions and UN agencies — altogether 2900 people from 137 countries. Large international donors have increased funding for microcredit, channelled through NGOs and

Microcredit Summit

MICROCREDIT
SUMMIT
CAMPAIGN

governments. They target women for reasons of cost-efficiency as well as equality, since repayment rates are higher among women.

The 1999 Microcredit Summit Meeting in Abidjan, Côte d'Ivoire, focused on four core themes: reaching the poor; reaching women; ensuring impact; and building financially self-sufficient microfinance institutions. It was reported that by September 1999, member programmes had reached over 12 million of the world's poorest people.

UNIFEM, as co-chair with UNDP of the UN Council of the Microcredit Summit, has been active in promoting a gender perspective. The most important contributions of the UN are building the institutional capacity of microfinance institutions (MFIs), strengthening their networks and alliances, advocating for increased resources, mainstreaming gender in microfinance and financial institutions and developing and sharing best practices in microfinance.

Microfinance schemes have been successful in increasing women's income levels and control over income in many of the world's poorest regions. Research by Linda Mayoux, for example, shows that they have improved perceptions of women's contribution to household income and family welfare and increased women's participation in decision-making in the household, resulting in overall improvements in attitudes towards women in the household and community (Mayoux 1998). However, as she demonstrates, drawing on evidence from Africa and South Asia, microfinance in itself is not the answer to the empowerment of poor women. Many women are disadvantaged by lack of access to complementary resources such as land and know-how, as well as continuing responsibility for subsistence production, which limits the time available for running a business.

"Credit is also debt"

— Susan Johnson and Ben Rogaly (1997)

Moreover, for some women and their families, microfinance programmes have had negative impacts. Impacts vary among women across schemes, and in some cases prove to be disempowering. For example, one study in Bangladesh found that among female borrowers, a majority reported an increase in verbal and physical aggression from male relatives after taking out loans (Pepall 1998). Other studies in Bangladesh have drawn attention to the fact that women run the risk of losing control of the loans to male relatives because they are culturally excluded from participating in markets outside their homes to buy inputs and sell outputs (Khondkar 1998). In some cases, women are not able to significantly increase incomes under their control or negotiate changes in gender inequalities within the household and community and may become dependent on loans to continue in low-paid occupations with heavier workloads.

The WomenWatch online working group on the Beijing Platform for Action generated a lively discussion of the pros and cons of microcredit for women in different regions. For example:

"In Nigeria this loan, small as it may be, has changed not only the economic capacity of the women who were forcibly evicted from their homes, but has also made them more active in the struggle for a just compensation for their demolished houses. With education and enlightenment campaigns introduced through projects such as micro-credit, women will become more involved in advancing their own rights."
— Social and Economic Rights Action Centre, Nigeria (UN 2000c)

"It is important to ensure that women use and have control over the money. Skills training and training in business management should be a part of these types of projects. Linking women to the market and giving them marketing facilities are also some important factors to be considered. These projects need to incorporate gender sensitivity and awareness training for whole families, as a woman's involvement with productive activities causes her extra burden in her existent reproductive activities."
— CARE, Bangladesh (UN 2000c)

"In our programmes we have advocated monitoring how the profit has been used within the household. My concern here is that women often do not have control of money within the household and men may take control of the credit funds. There are great benefits microcredit programmes can bring to women, as long as they are coupled with empowerment measures for women that ensure access and control of household finances and decision making in consultation with spouses."
— UNIFEM, Viet Nam (UN 2000c)

Ken Kobre

One of the contradictions of microfinance programmes is the tension between policies designed to increase the financial sustainability of microcredit institutions and strategies for women's empowerment. Financial sustainability requirements lead to pressure to cut costs to a minimum and have obliged many programmes to significantly reduce complementary support services. Services such as literacy programmes, business training and childcare services are often significant factors in both repayment rates and empowerment, allowing women to make real improvements to their economic and social situation. Ensuring complementarity between women's empowerment and the financial sustainability of the microcredit institution is critical, and must be strategically addressed and planned. The issue of women's access to markets for their products is particularly important.

Mayoux (1999) suggests several ways in which women's empowerment could be increased within microfinance programmes:

- the registration of assets used as collateral, or purchased with loans, in women's names or in joint names;
- the incorporation of clear strategies for women's graduation to larger loans;
- the provision of various loan options based on participatory consultation, including loans for non-traditional activities, health, education, housing, etc.;
- the provision of a range of savings facilities that include higher interest deposits.

Box 1: Mainstreaming Gender in Microfinance Institutions

Microfin-Afric
Microfin-Afric is a network of 45 microfinance and microenterprise organizations from 17 African countries that advocates for more inclusive policies on microfinance, nationally and internationally. Supported by UNIFEM and SU-TCDC (the UN Special Unit for Technical Cooperation among Developing Countries), the network facilitates the exchange of information among organizations working in this area, increases their credibility with their partners in development, and implements member-support programmes, including training. In addition, the network helps to highlight traditional African experiences in savings and credit, and provides data on funding directed to women and its impact on the overall situation of women.

The Microfin Afric network links sub-regional, national and local microfinance institutions to the global community in an effort to increase the voice, profiles and visibility of practitioners. In 1997 Microfin Afric reached out to 600,000 people, of whom 500,000 were women, and issued more than US$41,000,000 in credit.

ACCION International
A project to increase access to credit for women in the informal sector was initiated in 1992 by UNIFEM and ACCION International, an NGO network that provides credit and training to microentrepreneurs in Latin America and the United States. ACCION-affiliated NGOs, like most microfinance institutions, while committed to working with women, lacked the necessary capital and gender-sensitive methodology to support women with financial and business services. Although they sought to deliver microcredit and outreach to as many women clients as possible, they knew little about the differential impact that their delivery methodology and the microcredit they provided had on women and men. While women's participation rates were good – over 50 per cent in the region – there was little information on the quality of their participation and the impact of credit on the lives of the women clients. Information on women's savings behaviour, investment patterns, business decisions, training needs and non-credit barriers needed to be better understood.

Five inter-related components addressed these needs:
- research on characteristics of women entrepreneurs and how they operate their businesses;
- gender training for participating organizations and the network;
- improved financial services and increased access to such services for women;
- information disaggregated by gender;
- the extension of credit guarantees to allow access to credit for more women.

The most innovative aspects of the project include the use of standby letters of credit to enable local NGOs to raise capital locally and expand lending to reach thousands of new borrowers, and engendering intermediary microlending institutions and solidarity groups to promote women's capacity as entrepreneurs and producers. A survey on women's microenterprises and the situation of women clients in the informal sector resulted in a book entitled "Women's Microenterprises: Balancing the Double Day."

Sources: Microfin Afric Activity Report 1998; UNIFEM, "Microfinance Plus: A Project Experience in Latin America," mimeo, n.d.

Furthermore, there is a need to mainstream gender and empowerment concerns throughout all the activities of a microfinance programme. There is a difference in programmes where staff are gender-aware and empowerment issues are raised as a routine part of all interactions between staff and clients, and those where staff fail to question gender stereotypes or suggest ways in which women could overcome gender-based problems. Mainstreaming gender requires a review of norms and regulations from a gender perspective, integrating gender-equitable policies into services for both women and men; integrating gender and empowerment issues into client and staff training; and including indicators of women's empowerment in project evaluations.

UNIFEM supports a process of gender main-streaming in microfinance institutions to ensure that financial sustainability is combined with specific measures to support women's empowerment and to ensure that women's concerns inform international agendas on microfinance (see Box 1). Women's empowerment should have equal weight with institutional financial sustainability in determining resource flows to microfinance institutions. In support of this goal, UNIFEM organized a panel on Gender Issues in Microfinance at the 3rd Microcredit Summit in June 1999, emphasizing the need to include women's empowerment indicators in the design and evaluation of microcredit programmes. Without such indicators, there is a danger that women will be reduced from active participants in indigenous, participatory savings and credit schemes to passive recipients, dependent on new imported systems. Women's own indigenous, participatory systems also have an important contribution to make (see Box 2).

Whatever form microfinance takes, the ability of women to benefit depends upon their being able to access steadily growing markets in which they can sell their products at remunerative rates. This requires that women have not only management and marketing skills (see Box 3, p. 134) but also bargaining power within markets and an enabling macroeconomic environment, including the way in which markets are regulated. Without appropriate market development and anti-monopoly policy, small producers will tend to be out-competed by large businesses.

"Microfinance per se is not a panacea and other strategies for empowerment are also needed."

— Linda Mayoux (1998)

It is important that a focus on microfinance does not give rise to the illusion that poor women can pull themselves up by their own bootstraps and thus need less in the way of public services. In

Box 2: Women's Microfinance Schemes

Community-Based Savings and Credit Groups

Savings and credit groups (SCGs) provide an effective strategy for addressing women's day-to-day survival needs as well as providing a space in which women can organize to address local development issues. The savings and credit group is a custodian of women's savings. A central concern is to support the livelihood activities that sustain poor households.

In Maharashtra, India, a network of NGOs and women's collectives called Swayam Shikshan Prayog has been exper-imenting with new ways of learning for communities and organizations. The goal is to build capacity of savings and credit groups to access and manage resources so that they can stake a claim to participate in local decision-making processes that affect the allocation and management of resources. Swayam Shikshan Prayog has set up "learning laboratories" in two districts — Latur and Osmanabad — working with women's groups, savings and credit groups and local governing bodies on a variety of issues including construction, sanitation, local governance, credit and livelihoods. Learning activities, including site visits, dialogue meetings with state officials, study tours and information fairs, have helped expose women to new ideas and strategies, build self-confidence and create an enabling environment for experimentation and innovation. Their experiments include collective income-generating activities, setting up microenterprises, training women in microenter-prise activities, market surveys and credit planning for seasonal activities. A key question is how to move beyond mere sustenance to generating a surplus.

The network promotes strategic alliances with mainstream institutions such as government institutions, local authorities and banks. Members of the network also work to create institutional structures such as cooperatives, federations of savings and credit groups and information networks that respond to community-based solutions for accessing and managing resources.

Self-Help Groups in Tamil Nadu, India

Village women in Tamil Nadu are doing microfinance in a different way, through the formation of self-help groups that include semi-literate or illiterate village women. The women pool their household savings into a common fund, which is used to make loans to members on the basis of consensus. The rates of interest and the amount of the loan are decided by the group, which is typically composed of 15-20 village women who meet at least once a month. The government provides training in collec-tive decision-making while NGOs provide support in terms of keeping track of accounts and calculating interest, as well as group formation. Once the women have formed a cohesive group with financial discipline, the next stage is linking it to sources of institutional finance to enable it to provide funds for village-level economic activities. Since the whole process is entirely voluntary, the effects are truly long lasting at the grassroots. As of early 1999, there were 280,000 village women participating in 14,000 self-help groups in Tamil Nadu.

Sources: Gupta et al. 1998; Kumar 1999.

Ken Kobre

Box 3: Developing Women's Business Skills in Western Asia

UNIFEM is supporting a number of projects to equip women with the vocational and managerial skills to run their businesses. For example:

- "start your own business" workshops in Gaza and Syria which enable participants to meet with women who already run their own businesses and learn how to evaluate the market for their planned activities and how to deal with social constraints business women face;
- technical support (jointly with ILO) for the Directorate of Working Women, Ministry of Labour and Vocational Training, Yemen;
- development of training to improve women's skills in animal husbandry and fruit and olive tree cultivation in Jordan.

Source: UNIFEM Western Asia Regional Office Annual Report, 1999.

particular, it must be recognized that taking on loans introduces new risks into the lives of poor women. During periods of national financial crisis or recession, poor women are likely to be left with debt that is impossible to repay. Microcredit for poor women implies a need for more, not less attention to systems for social inclusion (social insurance, social protection). It also implies a need for macro-level national and international financial institutions to operate according to social criteria as well as financial criteria. Otherwise systemic risks generated at the macro-level cascade down to micro borrowers, who are poorly placed to absorb them.

Entering and Transforming Markets for Goods and Services

While the extension of markets is at the core of globalization, markets are organized in a variety of ways and women are differently positioned in relation to them. In some parts of the world, women are excluded by social norms from leaving their homes and going to market. In such cases, the challenge is to find a way of enabling women to participate.

One answer may be to bring the customers to women in their homes, as is done by Grameen Telecom Village Phone initiative in Bangladesh (see www.telecommons.com/villagephone). Village women use microcredit from the Grameen Bank to acquire digital GSM cellular phones and subsequently sell phone calls and phone services to other village women who come to their homes. The pilot phase involves 950 phones, but when the programme is complete, it is expected that there will be 40,000 phones in use. Rural women use the phones to make arrangements for the transfer of remittances from family members working in Dhaka and overseas. The lack of telephone connections in these areas makes this a profitable business.

In other parts of the world, where women do not face strong social norms of seclusion, they may confront other barriers in selling their products, including lack of transport, storage or information. Home-based women workers may be able to market the output through intermediaries, but they are usually in a very weak bargaining position. Lorraine Corner, UNIFEM Regional Programme Director for East and South East Asia explains:

A key issue here is while there is some commonality of interest between buyer and seller (both will benefit from a better quality product that can command a higher price) there is also a conflict of interest and an inherent inequality in the relationship. As a result the major benefits are likely to accrue to the buyer rather than the producer (Corner 1999).

Some women resolve this problem by establishing their own sales outlet, a space that is under their control. This aspiration was voiced by some of more than 80 women representing 33 Mayan women's groups from the Yucatan Peninsula in Mexico, who came together at the First Congress of Mayan Women in 1997. One of the women, Gloria Cauche Vazquez, explained the advantages of direct sales outlets:

This is what will enable us to improve our living standards.... We are trying to find a place that will function as a workshop as well as a shop... Our group, for example, has a piece of land... and we are seeing if we can build our premises there, since it would be a good location for selling... (UNIFEM 1997b).

Women in Peru have addressed this problem by establishing a House of Artisan Women store in Lima, where indigenous women's traditional handicrafts can be sold. With support from the Manuela Ramos Movement, an NGO based in Lima, and from UNIFEM, indigenous women have attended training workshops in producing and marketing for an urban market.

Many women know about local market opportunities, but lack information about how to enter international markets. UNIFEM has supported

Dennis Richardson

Gabriela Romanow

UNIFEM/Simone Buechler

Na Molay
Primer Congreso de Mujeres Mayas
Mayan Women First Congress

indigenous artisan women from Bolivia, Ecuador, Guatemala, Mexico and Peru in taking the first steps through an international trade fair held in Lima in 1998. By the end of the one-week fair, the 25 women artisans invited to attend had sold $33,500 worth of goods and better understood the financial value of their talents and their economic potential.

As well as access to international markets, women also need to learn how these markets are regulated, and how they can join together with other women to lobby governments, international trade unions, NGOs and fair trade organizations for forms of market organization that improve their bargaining power and protect their intellectual property rights (e.g., to their designs). This was among the goals of a UNIFEM-supported workshop that brought together women home-based embroidery workers in March 1999. Following the workshop, women set up an embroidery trade group within HomeNet, the international network of organizations of home-based workers. UNIFEM has helped women in other regions to appreciate the importance of the fine print of market regulations and to set up women's desks in important regional intergovernmental bodies that deal with international trade (see Box 4).

All of these dimensions — local marketplaces, international trade fairs, increased bargaining power and the ability to press for markets to be regulated in ways that are fair to women's small businesses — are addressed in the example of "shea butter," a multipurpose oil used in production of margarine, cosmetics and pharmaceuticals (see Box 5, p. 136). The shea butter case also illustrates the impact of changes in market regulations on women producers who wish to sell in international markets, since its export prospects have been substantially improved by changes in European Union regulations to allow its use as a substitute for cocoa butter in making chocolate.

Box 4: Market Regulations, Regional Trade Agreements and Gender Equality.

Trade Policy Harmonization in East Africa
An Inter-Governmental Authority on Development (IGAD) links Kenya, Uganda, Ethiopia, Djibouti, Eritrea and Sudan. A UNIFEM-supported Women's Desk will assist women's businesses operating in the regional market and enable them to benefit from trade policy harmonization. An IGAD Women in Business Forum was set up following a workshop in 1998.

Implementing Trade Policy in the Pacific
UNIFEM has been working to increase awareness of both government officials and gender trainers about the gender dimension of trade policy. In 1999 UNIFEM published a report on gender and trade in Vanuatu, Tonga, Fiji and Papua New Guinea as a step towards ensuring women's interests are represented when policy on international trade is developed. Inputs from women's groups have been solicited during consultations over the renegotiation of the Lomé Convention, which covers development and trade with EU countries.

Specialized Group on Women in the MERCOSUR
As a consequence of UNIFEM-supported studies to examine the gender implications of the Southern Cone Common Market Treaty (MERCOSUR) in Latin America, a regional high-level lobby group was set up to advocate for a gender equality commission to be located within the framework of MERCOSUR. This bore fruit in 1998 when the MERCOSUR Council of Ministers created a Specialized Group on Women, composed of representatives of national women's departments or offices and women's NGOs, which advises the Council of Ministers.

Aster Zaoude

Aster Zaoude

Box 5: Creating Women-Friendly Markets for Shea Butter

Shea nuts, from which shea butter is derived, come from a tree that grows wild in several African countries: Benin, Ghana, Mali, Burkina Faso, Côte d'Ivoire, Nigeria, Guinea, Togo, Cameroon, Chad and Central African Republic. Burkina Faso has 195 million shea trees that produce 25 per cent of the world's shea nuts.

Shea nuts are consumed locally and exported to Europe and Japan for the production of shea butter, which is used in chocolate, margarine, cosmetics and pharmaceuticals. Shea butter is also produced locally in Burkina Faso, with traditional methods by rural women who use it for cooking as well as for medicine, cosmetics and soap-making. There is a growing urban market for high-quality shea butter and its products within Burkina Faso and in neighbouring cities, along with a growing international market.

UNIFEM, in partnership with the Canadian Centre for Studies and International Cooperation, provides training on how to preserve shea nuts so that women can postpone the processing work until after the agricultural season without having the nuts spoil. Training also helps them ensure that the quality of the local butter meets international standards, even if it is produced in scattered, home-based or village-based units. By 1999, over 300 women in 25 associations had been trained in improved production techniques to meet the quality standards of international markets.

Liberalization policies have opened up new market opportunities. However, when production is scattered and producers are not well-organized, producers are less able to get a good price for their goods and more vulnerable to price fluctuations. To deal with this problem, UNIFEM has pioneered the development of a marketing strategy to link producers more directly to markets through five marketing centres, where women organize sales collectively, setting prices and negotiating directly with exporters. These sales points are linked to a marketing centre in the capital city, Ouagadougou, which serves women in the project along with other women producing shea butter.

To strengthen women's bargaining power, UNIFEM organized Shea Butter Trade Fairs in Ouagadougou in June 1998 and September 1999. The 1998 trade fair proved to be an excellent forum for product promotion, marketing and discussions with various partners. Regional and foreign buyers were invited, and discussion panels enabled women to raise their concerns before a prominent group of government officials, researchers, industrialists, technical experts and local traders, as well as similar groups from neighbouring countries.

After the 1998 fair, UNIFEM helped producers organize themselves in COFEM, a network that empowers them as a group to access larger markets and negotiate better prices. The cosmetic industry has been targeted as the key customer. This is a major breakthrough in the context of the long-standing monopolistic pricing imposed by the large foreign companies involved in the export of shea butter to the international food industries (chocolate makers, in particular).

The trade fair in 1999 was co-sponsored by UNIFEM and the Ministry of Women's Affairs and the Ministry of Commerce and assisted by the Chamber of Commerce and other national marketing institutions. The butter presented at this fair was better quality and women had made significant improvements in packaging. Butter produced by groups financed by UNIFEM were packaged with the same label, identifying each village. Participants presented new products made from shea butter, such as mosquito repellent, margarine and a variety of body creams, shampoos and other cosmetics, as well as ice cream made from shea fruit.

In the course of organizing around better marketing strategies, the women upheld a common basic price, which together with the quality improvements, enabled them to sell the butter at twice to three times the price obtained in 1998 (an increase from about 550 to 1250 CFA/kg). At the end of the fair, members of COFEM gathered the unsold stock and negotiated a common price with an exporter. For the first time, intermediaries were not able to intimidate the women into selling for less, so as to avoid transporting their butter back to the village.

OCCITANE, a French cosmetics enterprise known worldwide for its shea butter products, accepted an invitation to attend the fair. An agreement was reached whereby OCCITANE will purchase high quality shea butter at an improved price from the women in the UNIFEM supported projects, via a contract with CITEC, OCCITANE's main supplier in Burkina Faso.

The marketing centre was strengthened during the 1999 trade fair by the launch of a Website: www.fasonet.bf/karite. In April 2000, women from the project were invited to visit OCCITANE's factory in Manosque, France, to meet the women and men who further process the shea butter they produce.

Source: UNIFEM Regional Office, Senegal.

An important objective of these initiatives is to ensure that the changes in market regulations brought about by trade liberalization result in equal opportunities for women. Trade liberalization focuses on the abolition of quantitative controls on imports and the reduction of customs duties (tariffs) but it also often includes new regulations on intellectual property rights (patents, copyrights, etc.) as well as on health and safety. Liberalization permits new suppliers to enter markets, but this by itself does not create equal opportunities. Large and well-established businesses with well-developed information and political networks are likely to do better than small businesses that lack market information and lobbying clout. One of the things that large and well-established businesses are able to do is to influence the new market rules to their own advantage.

As stated by a UNIFEM regional study on the gender impact of trade, for example:

> *Disadvantaged groups are often prevented from having access to resources, information and policy development. Strong lobby groups that seek to entrench existing interests often frustrate and hijack the process and the implementation of new rules…*
>
> *The representation of the affected stakeholders, including consumers and women, and the extent to which they have access to information to make a knowledgeable and informed decision, will determine how trade policies and other resultant policies are shaped (UNIFEM 1999d).*

In addition to struggling for gender-aware regulations to counter existing inequalities in market access, however, women must also confront the new inequalities brought about by rapidly changing technology, especially in information and communications. The extent to which groups and individuals are able to take advantage of trade liberalization is strongly linked to their ability to control and use these new technologies.

Transforming Technology to Reshape Globalization

The vastly increased scope of access to information and speed of communication in the digital age is the second important dimension of globalization. Together with reduction in regulations, the new information and communications technologies (ICTs), especially the Internet, reshape the way that markets operate and production is organized. The danger is that just as with deregulation, these technologies will benefit mainly those who are already well placed in terms of their knowledge and skills.

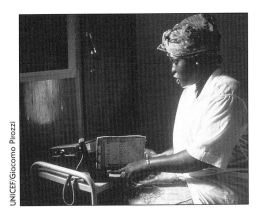

UNICEF/Giacomo Pirozzi

This was one of the findings of an innovative participatory research project UNIFEM supported on gender and new technologies conducted by the United Nations University Institute for New Technologies (UNU/INTECH) in partnership with women's NGOs in Asia. The director of the project, Professor Swasti Mitter, reports that the growth of transnational "teleworking" has opened up many new opportunities for women in the South, including data entry, medical transcription, geographical information systems and software production. But the women who are able to take advantage of these are generally well-educated and from higher income groups. Women with little or no education, especially older women, are losing out. As Mitter notes, there is "an age bias in the distribution of the benefits of globalization":

> *The work of UNU/INTECH in the context of China and Vietnam shows that globalization has brought new opportunities to young women with familiarity with English in new, service sector jobs, but has made a vast number of over-35-year-olds redundant, either because they are in declining industries, or have outdated skills (Mitter 1999).*

The project did not conclude that women's groups should oppose new technology, but rather that they need to strengthen their voice in policy dialogue so that they can press for improvements in training for women and for social protection for those who are negatively affected.

The Internet

With regard to the Internet, the 1999 Human Development Report drew attention to the wide inequalities both between and within countries in use of the Internet. Internet users command a wide range of knowledge and skills, including literacy, access to relevant information in a local language and the ability to utilize this information in ways that are meaningful and empowering. Men typically have greater access to equipment, time and money, and therefore more quickly acquire the necessary skills. The typical user is an English-speaking, university educated, high-income, young white man in a rich country. Poor women, especially those in poor countries, are most at a disadvantage.

Cost, while only one factor, is illustrative: in the United Kingdom, the annual cost of maintaining an Internet connection amounts to 2.7 per cent of per capita GNP, but in Argentina and South Africa it is 3.5 per cent and in Latvia it is 15.3 per cent of per capita GNP (Panos 1998). The problem here is not just lack of Internet hosts and personal computers, but also unequal access to televisions, telephone lines and mobile telephones. Even in the case of radios, there is still an imbalance between high-income countries and low-income countries, as shown in Table 6.1.

Improving Access to ICTs
To address these issues, and promote universal afford-able access, several developing countries have focused not on individuals but on communities (see Box 6). Innovative public access sites are being set up through "telecentres," located in community centres, public schools, libraries and women's centres, where people can obtain and share information through technologies such as computers, Internet, e-mail, faxes and telephones as well as through linkages between these technologies and more traditional media with broader outreach, such as community radio (see Box 7).

Telecentres are also becoming an important tool for education. One of the Commonwealth of Learning's "models for success" includes a literacy project that uses technology-based community learning centres to support literacy work in developing countries. Pilot projects to explore ways in which literacy programmes can benefit from information and communication technologies are being carried out in Bangladesh, India and Zambia. The objective for these learning centres is to provide training programmes that develop learner competencies in reading, numeracy and in the use of information and communication tools (see www.col.org/models/literacy.htm).

One constraint on the development of telecen-tres is the lack of reliable telephone connections, especially in rural areas. Mobile telephones may hold out more promise for the future as they become capable of transmitting e-mail and other forms of information.

Box 6: Women's Communications Network

The International Women's Communication Centre (IWCC) is an international network that came together in 1993 at a conference devoted to improving the communication network between grassroots women in Nigeria as well as in Africa as a whole.

IWCC-Nigeria is a locally based organization set up to disseminate information from the interna-tional network to Nigerian women at the grass-roots. In addition to weekly meetings to share information received over the Internet and workshops on topical issues, the group:

• prints local newsletters in local languages;
• distributes pamphlets to women on market day;
• broadcasts on the local community radio station;
• produces video documentaries on current issues;
• runs a free resource centre/library.

IWCC also serves as branch office to international NGOs such as Groots Super Coalition, Pan-African Women's Liberation Organization (PAWLO), International Alliance of Women Politicians, Help Women in Distress, Women's Voice on Radio Link, Global Alliance Against Trafficking in Women (GAATW), and WINGS Nigeria-Information Gathering on Women.

Source: Hajiya Limota Goroso Giwa, Global Knowledge for Development Internet Discussion.

Table 6.1: Indicators of ICT Availability, circa 1997

Income level	Radios per 1000 people	Televisions per 1000 people	Telephone main lines per 1000 people	Mobile telephones per 1000 people	Personal computers per 1000 people	Internet hosts per 10,000 people
High income	1300	664	552	188	269.4	470.12
Middle income	383	272	136	24	32.4	10.15
Low income	147	162	32	5	4.4	0.17

Source: adapted from World Bank, *World Development Report 1999/2000*, table 19, pp. 266-67.

Carol Barron

Box 7: WomensNet Community Radio Exchange

WomensNet, a joint project of SANGONet and the South African Commission on Gender Equality, seeks to enable the South African women's movement to take advantage of the potential for advancing women's struggles presented by ICTs, especially the Internet. The project is designed to help women's organizations to meet each other, find people, discuss issues, share resources and sharpen their tools for social activism.

The WomensNet Community Radio Project works with community radio stations, women's organizations and other media projects to create a space where community radio and women/gender orientated organizations can exchange information. The Website allows for "radio ready" information to be downloaded and aired and information to be posted online.

The project aims to:
- increase awareness of women's issues in community radio programming;
- develop capacity among women's groups to generate items for news and programming on community radio;
- improve information and communication skills of women's groups to help them deal with the media and to prepare radio-ready information for community radio.

WomensNet has created an Internet-based information clearinghouse to facilitate the dissemination of locally produced news about women and gender equality in South Africa. The Community Radio Exchange, a clearinghouse of radio-ready text and audio files for use in community radio stations, was formally launched on 29 March 2000 (see http://radio.womensnet.org.za).

Improving access is about more than a few more women "logging on." It is about ways to ensure that women who can log on, do so not only for themselves but also to transmit information from the Internet to women who cannot log on themselves (see Box 6 on IWCC). It is also about ensuring a two-way flow of information — not just from North to South — and in languages that are understood by more than the dominant cultures.

Thus improving access is part of a broader discussion on global knowledge, which focuses attention on human development obstacles faced disproportionately by women — ranging from lower income, education and training to gender roles and limited participation in decision-making — that impact upon their successful participation in the "knowledge society."

e-Campaigns

The Internet provides new opportunities to respond to situations such as humanitarian crises and violations of women's human rights (see Box 8). For organizations with limited budgets and no access to national media, it is an effective way to

e-Inclusion

In countries where strict cultural norms and traditions isolate women, the Internet has facilitated some women's access to knowledge and information. In Saudi Arabia for example, an Internet service provider — AwalNet — has created a special branch for women surfers, adding to the many "ladies only" services, such as banks, schools and shopping areas. Here women are able to use the Internet with the support of an all-female staff of computer experts (Sami 1999).

"[The Internet] whetted my appetite to keep up with the world...it gives you more confidence when you can keep up with the world...in knowledge, in culture. Why should we miss out?"

— Salwa Al-Qunaiber, census bureau computer operator (Sami 1999)

Box 8: Women's Human Rights Net

Women's Human Rights Net (whrNET) is a collaborative NGO initiative that links partner organizations and women's human rights advocates worldwide via the Internet. This dynamic resource is designed to be an integrated tool for women's human rights advocacy, networking, education and research. whrNET provides information in three main languages – English, French and Spanish – and serves as an on-line space for the exchange of information, the development of advocacy strategies and the provision of resources aimed at building capacity among women's human rights organizations and activists.

whrNET grew out of a 1997 meeting in Harare, Zimbabwe, where over 50 women's human rights leaders from nearly 20 countries gathered to develop strategies for strengthening advocacy, networking and capacity-building within the movement. whrNET is jointly sponsored and supported by its partner organizations and receives support from UNIFEM.

Source: www.whrNET.org.

communicate with audiences around the world, enabling them to get information out quickly and to avoid government censorship. It is especially useful for transmitting information requiring urgent action through electronic networks. Electronic campaigns illustrate how women are transforming the technical tool of the Internet into a political tool for advocacy in different regions from their different cultural perspectives.

An example is the Women in Black campaign in Serbia, where women used electronic networks to get the word out globally on what was happening to women during the civil war following the breakup of the former Yugoslavia in 1990 and to get support for their non-violent campaign. Similarly in Kosovo in 1998, women were able to tell the world of the atrocities as they were happening, as well as gain support and learn strategies from other women's groups for assisting the many women who were being traumatized by rape and other human rights violations.

"When the war in Yugoslavia-Kosovo broke out we developed a mailing list where all e-mails received regarding women in Kosovo and Belgrade were forwarded to newsgroups and our international members (around 300). [Our] mailing list strengthened the communication between women in the region and international activists and founders."

— Kristina Mihalec, Croatia, personal e-mail communication

UN DPI/Ron Da Silva

UNIFEM has actively supported the use of ICTs in campaigning against violence against women. An electronic discussion list (<end-violence>) brought together over 2000 participants to share views and strategies in 1998 and 1999. A global videoconference on International Women's Day in 1999, convened women policy-makers in the UN General Assembly and women's organizations, governments, development agencies and the general public around the world.

Communication via the Internet has played an important role in mobilizing and focusing criticism of the rules governing the global economy, such as the proposed Multilateral Agreement on Investment (MAI), which was withdrawn in part because of NGO Internet campaigns. E-mail also brought together many of those who protested at the World Trade Organization (WTO) meeting in Seattle in November 1999 against the undemocratic nature of WTO deliberations. Women's groups worldwide played an active role in both the campaign against the MAI and the NGO mobilization at the WTO meeting.

e-Commerce

According to the World Trade Organization, electronic commerce "can be both products which are bought and paid for over the Internet but are delivered physically, and products that are delivered as digitalized information over the Internet" (www.wto.org/wto/ecom/ecom.htm). The Internet offers women entrepreneurs access to a wider market faster and at a lower cost than do traditional market outlets. In some cases, women can also order products on-line. E-commerce training initiatives enable women vendors to develop relationships with interested partners and traders in many parts of the world. On-line sessions allow them to learn about marketing opportunities, explore ways to combine local and productive resources to meet large-scale demand with quality control, and even to design their own Web pages.

Some initiatives are making it possible for small and medium entrepreneurs and producers in the South to work within the framework of electronic commerce despite the difficulties of secure payments (necessitating the use of credit cards) and other logistical constraints. Producers can use the Internet to make initial contact with potential buyers and to show and advertise products. Then, through local Chambers of Commerce or business associations and NGOs, they can be contacted for an order. In India, for example, the Self-Employed Women's Association (SEWA) artisan support programme works with 6,000 women artisans from the Banaskantha district north of Gujurat. Over 3000 women artisans sell their products through their outlet, Banascraft, which illustrates digital images of their products (see www.banascraft.org/banascraft/sewa.htm).

PEOPLink, a fair trade organization, supports local artisans through digital cameras linked to the Internet and helps rural women market their products on-line. Such initiatives help women receive more for their products by eliminating the middle person who usually gets most of the profits from sales. The Virtual Souk

provides employment opportunities for women in the informal sector, facilitating inclusion of those who risk being left out of the benefits of the information technology because of lack of access and information. The concept of the Virtual Souk goes beyond the marketplace; it is a development tool designed to empower local artisans and NGOs through training and access to information and knowledge (see Box 9).

e-Consultation

The new technologies have made possible the inclusion of a broader spectrum of voices in policy-making. In preparation for the General Assembly review of progress in implementing the Platform for Action, in June 2000, an effort to guarantee broad participation and input from women around the world was carried out through WomenWatch, the UN Internet gateway to global information about women's concerns, progress and equality. WomenWatch, a joint initiative by the UN Division for the Advancement of Women, UNIFEM, and the International Research and Training Institute for the Advancement of Women (INSTRAW) held a series of e-mail Working Groups — the Beijing +5 Global Forum — from September to December 1999.

> "We have plenty of women's projects in this area but many remote villages can't get information on when there is an exhibition where they can bring their handicrafts."
>
> — Elizabeth Amuro, community development officer, Uganda (Opoku-Mensah 1999)

Box 9: e-Commerce Initiatives

PEOPLink trains local fair trade organizations to market their products on the Internet. Based on an earlier mail-order venture called Pueblo to the People, which marketed crafts from artisans in Latin America, it includes the novel marketing idea of presenting the lives of the artisans that created the products along with the products themselves. Typically PEOPLink will buy items for sale in bulk, so they can be shipped to customers quickly. The products are purchased in advance, allowing the producer to buy raw materials and supplies for creating more items. The site also allows wholesalers to buy on-line.

PEOPLink develops trading partner relationships via local NGOs that have links to grassroots groups such as craft cooperatives, widow groups, refugee associations and peasant leagues. Each NGO provides services to several of these grassroots groups, taking pictures of the artisans at work and the products for sale. They can also answer questions about products via e-mail.

PEOPLink supports its NGO trading partners with training - both in person and online - and via e-mail, and equips them with digital cameras. It trains partners on how to capture the images and edit them on computer in a format suitable for the Internet. The trading partners in turn provide training to the artisans and help to develop educational materials about their lives and work. Trading partners will also help groups set up their own Websites that are hosted by PEOPLink. The project has plans to expand and link with Oxfam America and the Smithsonian Institution's Folklife festival as well as to market handicrafts to museum stores and other retailers.

The Virtual Souk (or virtual market) is an initiative of the World Bank Institute (WBI), which links artisans with local development organizations to assist in marketing their products. The WBI provides management training and technical advice to the NGOs to enable them to create Websites and set up a commercial chain that includes pricing products, taking orders, delivering worldwide and handling all related financial aspects. The NGOs in turn deliver training in microenterprise management to participating artisans. Local designers are encouraged to interact with producers in order to protect traditional crafts while providing them with a contemporary commercial outlet.

The Virtual Souk is creating an Internet market for arts and crafts produced in the South and directed at global consumers. So far, artisans from Morocco, Tunisia and Lebanon participate in the Virtual Souk and 75-80 per cent of the artisan partners are women. Through the Virtual Souk it is envisioned that artisans will have better access to international markets and information, increase their income and help preserve their cultural heritage.

Sources: Barton Crockett, "Web crusade for global aid: PEOPLink pursues Net profits for the poor," www.PEOPLink.org/gen/press/98/09/29/msnbc; Gail L. Grant, "PEOPLink," www.PEOPLink.org/gen/press/99/06/23/commercenet; Azedine Ouerghi, 1999; www.elsouk.com/english/mainbazaar.htm.

Each Working Group addressed a critical area of concern from the Platform for Action, and discussed:

- policies, legislation, strategies and partnerships that have been successful in furthering women's equality;
- case studies, best practices and other examples of successful government, business and civil-society efforts;
- obstacles that remain and how they can be overcome.

Participants were from both the North and the South and included government representatives, activists, academics, private sector representatives and many others who shared their experiences and ideas for achieving women's equality. Inputs from all the Working Groups helped inform the March 2000 meeting of the Commission of the Status of Women (CSW) through their presentation as a "Conference Room Paper."

Policy and Regulatory Framework for ICTs

Although more women are gaining access to the new information and communications technologies, the rapid development and spread of these technologies, in languages and formats designed to fit the communication needs of their creators, means that many people, especially poor women in developing countries, are increasingly at risk of falling behind — both in the production and exchange of knowledge and information and in more and more aspects of everyday life, from shopping to paying household bills. In part, this is an issue of the concentration of ownership. The 1999 Human Development Report stated that in 1998, the top ten corporations controlled 60 per cent of total revenues in the computer industry and 86 per cent of the total in telecommunications. As a result:

> ...the technology, economics and culture of the Internet feel awfully American. The companies that have cashed in on the Internet, from newcomers like Amazon.com and Yahoo to the established technology suppliers like IBM, Sun Microsystems, Cisco and Microsoft, are American. By one estimate, United States corporations collect 85 per cent of the revenues from the Internet business and represent 95 per cent of the stock value of Internet companies (New York Times, 9 January 2000).

The implications are far-reaching, raising issues about women's ability to participate in creating and producing knowledge as well as accessing and consuming knowledge. This was one of the themes highlighted by the Global Knowledge Partnership, a

global coalition of development agencies, NGOs, governments and businesses focusing on knowledge for development, at a conference in March 2000. UNIFEM, along with women's networks from all regions, helped ensure the mainstreaming of a gender perspective in all areas, focusing especially on support to women entrepreneurs, women's participation in the ICT sector, and women as decision-makers in the regulatory sector. Other regulatory issues included protection of intellectual property rights in the context of traditional and indigenous knowledge, and protection of public cyberspaces in a sector that is being increasingly privatized.

Giney Villar/Women in Action #2

One forum where regulatory issues could be taken up from a gender perspective is the International Telecommunications Union (ITU) in Geneva, an institution within which governments and the private sector coordinate global telecom networks and services. In 1998, the World Telecommunication Development Conference established a Task Force on Gender Issues in the Development Sector aimed at ensuring that the benefits are made available to all women and men in developing countries on a fair and equitable basis. The ITU Development Sector also resolved to act as an enabling force for the development of an active network between various types of organizations of women involved in the information and telecommunication fields.

Gender Imbalances in Production and Use of Technologies

Many of the gender issues in relation to ICTs are similar to those that arise with other forms of technology: a fundamental gender imbalance between the viewpoint and knowledge of those who do the science and design and control the technology and those who use it and feel its impact. Contraception technology is a good example. The scientists who develop contraceptive technologies are disproportionately men, who do not look at the technologies from the point of view of users, who are mainly women. As Carmen Barroso and Sonia Corrêa (1995) show in the case of research on the contraceptive Norplant, gender issues arise at three critical points: the question of informed consent in medical trials, the assessment of efficacy and safety; and the understanding of the reasons why users often do not use the technology in the way envisaged by the scientists who developed it.

Informed consent is hindered by huge differences in initial knowledge and stereotypes that stigmatize poor women as incapable of understanding complex issues. Assessment of efficacy and risk is biased by a lack of scientific concern with effects that are not easily observed and measured: depression, loss of libido, interference with sexual life, menstrual irregularities, weight gain and permanent infertility. So-called user failure is misunderstood because it is not looked at from the point of view of the woman using the technology. The result is that scientific research in contraceptive technology is steered towards technologies that dramatically reduce women's chance of conceiving but which are not under women's control, leading to potential abuse of women's human rights.

The challenge is to improve communication between scientists and advocates for gender equality, as was achieved in the Norplant debate in Brazil in the 1980s, when what Barroso and Corrêa call "scientific isolation" was broken:

> *Many other actors voiced their opinions.*
> *This diversity of opinion, as well as the effort*
> *to make traditionally complex and obscure*
> *issues transparent, made the Norplant episode*
> *a moment of democratic communication...*
> *Citizens will be able to grasp the scope of the*
> *issues involved in scientific research only when*
> *they have access to basic information and*
> *through open communication (1995: 304).*

Mainstreaming Gender in Science and Technology
The goal is not only to encourage more women to do scientific research and design new technologies, but also to shift science and technology to being more people-centred. Prior to the Beijing Conference, UNIFEM supported the formation of an international network of NGOs working on issues of gender, science and technology known as the Once and Future Network (OFAN), which advocates for policies that enable women to play a more active role in redefining the direction of research and policy-making. The network was able to inform and influence the work of the UN Commission on Science and Technology for Development (UNCSTD), which in turn raised gender issues with government ministries dealing with science and technology. Since Beijing, UNIFEM has provided opportunities for both OFAN and the Gender Advisory Board of UNCSTD to work to implement a common agenda, most recently at the 1999 UNESCO World Science Conference in Budapest, where gender issues were raised by many of the national delegations.

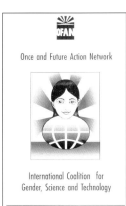

Once and Future Action Network

International Coalition for Gender, Science and Technology

In terms of information and communications, UNIFEM is working in partnership with NGOs on projects to improve women's access to, and mastery of, these new technologies, ranging from electronic sharing of information to initiatives for e-commerce and ICT policy. Activities include:

- *Policy:* making gender an explicit part of the agenda of ICT policy-making bodies and events and ensuring greater UN-system attention to progress made in the area of women and ICTs;
- *Learning:* consolidation of knowledge about key conceptual issues and successful project initiatives relating to gender equality and ICTs, and support for ongoing systematic sharing and incorporation of gender-related knowledge;
- *Projects:* pilot initiatives and replication — not only women-focused projects but also ways to integrate gender awareness and analysis into "mainstream" projects;
- *Resources:* identification of individuals and organizations available to help develop a gender-accountable agenda in the area of knowledge for development.

Transforming Economic Policy-Making

Many economists see their research as scientific, in the same way that physical scientists do, and argue that their policy advice is scientifically based. There are similar issues about mainstreaming gender in economic analysis and the technologies of economic governance based upon it. Not only do more women need to participate in discussions of economic analysis and policy, but the terms of the discussion also need changing.

At the beginning of the new millenium a vigorous debate is taking place about what kind of economic policy is required to ensure that poor people benefit from globalization, and what kind of global rules are required to regulate markets and guide the operations of international economic institutions. The 1999 Human Development Report made some suggestions about how to get globalization under social control and concluded:

> *Much debate is underway — but it is too*
> *narrrowly focused, too geographically*
> *unbalanced and driven too much by economic*
> *and financial interests. People in all parts of the*
> *world need to join in the debate and to make*
> *clear their interests and concerns (UNDP 1999).*

Women have been contributing to this debate and moving towards formulating women-led economic agendas that put social justice and care for people before making money. The challenge is to ensure that these are reflected in economic policy agendas at national and international levels.

BANCO MUNDIAL EN LA
Mira de las Mujeres

Critique of Stabilization and Structural Adjustment Policies
Since the late 1980s, women researchers have contributed to a critique of stabilization and structural adjustment policies that are a condition of access to International Monetary Fund (IMF) and World Bank loans. An initial focus on negative impacts on poor women was followed by a more nuanced critique which emphasized both the impact of these policies on gender relations and the impact of gender relations on the outcomes of these policies (Benería 1995). Groups such as Women's Eyes on the World Bank have analysed in detail the gender implications of the Bank's sectoral reform programmes in areas like health and education.

As a result of public pressure by NGOs and internal advocates, the World Bank has in recent years re-evaluated its position on gender and economic reform. The Bank has also set up an External Gender Consultative Group (EGCG) comprised of fourteen women from around the world who have experience at the operational, policy and research levels to advise it on gender issues. The consultative group includes experts on a wide range of development topics and from a broad spectrum of civil society including NGOs, women's organizations and academic and research institutions in Asia, Africa, Latin America, the Middle East, Europe, Central Asia and other OECD countries. More specifically, the objectives of the EGCG are:

- to provide a mechanism for disseminating information and discussing progress in implementing the Bank's gender policies and in responding to the Beijing Platform for Action;
- to provide a forum for discussing the concerns of the different sectors of civil society about the Bank's approaches to gender;
- to provide feedback to the Bank on lessons from NGOs and other organizations on promising approaches to gender;
- to promote and strengthen NGO-Bank cooperation on gender issues at the regional and country levels.

The External Gender Consultative Group held its first meeting in April 1996 with the president of the Bank, James Wolfensohn, the regional vice-presidents, chief economists, gender coordinators and staff from various sectors of the Bank. In this and subsequent meetings, staff are questioned about their policies and the integration of gender into the decision-making framework of the organization.

Assessments of the consultative group's effectiveness vary. The group itself continues to express both optimism about the Bank's willingness to talk about gender issues and reservations about lack of operational progress, especially at the country level. An independent assessment of the group's effectiveness by Women's Eyes on the World Bank argues that to date, the EGCG has not significantly influenced the Bank's conceptual framework in the area of macroeconomics. Forthcoming World Bank publications, including the Policy Research Report on Gender and Development, World Development Report 2000 and a report on Women and World Bank Adjustment Lending, are eagerly awaited to see if there are signs of new thinking. The IMF has a history of making policy behind closed doors, not even consulting with World Bank colleagues on many critical decisions. It has not engaged in any similar consultative exercises.

> "Officially, of course, the IMF doesn't 'impose.' It negotiates the conditions for receiving aid. But all the power on the negotiations is on one side — the IMF's — and the fund rarely allows sufficient time for broad consensus-building or even widespread consultations with either parliaments or civil society."
>
> — Joseph Stiglitz, former chief economist, World Bank, 4 April 2000

Towards a Different Approach to National Economic Policy
Women in different parts of the world have been taking initiatives to promote different, more gender-sensitive approaches to economic policy: improving the economic literacy of women's advocacy groups; securing more participation by women in economic policy processes; advocating a gender-sensitive approach to the design of economic recovery programmes; training policy-makers to look at economic issues from a gender perspective; undertaking research on the gendered impacts of macroeconomic policy at the local level; finding ways to "engender" macroeconomic analysis; and pressing for changes in global economic governance, especially changes in the WTO.

One initiative to improve the economic literacy of women's advocacy groups is the series of booklets produced by the Network Women in Development Europe (WIDE). These are written by women economists, who use imaginative approaches to communicate with women with no training in the field. Hilkka Pietilä analyses production through a series of diagrams, beginning with the theme of How the Cake is Cut. Nicky Pouw contrasts the HIStory of household economics with HERstory of how households operate economically, drawing upon the classic American story of Little Women. Irene van Staveren tells the story of the interaction between the commodity economy and the care economy, using diagrams and examples from the story, much used by economists, of Robinson Crusoe, who was shipwrecked alone on a small island and was necessarily a one-man economy. Lois Woestman provides a fresh look at markets and their place in society by describing them from the perspective of an extra-terrestrial visiting Planet Earth (see Box 10). Each booklet has a glossary of technical terms or a technical appendix and suggestions for how to use them in discussion groups.

Securing the participation of women in economic policy processes is the objective of the Council of Economic Empowerment for Women of Africa-Uganda Chapter (CEEWA-Uganda) and of the Center for Policy Alternatives in Washington DC. CEEWA-Uganda runs a programme on Women and Economic Decision-making that engages economists, planners, district councillors and parliamentarians in policy discussions concerning women and finance and women and agriculture. The Center for Policy Alternatives campaigns for a women-led economic agenda focusing on economic self-sufficiency for women and men, equal opportunities in entrepreneurship, affordable health care for all and better ways of supporting people in combining family and work responsibilities. It seeks to build an economic agenda from the bottom up to foster a new economy that bridges class and racial divides. In a national opinion survey to learn about women's economic policy concerns, the Center's Women's Voices Project (1996) found:

- time is also a big issue for women: 60% of women with children under age 19 worry about "having enough time to do everything you need to do and still spend time with your family"; 61% of all women under age 45 worry about this.
- women, more than men, believe that government can help solve problems; they strongly favour tax incentives to accomplish many of their goals, even if that means higher taxes.

UNIFEM produced a briefing kit called "Women in a Global Economy" for policy-makers advocating an approach to economic recovery in South-East and East Asia that focuses on removing the barriers to women's productive participation in the market economy, rather than encouraging women to return to their traditional roles in the unpaid domestic sector of the economy. It argues that policies to create new jobs should be sensitive to the different needs of men and women. Policy-makers should take into account the fact that most new jobs in public works projects are likely to be taken by men; and if these jobs require men to migrate and live away from home, a significant proportion of their incomes is less likely to be available for their families. Attention should be paid to the informal sector, where economic crises lead to increasing numbers of participants, putting downward pressure on women's wages and working conditions. The overall message is that

Box 10: Markets on Earth versus Markets on Venus

Economists often tell parables to provide an intuitive understanding of economic processes. They also often compare what does happen with hypothetical alternatives. In the spirit of this tradition, Lois Woestman discusses the way that markets work by comparing those on earth with the way she imagines they might operate on the more gender-sensitive planet of Venus.

Earth

Real markets are to some extent efficient at encouraging innovation and matching up supply of goods with demand for them. However...the common definition of efficiency...fails to consider the fact that production for money uses things that are not calculated into their costs. As well as natural resources these include unpaid labour which helps to provide healthy, productive paid workers, and which absorbs the shocks to society that are inherent in modern markets' design and functioning on earth.

Venus

We too use markets for some of our provisioning processes because we share the conviction with Earthlings that they are one of many ways of encouraging innovation. However, we reserve the use of markets for provisioning processes that are non-essential.

Provision of health, education and a minimum subsistence income are provided to every Venusian....Rather than it being considered a drudgery, we prize the time we spend taking care of our young and our elderly, and adults share this time equally.

Source: Woestman 1998: 22-23.

Box 11: Rethinking Sectoral Policy to Account for Women

Nalini Burn, an economist from Mauritius, has used this exercise in workshops in several parts of Africa. She divides the participants into a number of mixed groups, men and women, from international organizations, government and NGOs and asks them to consider the following statement and answer the following questions:

"Women carry more on their heads and backs than the entire inland transport system in this country."

1. How would you verify this statement? Give details.
2. What is your answer? Give reasons for it.
3. What are the factors that account for this situation?
4. What are the effects and impact?

Burn reports that the exercise provokes a journey of discovery. The usual statistics for the transport sector make no mention of women's time and energy as a means of transport. But every day, participants see women loading bundles on their heads and carrying small children on their backs. Once this disjuncture is recognized and explored, a whole new way of analysing transport policy and identifying the indicators required to design, monitor and evaluate transport policy starts to be created. She suggests that one important indicator of women's progress would be charting movement towards the goal of women no longer being a means of transport and instead being able to use their time and energy for learning, other forms of creative work, and playing, resting and dreaming.

Source: Personal communication from Nalini Burn.

economic recovery programmes should be designed in ways that directly support women's incomes and do not assume that income will "trickle down" from men to women and children.

Policy-makers are often more receptive to messages about the need to redesign economic policy when they have a better understanding of how gender influences resource allocation, gained through a new look at old questions (see Box 11). More detailed information about the gendered impact of policy is provided by research on the micro-level impacts of macroeconomic policy, such as that conducted by GERA, the Gender and Economic Reform in Africa programme, launched in 1996 (see Box 12). GERA grew out of an initiative at the North-South Institute in Ottawa, Canada but since 1999 has been hosted by the Third World Network in Accra, Ghana. Its management committee is made up of women from all parts of Africa.

To influence economic policy it is also necessary to speak the language of economics, but to inflect it in new ways. This was one of the objectives of the Asia-Pacific Economic Cooperation (APEC) Project on Linkages Between Paid and Unpaid Work in Human

Box 12: Selected GERA Research Projects

• Impact of Currency Devaluation on Men and Women in a Semi-Urban Area in Burkina Faso

Burkina Faso's currency devaluation has affected sectors of the population differently, depending on where they live and their gender. By examining the effects on the gender division of labour within the home and on male-female relations, the project will develop policy recommendations and an action plan to make control over productive resources more equitable.

• Financial Sector Reforms and Women's Survival Strategies in Cameroon

This project will investigate how women's access to financial services has been affected by recent financial sector reforms. Through participatory research, the project team will identify the specific financial obstacles women face, then design and implement training programmes to promote sustainable financial institutions for women.

• Improving the Bank of Uganda's Credit Programme

Women dominate the small and microenterprise sector of Uganda and run their enterprises within the limited financing that microfinancing institutions offer. Because women are at a clear disadvantage in formal financial institutions, this study will examine current Bank of Uganda lending policies, processes, and programmes from a gender perspective.

• Economic Liberalization and Women in the Informal Sector of Rural Nigeria

Both quantitative and qualitative research will be conducted to examine the impact of economic liberalization policies on the output, income, savings, and investment of microenterprises owned by rural women. The project will analyse how women have been able to gain access to resources, appropriate technology and other needs; how enterprise performance has influenced women's roles in rural households; and what prevents women from responding appropriately to changing economic incentives.

Source: GERAlinks Newsletter, various issues.

Resource Policy, which explored how economic policy could become more effective by recognizing that people undertake unpaid as well as paid work. The project covered nine economies: Australia, Canada, Indonesia, Korea, Malaysia, Philippines, Chinese Taipei, Thailand and the United States, and highlighted linkages between unpaid work and economic cycles that are often overlooked (see Box 13). A key recommendation is to broaden the agenda for human resource development to include all kinds of labour, paid and unpaid, formal and informal. Among other steps for governments to consider are:

- reform of the tax system and social security policies to eliminate the concept of the sole breadwinner in a two adult family;
- maternity, paternity and child-care leave for both women and men;
- provision for family-friendly workplaces and social support structures;
- provision of quality, affordable child- and elder-care services;
- financial support of enterprises, such as tax rebates, to encourage them to provide social services for employment.

Box 13: Linkages Between Economic Cycles and Unpaid Work in Canada

Public and private sector goods and services can replace unpaid care work. Alternatively, when household income or public provision fall, unpaid caring work may increase to compensate. A number of tracking projects are underway in Canada which will throw more light on this. One is the Elliot Lake Tracking Study (ELTS) which examines the impact of retrenchment on workers, families and communities. It has found evidence that unpaid work in the domestic sector does increase to make up for shortfalls in income.

An alternative to public provision is the NGO sector, especially the voluntary component. Governments in Canada have continually called on the NGO sector to fill the gaps left by cut-backs in public provision. However, a report by GPI Atlantic (1999) shows that the number of hours of volunteer work per capita declined by 4.7 per cent between 1987 and 1997 — a loss of 110.2 millions of hours. This appears to be related to economic restructuring. Due to falling real incomes, many people are obliged to spend more time in paid work. In particular, university graduates, who were in the past disproportionately contributors to volunteer work, are most affected by the squeeze on time.

Source: Bakker 1999.

National Economic Policy and Global Economic Governance

Globalization has transformed the national economic policy environment. Either for internal political reasons or to comply with conditions for loans from the World Bank and the IMF, governments have opened up their markets for goods, services and capital to the international economy. As a result, they now have to pay more attention to the sentiments of dealers in international financial markets than to the sentiments of their own citizens. Unfortunately, the time horizons of participants in international financial markets are measured in hours and even minutes, rather than the decades of a human life. Moreover, flows of money are quickly reversible, whereas the flow of a human life is not. The result of liberalization of international capital markets has been an increase in volatility and economic instability and new constraints on the extent to which macroeconomic policy can be used to promote social justice (UN 1999b).

Gender Inequality, Economic Growth, Market Liberalization

Some of the implications for gender equality have been explored by an International Working Group on Gender, Macroeconomics and International Economics, comprising men and women economists from a variety of countries, North and South, who have conducted empirical and theoretical research, published in a special issue of the journal *World Development* edited by Grown et al. (2000).

Exploring the relationship between gender inequality, economic growth and liberalization of trade and investment, the editors note that four scenarios are possible (see Chart 6.1, p. 148): win-win (low gender inequality, high economic growth); win-lose (low gender inequality, low economic growth); lose-win (high gender inequality, high economic growth); and lose-lose (high gender inequality, low economic growth). Different outcomes are related to the structure of the economy being considered (e.g., industrialized; semi-industrialized; agricultural; degree of openness to world economy) and to the dimension of gender inequality being considered (e.g., health, education, labour market). World Bank research has revealed mainly win-win outcomes in which low gender inequality and high economic growth go together (Dollar and Gatti 1999; Klasen 1999). This research measures gender inequality primarily in terms of education and health variables and has been used to make a case for reducing gender inequality on efficiency grounds.

Research by members of the International Working group, using different measures of gender equality, reveals a different picture. Seguino (2000) focuses on the gender gap in earnings and finds that for open semi-industrialized economies (1975-1995), economic growth was higher where the gender gap in earnings

Chart 6.1: Gender Inequality and Economic Growth

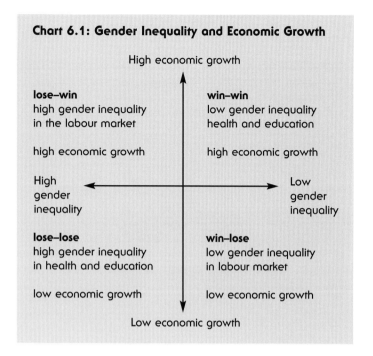

The policy implications of this analysis are twofold:

- first, while globalization permits some dimensions of gender inequality to continue to be addressed at the national level (e.g., health, education), it makes it more difficult to tackle other dimensions of gender inequality (e.g., labour-market inequality) at this level;
- second, more concentrated efforts are needed at the international level to develop a harmonized framework for labour-market equality.

Mainstreaming Gender in the Ministry of Finance
The ways in which national economies are analysed and policy is made need transforming. Two frameworks for doing this are presented in the special issue of *World Development* (2000).

Gita Sen (2000) offers a strategy for gender mainstreaming in finance ministries, drawing upon previous work for the Commonwealth Secretariat. She identifies a fundamental constraint in the way that finance ministries operate: they do not deal directly with people but with monetized variables, such as aggregate national income and expenditure, and the aggregate money supply. Three possible points of entry, she suggests, are:

- short-run macroeconomic management, which focuses on budget deficit, the balance of payment deficit and debt;
- structural reforms such as trade liberalization and privatization of public sector enterprises and services;
- financial liberalization and its link to microcredit.

Sen proposes a matrix (see Table 6.2) linking these three dimensions with three gender issues: the differential impact of policies on the well-being of women and men; the implications for human

was higher (i.e., a lose-win scenario). This does not mean that gender equality objectives should not be pursued. Rather, it shows that some types of growth do not diminish gender gaps in the labour market, even though the absolute incomes of women may increase. Braunstein (2000) develops a theoretical model to show how outcomes depend on whether the economy is subject to low or high capital mobility, and how far women are under patriarchal authority, with male support for the costs of raising families, or are autonomous, but still bear much of the costs of raising families on their own. She shows that in open economies where capital is highly mobile, policies that successfully promote greater autonomy for women can lead to an increase in national income (win-win); but those that increase women's bargaining power in the workplace can have a negative impact on national output (win-lose) if the response of capital is to move to other locations.

Table 6.2: Analytical Matrix of Interactions Between Gender and the Finance Ministry

Engendering dimensions ➡ Finance ministry's roles ⬇	Differential impact on the well-being of women and men	Human reproduction/ the "care economy"	Gender power relations
Short-run macroeconomic management			
Structural reforms			
Financial sector reforms/ liberalization			

Source: Sen 2000.

reproduction of the "care economy"; and for gender power relations (the relative degree of political voice, social/cultural value, and access to and control over economic resources held by women and men). The matrix is envisaged as a tool for use within finance ministries to enable officials to understand how their fiscal and monetary policies and privatization and liberalization measures impact on gender equality and women's empowerment; and how in turn gender relations impact back upon the economic efficiency and stabilization concerns of the finance ministries.

Sen presents some ideas about likely interactions, drawing upon research on structural adjustment and gender equality, including a 1995 issue of *World Development* on Gender Adjustment and Macroeconomics (Çağatay et al., eds. 1995). These ideas provide a starting point for finance ministries, which with the assistance of local gender experts could gradually fill in information for their own particular economy. The use of the matrix is not envisaged as a one-off exercise, but as an ongoing endeavour that can be enriched as more information becomes available, and which will provide a framework for sustaining the attention of officials to gender issues. It would need to be complemented by a system of incentives and disincentives (through performance appraisal systems) so that finance ministry officials find it in their interest to take gender seriously.

In working with such a matrix, Ministry of Finance officials could draw upon some of the other work of the International Working Group on Engendering Macroeconomics and International Economics, such as:

- computable general equilibrium models incorporating gender variables;
- gender analysis of the East Asian financial crises;
- gendered bargaining models.

Incorporating gender variables into general equilibrium models, for example, Arndt and Tarp (2000) explore the implications of changing technology and marketing structures on the agricultural sector in Mozambique while Fontana and Wood (2000) examine the gendered effects of changes in trade policies in Bangladesh. The results can be entered into the matrix in Chart 6.2, in the rows that identify the interaction of gender issues with short-run macroeconomic management and with structural reforms. Gendered bargaining models, such as that provided for Sub-Saharan Africa by Warner and Campbell (2000) could be used to fill in the row under gender power relations in the last column of the matrix. And gender analyses of effects of the East Asian financial crises could be used in several ways. For example, Lim (2000) finds a differential impact on employment, with male unemployment rising more than female

United Nations/Jackie Curtis

UNIFEM

unemployment, resulting in increased female labour-force participation and longer working hours for women. This information could be used to fill in the row about the interaction between short-run macroeconomic management and gender issues. Floro and Dymski (2000) analyse the crisis to draw conclusions about the gender implications of financial market liberalization, which could be used in considering the last row of the matrix on financial liberalization.

Promoting Social Dialogue on Macroeconomic Policy

Elson and Çağatay (2000) extend the idea of a policy matrix linking gender issues and national economic policy to encompass proposals for a broad social dialogue about the social content of macroeconomic policy and reshaping it to promote social justice (see Table 6.3, p. 150). They look at the issue from the perspective of the implications of macroeconomic policies for poor women, and identify three forms of bias that need to be avoided if macroeconomic policies are to promote improvements in the position of poor women.

The first is *deflationary bias*, the bias that overemphasises deflating the economy by reducing public expenditure and raising interest rates whenever financial markets show signs of concern about rising inflation or whenever short-term capital leaves the country. Such austerity measures are sometimes called for – but not without a careful analysis of the nature of the problems an economy is experiencing. There is, for instance, no clear evidence that low rates of inflation (below 15-20% a year) have a negative impact on growth rates (A. Sen 1998). There is clear evidence that using deflation to deal with problems caused by inappropriate financial liberalization makes the position of poor people, and poor women in particular, worse – as the financial crises in South-East Asia have shown (World Bank 1998).

The second is *commodification bias*, the bias that turns as many public services as possible into commodities, to be sold to the public by newly

Table 6.3: The Left Hand Side of the Balance Sheet: A Matrix for Macroeconomic Policy

Activities of Different Social Interests	Macroeconomic Prerequisites for Social Justice		
	Avoidance of deflationary bias	Avoidance of commodification bias	Avoidance of "male breadwinner" bias
Government national, provincial, local			
Other political parties			
Civil society organizations e.g. • advocates for rich households • advocates for poorer households • advocates for women's advancement • environmentalists • trade unions			

Private sector
Local: big, small and microbusiness associations
 	
Global: TNCs
          financial
          institutions
              •retail
              •wholesale			

IMF, World Bank other multilateral and bilateral institutions			

Source: Elson and Çağatay 2000.

privatized businesses, or to be delivered by a public sector operating on business principles and levying user fees for its services. There may be good arguments for privatization and business principles in the case of some products formerly produced in the public sector — textiles or steel for instance — though even here privatization often frequently fails to deliver the promised increases in efficiency. But in the case of health, education and social security, the replacement of citizen entitlements secured through the public sector by market-based entitlements to buy from the private sector polarizes societies. It excludes poor women from the prospect of access to social support for unpaid care work.

The third is *"male breadwinner bias,"* which sees women as dependents of men and constructs what public services and social protections remain upon the principle that men are the breadwinners and direct possessors of citizen entitlements, while women can get access only as dependents of men.

This bias predates the other two, and is often still to be found in the policy alternative put forward by those who are opposed to deflationary bias — but do not look at the economy through women's eyes.

Macroeconomic policy is more and more marked by these three biases (see UN 1999b), but not solely due to finance ministry policy. Much of the pressure that creates deflationary and commodification bias comes from global institutions, such as the World Bank and the IMF, and the globalized private sector, especially transnational corporations and international financial corporations. But there are national-level NGOs reinforcing these biases, including organizations that act as advocates for the rich, who benefit, as owners of financial assets, from these biases. In addition, a male breadwinner bias may come from organizations that also fight for social justice, such as trade unions, or may be reinforced by fiscal decentralization to provincial and local

WEDO/Rosa Lizarde

governments where officials and politicians hold out-of-date ideas about the reality of men's and women's lives.

The policy matrix in Table 6.3 is envisaged as a framework for a dialogue among a wide range of social actors (examples are listed in the left side of the matrix). A key objective is to open up macroeconomic policy-making to consultation, in the way that many other areas of policy are being opened up. As with the matrix proposed by Sen, the boxes have to be filled in at the country level, drawing on country-specific evidence. But some general guidelines are possible. For instance, to avoid deflationary bias, do not automatically assume that:

- low unemployment is a sign that rising prices will automatically follow and that interest rates must be raised to avoid this;
- lower taxes are better than higher taxes, and that all reductions of budget deficits should come by means of cutbacks in expenditure.

Moreover, the dialogue could usefully be guided by the provisions of the International Covenant on Economic, Social and Cultural Rights (ICESCR), as the three biases to which macroeconomic policy is subject could well be in violation of the covenant. Two main obstacles to social dialogue are:

- the IMF, which does not have a consultative approach to economic policy-making;
- owners of large-scale financial assets who can, and do, exercise their option to exit from an economy rather than engage in a mutual voicing of views about the economic policies appropriate for promoting social justice.

The Global Financial Context

Singh and Zammit (2000) take up the issue of gender dimensions of international capital flows and show why it is important for women to begin articulating their ideas about how the global financial system should be changed and what the new global financial architecture should contain. Women have

---

Box 14: The Informal Working Group on Gender and Trade (IWGGT)

The Informal Working Group on Gender and Trade is a group of individuals and representatives from development NGOs, advocacy organizations and trade unions who share a concern about the impact of globalization, especially trade liberalization, on women and who work to ensure that international trade policy-makers build a gender analysis into their trade policies and procedures.

The Informal Working Group on Gender and Trade developed out of the Women's Caucus convened at the first Ministerial Meeting of the World Trade Organization in Singapore in 1996. Administered through a partnership arrangement between the International Coalition for Development Action (ICDA) and the Network Women in Development Europe (WIDE), it includes:

- Alt-WID, Alternative Women in Development (US)
- CAFRA, Caribbean Association for Feminist Research and Action
- CEEWA-K, Council for Economic Empowerment for Women of Africa – Kenya Chapter
- CIIR, Catholic Institute for International Relations (UK)
- Education International (EI)
- Gambia Women Finance Association
- ICDA, International Coalition for Development Action
- ICFTU, International Confederation of Free Trade Unions
- K.U.L.U., Women and Development (Denmark)
- OXFAM-Ireland
- SEWA, Self Employed Women's Association (Nepal)
- WIDE, Network Women in Development Europe
- WWW, Women Working World Wide (UK)
- WEDO, Women's Environment and Development Organization (US)

Source: Hale, ed. 1998.

---

not yet done much work on this dimension of global economic governance, perhaps because, unlike trade liberalization and the WTO, there is no World Financial Organization on which to focus attention.

Global Economic Governance and the WTO

Women's organizations have been arguing for at least five years that *world trade is a women's issue*. In 1996, during the Ministerial Meeting of the World Trade Organization in Singapore, women at the parallel NGO forum set up an Informal Working Group on Gender and Trade (see Box 14), and member organizations have subsequently produced a number of publications (Hale 1998; Haxton and Olsson 1999; Vander Stichele 1998). In preparation for the WTO meeting in Seattle in 1999, both DAWN and WEDO produced briefing papers (Williams 1999; WEDO 1999). Many women joined the protests in Seattle to challenge the destructive aspects of globalization.

These organizations share the widespread concerns about the undemocratic and non-transparent character of WTO procedures and the unequal distribution of the benefits of trade liberalization. In particular, women's NGOs have documented how women have lost their livelihoods as a result of trade liberalization. CEEWA, cites the case of Cotilda, a single mother with five children :

She is counselled, equipped with skills in leather shoe manufacturing, given a loan, assisted with marketing information, and given a second loan on her business. She is given a third loan to purchase equipment. Government policies on...trade liberalization find Cotilda unprepared. She cannot explain why her shoes no longer sell. The market is flooded with cheaper inputs [and she becomes] unemployed (Kiggundu 1998).

Trade liberalization produces winners as well as losers, however (Fontana et al. 1995; UN 1999b). The expansion of manufacturing exports creates more employment opportunities for women in the South, and in so doing tends to reduce some dimensions of gender inequality. Moreover, women as managers of household budgets gain when trade liberalization reduces the price of everyday goods they have to buy.

Much more serious is the issue of whether WTO policies concentrate losses among the poorer groups and gains among the richer groups. Recent research at the World Bank suggests that this is the case. Openness to the world economy was found to be negatively correlated with income growth among the poorest 40 per cent of the population but strongly and positively correlated with growth among higher income groups. The costs of adjusting the trade reform have thus been borne by the poor (Lundberg and Squire 1999).

Moreover, there are indications that the WTO rules regarding what governments may and may not do may hinder governments in protecting those most vulnerable to the downside of trade liberalization and in building up their economic capacity so that they can take advantage of trade in the future. This is because the WTO agenda goes far beyond the reduction of import quotas and tariffs. It identifies and seeks to reduce a wide range of "barriers to trade," including regulations on foreign investment, environment protection, health and safety standards, laws on the ownership of natural resources and of systems of knowledge and new technology, and systems for placing government contracts and designing and operating social security systems.

For instance, there are moves within the WTO to extend the Government Procurement Agreement, which would restrict the ability of govern-ments to award contracts on social and environmental as well as economic grounds. This would, among other things, jeopardize schemes such as that operated by the US government that allocates 5 per cent of the total value of major federal government contracts and subcontracts to women-owned small businesses. In 1997, this allocation was worth US$5.7 billion and more than half went to small businesses owned by women of colour. It would also put at risk the scheme whereby Telkom, the South African telecommunications parastatal, makes it easier for women's small businesses to tender for contracts by providing them with advice and exemptions from paying the customary performance guarantees. Such government support for women's small businesses is understood within the WTO agenda as a restriction on trade, not a policy for trade development (WEDO 1999).

Among the most important ways in which the WTO has extended the idea of barriers to trade is through the Trade Related Intellectual Property Rights (TRIPS) Agreement, the starting point of which is the infringement of patents, trademarks and copyrights. Patents, trademarks and copyrights convey property rights over knowledge and innovations. But TRIPS does not only deal with problems of counterfeiting or copying; rather, it enables a patent to be obtained if the patent seeker adds anything, however small, to existing knowledge. The provision enables multinational corporations to appropriate the knowledge of women and indigenous healers and farmers in developing countries without adequate recompense. One example is the experience of women farmers in India, who for many years have used the indigenous Neem plant as a pesticide and fungicide. There are now more than 35 patents on Neem as a pesticide registered in the United States and Europe and market prices have risen considerably, reducing the access of local communities in India (WEDO 1999).

The agenda of eliminating trade barriers carries with it the implication that markets are the most appropriate way of organizing all forms of resource allocation; and that private property rights needed by markets to function are the most appropriate forms of ownership. It drives the whole system of entitlements towards one that is market-based. It increases the scope for the operations of

WEDO/Rosa Lizarde

Box 15: Gender Issues in the WTO Agenda

DAWN (Development Alternatives for Women in a New Era) presents a gender analysis of the World Trade Organization in a 1999 discussion paper entitled "Free Trade, or Fair Trade?" Among the issues it raises are the following:

The Agreement on Agriculture (AOA): a review of AOA should seek to remedy and remove imbalances so as to benefit women and small farmers. AOA has severely impacted women farmers in Asia and Africa. Women farmers who traditionally produce food and vegetables are unable to compete with inflows of cheap, heavily subsidized products from the North. Furthermore, the food security impact of implementing the AOA has not been widely recognized and adequately dealt with. It is therefore imperative that developed countries follow through on their commitments to liberalize agriculture. A review of AOA should put greater emphasis on eliminating export subsidies and export restraints by the European Union and the United States. It should be gender sensitive and provide mechanisms to promote and ensure food security as an important non-trade concern.

The General Agreement on Trade in Services (GATS): poor people's access to water, schooling and reasonable and affordable health care must be protected. GATS includes not only information and communication sectors but also medical/health, education, human services and public services. GATS therefore has implications for health care/health standards, job security and conditions of work for a large number of people.

Women workers tend to dominate in the public sector as well as the middle and lower rungs of almost all service sectors. Many other areas of service in developing countries rely on women's labour. Before extending the GATS into energy, mail/courier services, maritime and air transportation and environmental services, gender-sensitive impact assessments should be made in each area to ascertain the potential impact on the cost and access to services for the poor and on women workers in the service sector.

An area that has been grossly neglected is the issue of the movement of natural persons. Though developing countries have argued for symmetry between the movement of capital and labour through the inclusion of provisions on the movement of natural persons in the GATS, developed countries have not been willing to discuss this issue and it has so far remained on the back-burner. However, this is an issue of central importance to the lives of migrant women whose rights and working conditions need to be protected and ensured.

Trade Related Intellectual Property Rights (TRIPS): there should be no patents on life and attention should be paid to the recognition of the traditional knowledge of women and men in agriculture, healing and the preservation of nature. Indigenous knowledge and cultural heritage have collectively evolved through generations and no single person can claim invention or discovery of medicinal plants, seeds or other living things. In this regard the Convention on Bio-Diversity should have precedence over TRIPS. Secondly, article 27.3(b), which makes an artificial distinction between plants, and animals and microorganisms, and between essentially biological and microbiological processes, should be amended as per the recommendation of the Africa Group. Finally the developing countries' call for operationalization of mechanisms to promote technological innovation in the South and to accelerate the transfer of technology should also be given priority treatment in the negotiations.

Trade Related Investment Measures (TRIMS): developing countries should be exempt from the prohibition on local content and foreign balancing requirements. The objective of trade should be to promote development, which requires governmental assistance to build the capacity of small and medium enterprises. Investment is an area with important implications for women. First, in many of the countries of the South, foreign direct investment is highly female-intensive as it relies on the labour of women in export manufacturing, and in some places, in commercial agriculture. Second, women entrepreneurs in the micro and small business sector may require special assistance from governments to produce goods and services or to protect the markets for the goods that they produce. Third, TRIMS, like all other WTO provisions, must be reviewed in the context of the foreign exchange and foreign debt constraints on developing countries, particularly the least developed countries. Lastly, there should be no attempt to expand the scope of TRIMS until the working group on investment has completed its work.

Government Procurement: particular attention should be paid to the possible negative impact of liberalization of government purchases on small to medium-sized businesses, especially those owned by women. Additional attention should paid to the possible secondary and tertiary impacts of liberalization of government procurement on the microenterprise sector, which is dominated by women in many of the poorest countries. Since a working group is currently deliberating this matter, there should be no attempt to broaden the scope of the issue, including discussions about transparency of government procurement process, until it has completed its report. The working group also needs to undertake a gender-sensitive assessment of this issue including its implications for the delivery of public services and the potential impact on public sector workers.

Source: Williams 1999.

already-powerful international businesses and elevates economic competitiveness above all other goals. In fact, this enlargement of the range of what are considered "barriers to trade" potentially brings all of domestic economic and social policy within the purview of the WTO Trade Policy Enforcement Mechanism. This mechanism is widely recognized as tilted in favour of rich countries that can afford teams of expensive lawyers well versed in international trade law.

Criticism of the WTO is not the same as rejecting international trade, which carries benefits as well as pitfalls for economies in developing countries.

> *Trade is an important tool in the process of economic development of Southern economies. For least developed countries, trade is also an important tool for promoting development that is anchored in security and rural livelihoods. Trade rules are therefore important but cannot take precedence over human rights and environmental sustainability* (Williams 1999: 1).

Thus the issue is one of slowing the operation of the WTO agenda for a period of review, repair and reform, so as to create a global trading system that promotes fair trade as an adjunct to social justice rather than limitless trade as an adjunct to corporate profit. Some of the issues that review, repair and reform needs to consider from the perspective of poor women are identified in Box 15.

Gender Justice and Economic Justice

Women are starting to bring together ideas on gender justice and economic justice in the context of the five-year review of the UN conferences of the 1990s. For example:

- women from a variety of NGOs formed an Economic Justice Caucus during the Beijing +5 Preparatory Commission in March 2000 and produced a Declaration for Economic Justice and Women's Empowerment;
- supported by WEDO and UNIFEM, the Women's Caucus worked throughout the Copenhagen +5 Preparatory Commission in April 2000 to make the links between the implementation of the Beijing Platform for Action and the Copenhagen Platform of Action.

There is a need to bring together these initiatives, and all the other practical and policy-research initiatives discussed in this chapter in a global campaign for economic justice with a women's face.

The purpose of this campaign would be to make visible the links between rights for women and economic justice for poor countries relative to rich countries and poor people relative to rich people. A global campaign could build a worldwide coalition for change, using the resources of the Internet, and including UN agencies such as UNIFEM, women's organizations and businesswomen committed to social and environmental sustainability. It should link up with both the operationalization of the UN Development Assistance Framework and women's desks or units within regional economic agreements. It should build the capacity of women's bureaus or departments and harness the energies of gender-aware economists; it should engage the interest and support of journalists in all media.

Such a campaign should seek the commitment of governments, businesses, and international economic institutions for an approach to economic life that:

- recognizes the need for economic democracy as well as political democracy;
- recognizes that compliance with the International Covenant on Economic, Social and Cultural Rights is as important as compliance with the International Covenant on Civil and Political Rights;
- does not assume that growth and equality can be separately pursued, using separate policy instruments;
- does not wait until the next financial crisis to put in place a set of global economic rules that promote equality and security, and enable both women and men to combine paid work outside their homes with unpaid care work in their homes.

Conclusion

Reshaping globalization to promote the progress of women along the lines discussed in this chapter will not just promote gender equality; it will also promote poverty reduction, human development and the realization of human rights. This is because women and their organizations are pressing for new ways of organizing global interconnections that are more inclusive and more fully human; which recognize people as providers of care for one another and not just producers of commodities; which recognize that it is essential to subject markets to socially negotiated regulations and to understand values as well as prices. Of course, there will have to be changes in global power structures, and these are not easy to bring about in a world that daily concentrates economic power in fewer hands. But globalization has also put new tools at our disposal to mobilize global alliances for change around women-led economic agendas.

Annex: Technical Notes

Geographical Coverage

Data is presented following the list of countries and their geographical area classification used by the United Nations Statistics Division, in compiling *The Worlds Women 2000: Trends and Statistics*. In common with comparable UN and World Bank reports, this report does not include the following small countries, territories, islands and states owing to problems of data accessibility: American Samoa, Andorra, Antigua and Barbuda, Aruba, Bermuda, Dominica, East Timor, French Guyana, French Polynesia, Gaza Strip, Grenada, Guadeloupe, Guam, Kiribati, Leichtenstein, Macao, Marshall Islands, Martinique, Micronesia (Federated States of), Monaco, Netherlands Antilles, New Caledonia, Palau, Puerto Rico, Saint Kitts and Nevis, Saint Lucia, Saint Vincent and Grenadines, San Marino, São Tome and Principe, Solomon Islands, U. S. Virgin Islands.

The designations do not imply the expression of any opinion on the part of UNIFEM concerning the legal status of any country, territory or area of its authorities, or concerning the delimitation of its frontiers or boundaries.

Databases and Statistical Yearbooks

The major data source for this report is the Women's Indicators and Statistics Database (Wistat)-CD-ROM, version 4, produced by UN Statistics Division (UN Statistical Yearbook; Website: www.un.org/depts/unsd), which presents data in EXCEL files, facilitating use of the data for construction of charts and tables. In addition, several other UN and other international databases have been used:

- United Nations Educational, Scientific and Cultural Organization (UNESCO) Educational Statistics. Website: http//unescostat.unesco.org UNESCO Annual Statistical Yearbook

- International Labour Office (ILO) Laboursta database, Website: www.ilo.org ILO Labour Statistics Yearbook (various years)

- The Human Development Report CD-ROM: This database provides internationally comparable statistics on 300 indicators for 174 countries, and full text of Human Development Reports from 1990-1999.

- Human Development Report (various years). Website: www.undp.org/hdro

- World Income Equality Database, Beta 3, 8 November 1999. United Nations University, World Institute for Development Economic Research – United Nations Development Programme (UNU/WIDER-UNDP). Website: www.wider.unu.edu/wiid/wiid.htm

- Inter-Parliamentary Union (IPU). Website: www.ipu.org

- World Bank Gender Statistics GenderNet. Website: genderstats.worldbank.org

- World Bank World Development Indicators. Website: www.worldbank.org/data /wdi2000/index.htm

- Organisation for Economic Co-operation and Development (OECD) Statistics for OECD countries. Website: www.oecd.org/ statlist.htm Statistics for developing countries Website: www.oecd.org/dac/indicators/htm/list/htm

Chapter 3 Indicators

Gender Equality in Education (Chart 3.1, Table 3.1, Chart 3.2)

The indicators all pertain to secondary education and are: the ratio of girls' net enrolment ratio to boys' net enrolment ratio (Chart 3.1); the girls' net enrolment ratio (Table 3.1); and the change in girls' net enrolment ratio (Chart 3.2). Data for the first two indicators are for 1997; change is measured using an index with base 1985=100. The data comes from special tabulations prepared by the UN Educational, Scientific and Cultural Organization (UNESCO) for the Human Development Report Office and presented in the *Human Development Report 1999*, table 25, pp. 229-32. Since these tabulations do not include all countries, they are supplemented with the latest available data for the female gross enrolment ratio obtained from the UNESCO Website: unescostat.unesco.org. Estimates of progress are not provided for countries for which net enrolment ratios are unavailable.

The primary sources of enrolment data are national ministries of education, which collect the data from schools. The reliability of data varies according to the effectiveness of record-keeping in each school. Where resource allocation to schools depends upon enrolment numbers, there may be an incentive to over-report enrolment. Accurate calculations of enrolment ratios also depend upon estimates of the population of school-age children, the reliability of which is variable.

The enrolment indicator selected by the OECD to measure progress towards empowerment of women is the combined primary and secondary gross enrolment ratio for girls as a percentage of the combined primary and secondary gross enrolment ratio for boys. The UN indicator framework uses net enrolment ratios and treats primary and secondary education separately since the gender gap may be very different and may be subject to different influences at the primary and secondary levels.

Gross enrolment ratios measure the number of children enrolled in primary or secondary school as a percentage of the total number of children in the relevant age group for that level. These ratios can be greater than 100 per cent because many children of secondary school age may still be attending primary school, while young people who are past the normal age of completion of secondary school may still be attending secondary school if they have not yet attained the desired qualifications. Net enrolment ratios show the number of children enrolled at a schooling level who belong to the relevant age group, expressed as a percentage of the total number of children in that age group. Net enrolment ratios are better indicators and are used here whenever possible.

Gender Equality in Employment (Table 3.2, Chart 3.3)

The UN indicator for gender equality in employment is women's share of paid employment in industry and services. The figures used in Table 3.2 and Chart 3.3 are calculated from raw data provided in the ILO statistical database (www.ilo.org). The ILO defines paid employment as that which relates "solely to employees (wage earners and salaried employees) in employment" (ILO Labour Statistics Yearbook, 1998). Non-agricultural economic activities (industry and services) are defined according to the International

Standard Industrial Classification (ISIC) and include mining and quarrying; manufacturing; electricity, gas and water; construction and services (both private and public sector). Because of an absence of up-to-date data, this indicator is presented for the 1990s (any year available) and the 1980s (any year available). The country coverage for this indicator is low in some regions of the world, especially Sub-Saharan Africa.

There are differences in ILO's presentation of data over time. Up to and including 1995, the raw data is presented as an aggregate for paid employment in non-agricultural activities. For some countries, the data is disaggregated by sex, but for others only the total is given. From 1997 onwards, for some countries the raw data is presented disaggregated by separate non-agricultural economic activities, according to the one digit level of the ISIC, and has thus to be reaggregated to construct the chosen indicator. Again, for some countries the data is disaggregated by sex, but for others only the total is given. In all cases, sectoral coverage is often incomplete. Where aggregate data is presented there are often footnotes indicating that the aggregate figures cover only selected non-agricultural activities. Where the data are presented in disaggregated form, there is no data for some of the subsectors. Another problem is inconsistencies between the yearbooks and the online database; and internal inconsistencies within a given table, for example, the sum of male and female employment does not always equal total employment in some cases.

The data is supplied by national governments, which collect it from a variety of sources: labour-related establishment surveys; official estimates; insurance records; labour force surveys; labour-related establishment censuses; administrative records and related sources. This creates problems of compatibility; for example, the figure for Turkey seems very low, given the country's level of industrialization. This is because the primary data source is insurance records and many women workers are not covered by such insurance.

Gender Equality in Political Representation (Table 3.3, Chart 3.4)
The primary source of data for women's share of seats in parliaments or national legislatures is the Inter-Parliamentary

Union (IPU), and is supplied from surveys of parliaments in 177 countries. The data reported in Table 3.3 and Chart 3.4 is taken primarily from the IPU Website for 25 January 2000; data for Botswana, Indonesia, Panama, Pakistan, Thailand and Togo, absent from the IPU data, is from *Human Development Report 1999*, table 3, pp. 142-44, which presents information as of 1 February 1999.

A number of countries have both upper and lower chambers of parliament (bicameral legislatures): Algeria, Argentina, Australia, Austria, Bahamas, Barbados, Belarus, Belgium, Belize, Bolivia, Bosnia and Herzegovina, Brazil, Burkina Faso, Cambodia, Canada, Chile, Colombia, Croatia, Czech Republic, Dominican Republic, Ethiopia, France, Fiji, Gabon, Germany, Haiti, India, Ireland, Italy, Jamaica, Japan, Jordan, Kazakhstan, Kyrgyzstan, Lesotho, Liberia, Malaysia, Mauritania, Mexico, Morocco, Namibia, Nepal, Netherlands, Nigeria, Paraguay, Philippines, Poland, Portugal, Romania, Russian Federation, Senegal, South Africa, Spain, Swaziland, Switzerland, Thailand, Trinidad and Tobago, Uruguay, United Kingdom, United States, Venezuela, Yugoslavia. In such cases the procedure used in the *Human Development Report* is followed and data in the tables usually refer to women's share of the seats in the combined chambers (number of women in lower house plus number of women in upper house divided by total number of seats in lower house plus upper house). In a few cases, complete data are available only for women's share of seats in the lower chamber: in Cambodia, Ethiopia and Haiti the IPU Website provides no data for women in the upper chamber; in South Africa the IPU Website data for the upper chamber is incomplete; and in the United Kingdom the upper house is currently undergoing reconstruction. In these cases, data in this report refer only to the lower house.

The IPU Website does not provide time series data. Data for 1987 is taken from *The World's Women 1995: Trends and Statistics*, table 14, pp. 171-75, and includes data only for women's share of seats in the lower chamber of bicameral parliaments. The primary source of this data is IPU, *Distribution of Seats between Men and Women in the 144 National Assemblies*, Series Reports and Documents No 14 (Geneva 1987).

Progress of Women Scoreboard (Table 3.5)

Education variable
Change in secondary level female net enrolment ratio, 1985-1997 (1985=100) (Chart 3.2)

+ index in 1997 was 106 or more
= index in 1997 was in range 105 to 95
- index in 1997 was 94 or below
? no data available

Employment variable
Change in female share of paid employment in industry and services, early 1980s to mid 1990s (Chart 3.3)

+ increase of 2 or more percentage points
= change in range of +1.9 to –1.9 percentage points
- fall of 2 or more percentage points
? no data available

Parliament variable
Change in women's share of seats in national parliament, 1987-2000 (Chart 3.4)

+ increase of more than 1 percentage point
= change in range +1 percentage point to –1 percentage point
- fall of more than –1 percentage point
? parliament was not in existence for one or the both of the chosen dates

Economic growth variable
Change in real per capita income, 1985-1997 (measured in 1987 US $)

+ increase of more than 0.5 percent point
= change in range +0.5 to –0.5 percentage points
- fall of more than -0.5 percentage point
? no data available

The data source for real per capita income is the Human Development Report CD-ROM. The calculation of growth rates uses a model of continuous, exponential growth between two points in time. The equation used for the calculation is as follows:

$r = \ln(p_n/p_1)/n$
r = growth rate
ln = natural logarithm operator
p_n = GDP per capita, 1985

$p1$ = GDP per capita, 1997
n = number of years in the period, 12

Income equality variable
The gini coefficient indicates the degree of equality in distribution of national income among households. A lower value means greater equality. The source is the UNU/WIDER-UNDP World Income Inequality Database, Beta 3, 8 November 1999. Change is calculated between 1980s and 1990s.

+ decrease of more than –2 percentage points, i.e. greater equality
= change in range -2 to 2 percentage points
- increase of 2 or more percentage points, i.e. less equality
? no data available

Debt reduction variable
Change in the ratio of external debt to GNP between 1985 and 1997. The source for external debt ratio data is the Human Development Report CD-ROM. The change is calculated in terms of the ratio of 1997 debt ratio to 1985 debt ratio.

+ an improvement, ratio is less than 1
= no change, ratio is equal to 1
- a deterioration, the ratio is greater than 1
? no data available

Chapter 4 Indicators

Unpaid Family Workers and Employers/Own-account Workers (Table 4.1, Chart 4.1, Chart 4.2)
According to International Classification of Status in Employment (ICSE-1993): *employer* refers to a person who operates his or her own enterprise, or engages independently in a profession or trade, and hires one or more employees; *own-account worker* refers to a person who operates his or her own-enterprise, or engages independently in a profession or trade, and hires no employees; *unpaid family worker* usually refers to a person who works without pay in an economic enterprise operated by a related person living in the same household.

This report draws upon the Wistat database, which provides raw data for economically active population by status in employment, disaggregated by sex, using data supplied by ILO.

The primary data is collected by national governments via labour-force surveys and labour-related establishment surveys. Comparisons are complicated by differences in the ways in which people, especially women, are assigned to the categories of own-account worker and unpaid family worker. The latest data available refers to early or mid-1990s. Data for 1980s mostly refers to the early 1980s, with few exceptions from the late 1970s.

Female Share of Administrative and Managerial Positions (Chart 4.3)
The International Standard Classification of Occupations was revised during the period (mid 1980s to mid 1990s) covered by Chart 4.3. Data for the mid 1980s is based on ISCO-1968. While some countries switched to ISCO-88 immediately after its publication in 1990, the following countries listed in Chart 4.3 continued to use ISCO-68: Egypt, Niger, Swaziland, Bahrain, Syria, Turkey, Bangladesh, Hong Kong, Malaysia, Pakistan, Philippines, Thailand, Barbados, Belize, Chile, Colombia, Ecuador, Haiti, Honduras, Panama, Paraguay, Uruguay, Venezuela, Canada, Finland, Japan, Norway.

The source of data, with few a exceptions, is ILO Website "laboursta" database. However, for Ethiopia, Brunei Darussalam, Iran, Bulgaria, France and Luxembourg, the source is Wistat version 4, because data was unavailable from "laboursta."

One complication is that a number of countries combine the category of administrative and managerial positions with the category of clerical and related workers. As far as possible, countries which do this have been excluded from Chart 4.3.

Gender Gap in Wages (Table 4.2, Chart 4.4, Chart 4.5)
Wages refer to remuneration paid to employees for the work they have carried out. The source of data is the Wistat database, which draws upon data from ILO, and ECLAC 1998.

Wistat provides female wages as a percentage of male wages for 38 countries in manufacturing and 25 countries in industry and services for circa 1997, and for 29 countries in manufacturing and 27 countries in industry and services for circa 1980. The indicator for manufacturing in Costa Rica proved to be

erroneous and was recalculated from raw data in the ILO laboursta database. Wistat data for Hong Kong and Bangladesh is not used in this report because it refers to wage rates rather than earnings.

Wistat data may refer to hourly, weekly or daily earnings. The primary sources of data vary: Egypt, Iceland, Latvia, Lithuania, Hungary, Ukraine, Denmark, Finland, New Zealand, Luxemburg, Swaziland are from "labour-related establishment censuses"; Jordan, Cyprus, Sri Lanka, Thailand, Korea, El Salvador, Sweden, Norway, Greece, Belgium, Ireland, Germany, United Kingdom, Switzerland, Portugal, Netherlands, France are from "labour related establishment survey"; Malaysia and Myanmar from "establishment survey"; Turkey and Austria from "insurance records"; Paraguay is from "administrative records." As the Wistat technical notes point out: "International comparison of wage ratios presented here must be made with great caution. As indicated above, the coverage, definitions and methods of compiling wage statistics differ significantly from country to country. Disaggregation of statistics by sex is available for only few countries and may be based on a narrow segment of the population." Many developed countries with capacity to produce detailed labour-market data are not included in the Wistat database, e.g., United States, Canada, Japan.

Neither Wistat nor recent ILO yearbooks include the data provided by ECLAC (1998, table 39, p. 303) for 17 Latin American countries on women's monthly labour income as a percentage of men's monthly labour income (calculated on the basis of value per hour worked, expressed in terms of the poverty line for urban and rural areas). Thus it is not strictly comparable with the Wistat/ILO data, and it is likely to include income from self-employment as well as wage employment; it also refers to geographical area rather than industrial activity. Nevertheless, there is likely to be considerable overlap between urban areas and industry and services categories. Therefore, this report includes the ECLAC indicator derived from urban household surveys for urban areas for Argentina, Bolivia, Chile, Colombia, Dominican Republic, Ecuador, El Salvador, Guatemala, Honduras, Mexico, Panama, Uruguay, Venezuela.

Prevalence of Violence Against Women by an Intimate Partner (Table 4.5)
The indicator presented in Table 4.5 is the percentage of adult women who have been physically assaulted by an intimate partner in the past 12 months, in the current relationship or ever (in any relationship). Physical assault excludes psychological, verbal, sexual abuse and rape. However, data from Barbados, Uruguay, Canada, New Zealand, Barbados, Switzerland refer to both physical and sexual abuse. It is important to note that the definition of physical violence varies substantially from study to study. Physical violence refers to violence at least at the level of physical contact. Some studies define physical contact as "more than slaps," which would exclude pushes and slaps. Some studies define it as "at least at the level of hitting"; in this case it includes slaps but excludes pushing and shoving. Of 32 studies included in Table 4.5, 12 have national coverage (figures in brackets give the sample size): Egypt (7121), South Africa (5077) Korea (707), Philippines (8481), Barbados (264), Colombia (6097), Paraguay (5940) (except Chaco region), Australia (6300), Canada (12300), Netherlands (1016), Switzerland (1500), United States (8000), New Zealand (2000), Moldova (4790). The remaining 18 studies cover selected cities or regions within the country.

This report draws upon studies from the World Health Organization (WHO) database developed and maintained by WHO- Violence and Injury Prevention Unit in collaboration with the Johns Hopkins School of Public Health, and the report on *Ending Violence Against Women,* published by the Johns Hopkins School of Public Health in collaboration with the Center for Health and Gender Equity (CHANGE) (Website: www.jhuccp.org). While the WHO database includes 36 studies, with sample size ranging from 111 to 12,300, the Johns Hopkins Report includes the same 36 plus an additional 13, which together have a sample size ranging from 97 to 12,300.

These studies include unpublished data such as academic theses, dissertations and local NGO information. The John Hopkins Report specifies that the respondents in all the studies are women except in the case of Thailand and New Zealand where the respondents are all men or married/partnered men reporting their own violence against women. There are some discrepancies between the two databases; for instance, sample sizes reported for South Africa, Netherlands and Paraguay for the same surveys do not match. Table 4.5 does not include every entry in the two databases since there are multiple entries for several countries. In such cases the entry providing the most comprehensive coverage, in terms of geographical coverage and sample size, is selected.

Prevalence of HIV/AIDS (Table 4.6)
The percentages of women and adults living with HIV/AIDS refer to all people alive with HIV infection at the end of 1997, whether or not they have developed symptoms of AIDS.

Table 4.6 draws upon the Wistat database, which presents data from the *Report on the Global HIV/AIDS Epidemic,* June 1998 issued by the United Nations Programme on HIV/AIDS (UNAIDS) and the World Health Organization (WHO). The primary source of data is the individual country Epidemiological Fact Sheets for 1997, which are prepared through the collaborative efforts of UNAIDS, WHO and national AIDS programmes or other national authorities. Regional estimates have been released in *Aids Epidemic Update: December 1999* published by UNAIDS/WHO. Updated country-level estimates will be released during the HIV/AIDS conference in summer 2000.

Bibliographic Note

This report draws upon a number of works not explicitly cited in the text:

Chapter 2

Elson, Diane. 1991. "Male Bias in Macro-Economics." In Diane Elson, ed., *Male Bias in the Development Process.* Manchester: Manchester University Press.

_____ and Jasmine Gideon. 1999. "The International Convenant on Economic, Social and Cultural Rights and the Empowerment of Women," background paper, *Progress of the World's Women 2000, A UNIFEM Report.*

International Labour Office. 1999. *Decent Work.* Geneva.

International Women's Tribune Centre. 1998. *Rights of Women.* New York: IWTC.

Khor, Martin. 1995. "Briefing for the Social Summit." Third World Network, Penang.

UNIFEM and UNICEF. 1995. *Convention on the Elimination of All Forms of Discrimination Against Women: A Handbook.* New York: UNIFEM and UNICEF.

Women, Law and Development International and Human Rights Watch Women's Rights Project. 1997. *Women's Human Rights Step by Step.* Washington, DC: Women, Law and Development International.

Chapter 5

Bakker, Isabella and Diane Elson. 1998. "Engendering Budgets." In *Alternative Federal Budget 1998.* Ottawa: Canadian Centre for Policy Alternatives.

Bakker, Isabella. 1998. *Unpaid Work and Macroeconomics: New Discussions, New Tools for Action.* Ottawa: Status of Women Canada.

_____. 1994. *The Strategic Silence: Gender and Economic Policy.* London: Zed Books and the North-South Institute.

Barrientos, Stephanie, Sharon McClenaghan and Liz Orton. 1999. *Gender and Codes of Conduct: A Case Study from Horticulture in South Africa.* London: Christian Aid.

Elson, Diane. 1999. "Why Gender Sensitive Budgets?" In Isabella Bakker, ed., *Pro-Poor, Gender- and Environment-Sensitive Budgets.* New York: UNDP/SEPED.

International Confederation of Free Trade Unions. 1997. *Labour and Business in the Global Market.* Brussels: ICFTU.

Mather, Celia. 2000. can Companies Be "Good Citizens"? An Overview of Current trends in Corporate Responsibility." Draft report for UN Non-Governmental Liaison Service, Geneva.

References

Agarwal, Bina. 1996. "From Mexico 1975 to Beijing 1995," *Indian Journal of Gender Studies,* Vol.3, no.1.

_____.1995. "Gender, Property and Land Rights: Bridging a Critical Gap in Economic Analysis and Policy." In Edith Kuiper and Jolande Sap, eds., *Out of the Margin: Feminist Perspectives on Economics.* London and New York: Routledge.

_____. 1994. *A Field of One's Own: Gender and Land Rights in South Asia.* Cambridge: Cambridge University Press.

AMRC (Asia Monitor Resource Center). 1997. *Asian Labour Update* (Hong Kong) 24. April-June.

Arndt, Channing and Finn Tarp. 2000. "Agricultural Technology, Risk, and Gender: A CGE Analysis of Mozambique," *World Development,* Vol.28, no.7.

Arriagada, Irma. 1998. *The Urban Female Labour Market in Latin America: The Myth and the Reality.* Santiago, Chile: ECLAC.

Bakker, Isabella. 1999. "Toward Social and Economic Sustainability: Linkages between Paid and Unpaid Work in Canada," paper presented at APEC Human Resources Development Working Group Conference on Linkages Between Paid and Unpaid Work in Human Resource Policy, Hong Kong, China.

Balakrishnan, Radhika. 1999. "Capitalism and Sexuality: Free to Choose?" In Patricia Jung, Mary Hunt and Radhika Balakrishnan, eds., *Good Sex: Feminist, Religious and Crosscultural Perspectives.* New Brunswick, NJ: Rutgers University Press.

Balgos, Cecile C.A., ed. 1998. *Investigative Reports on Filipino Women in the 1990s.* Manila: Philippine Center for Investigative Journalism.

Bardhan, Kalpana and Stephan Klasen. 1999. "UNDP's Gender-Related Indices: A Critical Review," *World Development,* Vol.27, no.6.

Baulch, Bob. 1996. "The New Poverty Agenda: A Disputed Consensus," *IDS Bulletin,* Vol.27, no.1.

Barroso, Carmen and Sonia Corrêa. 1995. "Public Servants, Professionals, and Feminists: The Politics of Contraceptive Research in Brazil." In Faye Ginsburg and Rayna Rapp, eds., *Conceiving the New World Order: The Global Politics of Reproduction.* Berkeley: University of California Press.

Benería, Lourdes. 1999. "The Enduring Debate over Unpaid Labour," *International Labour Review* (Geneva), Vol.138, no.3.

_____. 1985. "Toward a Greater Integration of Gender in Economics," *World Development,* Vol.23, no.11.

_____. 1982. "Accounting for Women's Work." In Benería, Lourdes, ed., *Women and Development: The Sexual Division of Labor in Rural Societies.* New York: Praeger.

Bhatia, Bela and Jean Dreze. 1998. "For Development and Democracy," *Frontline* (India), March 6, 1998.

Bisnath, Savitri and Diane Elson. 1999. "Women's Empowerment Revisited," background paper, *Progress of the World's Women 2000, A UNIFEM Report.*

Block, Jennifer. 2000. "Workers Win One," *Ms. Magazine,* February/March.

Braunstein, Elissa. 2000. "Engendering Foreign Direct Investment: Family Structure, Labor Markets and International Capital Mobility," *World Development,* Vol. 28, no.7.

Budlender, Debbie, ed. 1999. *Engendering Budgets: The Southern African Experience.* Harare: UNIFEM.

_____. 1996/97/98/99 *First, Second, Third and Fourth Women's Budgets* Capetown: IDASA.

_____ and Rhonda Sharp. 1998. *How to Do a Gender-Sensitive Budget Analysis: Contemporary Research and Analysis.* Canberra and London: Australian Agency for International Development and the Commonwealth Secretariat.

Bulbeck, Chilla. 1998. *Re-Orienting Western Feminisms: Women's Diversity in a Postcolonial World*. Cambridge: Cambridge University Press.

Burns, Maggie, Maya Forstater, Adrienne Mong, Diane Osgood, and Simon Zadek. 1999. *Open Trading: Options for Effective Monitoring of Corporate Codes of Conduct*. London: New Economics Foundation.

Çağatay, Nilüfer. 1998. "Gender and Poverty." Working Paper no. 5, UNDP, Social Development and Policy Division, New York.

Çağatay, Nilüfer, Diane Elson, and Caren Grown. 1995. "Introduction: Gender, Adjustment and Macroeconomics," *World Development*, Vol.23, no.11.

Canadian International Development Agency (CIDA). 1996. *Guide to Gender-Sensitive Indicators*. Hull: Women in Development and Gender Equity Division.

Carr, Marilyn, Martha Chen and Renana Jhabvala, eds. 1996. *Speaking Out: Women's Economic Empowerment in South Asia*. London: Intermediate Technology Publications.

Caspar, Lynne, Sara McLanahan and Irwin Garfinkel. 1994. "The Gender Poverty Gap: What Can We Learn from Other Countries?" *American Sociological Review*, Vol.59.

CAW (Committee for Asian Women). 1998. *Asian Women Workers Newsletter* (Hong Kong), July.

Charmes, Jacques. 1998. "Informal Sector, Poverty and Gender: A Review of Empirical Evidence." Background paper for World Bank, *World Development Report 2000*, Washington, DC.

Choices: A Coalition for Social Justice. 1998. *Show us the Money! The Politics and Process of Alternative Budgets*. Winnipeg: Arbeiter Ring.

Commonwealth Secretariat. 1999. *Gender Budget Initiative Kit*. London: Commonwealth Secretariat.

_____. 1998. *Gender Mainstreaming: Commonwealth Strategies on Politics, Macroeconomics and Human Rights*. London: Commonwealth Secretariat.

Corner, Lorraine. 1999. "Analysis of Approaches to Strengthening Homeworkers & Micro-Enterprise: A Gender Perspective," paper prepared for *Gender and Globalization: Empowering Women in Homework & Micro-enterprise to Meet the Challenges of the Market*. New York: UNIFEM.

Davis, Susan. 1996. "Making Waves: Advocacy by Women NGOs at UN Conferences," *SID WID Development* 1996:3, pp. 42-45.

Day, Shelagh and Gwen Brodsky. 1998. *Women and the Equality Deficit: The Impact of Restructuring Canada's Social Programs*. Ottawa: Canada Status of Women.

Demery, Lionel, Shiyan Chao, Rene Bernier and Kalpana Mehra. 1995. "The Incidence of Social Spending in Ghana," World Bank Poverty and Social Policy Discussion Paper, Washington, DC.

Dollar, David and Roberta Gatti. 1999. "Gender Inequality, Income, and Growth: Are Good Times Good for Women?" Policy Research Report on Gender and Development, Working Paper Series, no.1, The World Bank, Washington, DC.

Dollar, David, Raymond Fisman and Roberta Gatti. 1999. "Are Women Really the 'Fairer' Sex? Corruption and Women in Government," World Bank Working Paper Series, no.4, Washington, DC.

Dreze, Jean and Amartya Sen. 1989. *Hunger and Public Action*. Oxford: Clarendon Press.

Economic Commission for Latin America and the Caribbean (ECLAC). 1999a. *Social Panorama of Latin America. 1999* ed. Santiago, Chile: ECLAC.

_____. 1999b. *Participation and Leadership in Latin America and the Caribbean: Gender Indicators*. Santiago, Chile: ECLAC.

_____. 1998. *Social Panorama of Latin America, 1998*. Santiago, Chile: ECLAC.

_____. 1993. *Social Panorama of Latin America, 1993*. Santiago, Chile: ECLAC.

_____. 1998. "Integrating Gender Issues into National Budgetary Policies and Procedures: Some Policy Options," *Journal of International Development*, Vol.10, pp. 929-41.

Elson, Diane and Nilüfer Çağatay. 2000. "The Social Content of Macroeconomic Policies," *World Development*, Vol.28, no.7

Equality Now. 1999. *Words and Deeds: Government Actions Five Years After the Beijing Conference*. New York: Equality Now.

European Union. 1999. *Joint Employment Report 1999*. Brussels: European Union.

Evans, Alison and Kate Young. 1988. "Gender Issues in Household Labour Allocation: The Case of Northern Province, Zambia," ESCOR Research Report, Overseas Development Agency, London.

Fukuda-Parr, Sakiko.1999. "What Does Feminization of Poverty Mean? It Isn't Just Lack of Income," *Feminist Economics*, Vol.5, no.2.

Floro, Maria and Gary Dymski. 2000. "Financial Crisis, Gender, and Power: An Analytical Framework," *World Development*, Vol.28, no.7.

Folbre, Nancy. 1994. *Who Pays for the Kids? Gender and the Structures of Constraint*. London and New York: Routledge.

Fontana, Marzia and Adrian Wood. 2000. "Modelling the Effects of Trade on Women, at Work and at Home," *World Development*, Vol.28, no.7.

Fontana, Marzia, Susan Joekes and Rachel Masika. 1998. *Global Trade Expansion and Liberalisation: Gender Issues and Impacts*. London: DfID.

Food and Agricultural Organization. 1996. *Rome Declaration on World Food Security and World Food Summit Plan of Action*. Rome: FAO.

Gálvez, Thelma. 1999. "Aspectos económico de las equidad de género," paper presented at 8th Regional Conference of Women in Latin America and the Caribbean, Lima, Peru.

Goldschmidt-Clermont, Luisella and Elisabetta Pagnossin-Aligisakis. 1995. "Monetary Valuation of Unpaid Work." In *International Conference on the Measurement and Valuation of Unpaid Work, Proceedings*. Ottawa: Statistics Canada.

GPI Atlantic. 1999. "The Economic Value of Civic and Voluntary Work in Nova Scotia," unpublished paper, Halifax, Nova Scotia.

Grown, Caren, Nilifür Çağatay and Diane Elson. 2000. "Introduction: Growth, Trade, Finance and Gender Inequality," *World Development*, Vol.28, no.7.

Guerrero, Margarita. 2000. "Towards International Guidelines in Time-Use Surveys: Objectives and Methods of National Time-Use Surveys in Developing Countries," Seminar on Users and Producers of Household Surveys and Time-Use Surveys, Havana, Cuba.

Gupta, Surunjana, Prema Gopalan, Sandy Schilen, and Gayatri A. Menon. 1998. *Visiting Alternatives: An Inter-State Study Tour on Savings and Credit*. Mumbai, India: Prayog Swayam Shikshan.

Gurumurthy, Anita. 1998. *Women's Rights and Status: Questions of Analysis and Measurement*. UNDP Gender in Development Monograph Series, no.7. New York: UNDP.

Hale, Angela. 1997. *Company Codes of Conduct*. Manchester: Women Working Worldwide.

Hale, Angela. ed. 1998. *Trade Myths and Gender Reality: Trade Liberalisation and Women's Links*. Uppsala: Global Publications Foundation.

Haxton, Eva and Claes Olsson, eds. 1999. *Gender Focus on the WTO*. Uppsala: Global Publications Foundation.

Heyzer, Noeleen. 1999. "The Asian Financial Crisis: Causes, Consequences and Ways Forward," Online Development Forum, World Bank, Washington, DC; www.worldbank.org/devforum/speaker-heyzer.html.

_____. 1994. "Introduction: Market, State and Gender Equity." In Noeleen Heyzer and Gita Sen, eds., *Gender, Economic Growth and Poverty*. Kuala Lumpur: Asian and Pacific Development Centre.

Hilkka, Pietilä. 1998. *How the Cake Is Cut: Production and Economic Well-Being*. Brussels: WIDE, Network Women in Development Europe.

Hide, Richard. 1997. "Fairly Traded and Organic Coffee: Twin Trading's Experience and Perspectives," presentation to the 15th Coffee International Conference and Exhibition.

Hill, Anne and Elizabeth King. 1995. "Women's Education and Economic Well-being." *Feminist Economics*, Vol.1, no.2.

HomeNet Newsletter. Autumn 1998. Leeds.

Hurt, Karen and Debbie Budlender, eds. 1998. *Money Matters: Women and the Government Budget*. Cape Town: Institute for Democracy in South Africa.

ICEM. 1997. "Key Occupational, Health, Safety and Environmental Issues and Developments at the International Level in the Chemical Sector," ICEM World Chemical Industry, Hanover, Germany.

INSTRAW. 1995. *Measurement and Valuation of Unpaid Contribution: Accounting through Time and Output*. Santo Domingo: INSTRAW.

International Civil Service Commission (ICSC). 1998. *Gender Balance in the United Nations Common System: Progress, Prognosis, Prescriptions*. New York: ICSC.

International Labour Organization (ILO). 1999. *Key Indicators of the Labour Market (KILM)*. Geneva: ILO.

International Union of Local Authorities (IULA). 1998. "Worldwide Declaration on Women in Local Government," Harare.

International Women's Tribune Centre (IWTC). 2000. *Preview 2000*, no.3. February.

_____. 1999. *Preview 2000*, no.2. May.

Ironmonger, Duncan. 1996. "Priorities for Research on Nonmarket Work," *Feminist Economics*, Vol.2, no.3.

Jain, Devaki. 1999. "Nuancing Globalisation or Mainstreaming the Downstream, or Reforming Reform," Nita Barrow Memorial Lecture, Centre for Gender and Development Studies, University of West Indies, Barbados.

Jain, Devaki and Samia Ahmad. 1999. "Towards Just Development: Identifying Meaningful Indicators," a working paper for UNDP (South Africa).

Jamaica Employees Federation and Centre for Gender and Development Studies, University of the West Indies (UWI). 1995. "Report to the Symposium on Optimising the Contribution of Women to the Jamaican Workplace," University of West Indies, Jamaica.

Jenkins, Rob and Anne Marie Goetz. 1999. "Accounts and Accountability: Theoretical Implications of the Right-to-Information Movement in India," mimeo, Institute for Development Studies, Sussex.

Jessop, Bob. 1997. "Capitalism and Its Future: Remarks on Regulation, Government and Governance," *Review of International Political Economy*, Vol.4, no.3.

Johnson, Susan and Ben Rogaly. 1997. "Microfinance and Poverty Reduction," Oxfam, Oxford, UK.

Kabeer, Naila. 1999. "Resources, Agency, Achievements: Reflections on the Measurement of Women's Empowerment," *Development and Change*, Vol.30, no.3.

Kardam, Nuket and Yakin Ertürk. 1999. "Expanding Gender Accountability? Women's Organizations and the State in Turkey," *International Journal of Organization and Behavior*, Vol.2, nos.1&2.

Kensington Welfare Rights Union. 1999. *Poor People's Human Rights Report on the United States*. Philadelphia: Kensington Welfare Rights Union.

Khondkar, Mubina. 1998. "Women's Access to Credit and Gender Relations in Bangladesh," Ph.D. thesis, University of Manchester, UK.

Kiggundu, Rose. 1998. "Women and Trade: The Case of Uganda." In Angela Hale, ed., *Trade Myths and Gender Reality: Trade Liberalisation and Women's Lives*. Uppsala: Global Publications Foundation.

Kimmel, Michael. 2000. "What About the Boys? What the Current Debates Tell Us, and Don't Tell Us, About Boys in School," Keynote presentation, 6th Annual K-12 Gender Equity in Schools Conference, Wellesley College, Center for Research on Women, Wellesley, MA.

Klasen, Stephan. 1999. "Does Gender Inequality Reduce Growth and Development? Evidence from Cross-Country Regressions," background paper for World Bank Policy Research Report on Gender and Development, Washington, DC.

Kumar, Anusya. 1999. "Small Steps in Tamil Nadu," *Business India*, 8-21 March.

Lazo, Lucita. 1999. "Counting Paid and Unpaid Work: The State of the Art in the Asia-Pacific Region," paper presented at APEC Human Resources Development Working Group Conference on Linkages Between Paid and Unpaid Work in Human Resource Policy, Hong Kong, China.

Licuanan, Patricia B. 1999. "Monitoring and Evaluation Strategies for the Empowerment of Women," paper prepared for the ESCAP High Level Intergovernmental Meeting to Review Regional Implementation of the Beijing Platform for Action, Bangkok, October.

Lim, Joseph Y. 2000. "The Effects of the East Asian Crisis on the Employment of Women and Men: The Philippine Case," *World Development*, Vol.28, no.7.

Lundberg, Lars and Lyn Squire. 1999. "Inequality and Growth: Lessons for Policy," mimeo, World Bank, Washington, DC.

Maddock, Sue and Diane Parkin. 1993. "Gender Cultures; Women's Strategies and Choices at Work," *Women in Management Review*, Vol.8, no.2.

Madeley, John. 1999. *Big Business, Poor People: the Impact of Transnational Corporations on the World's Poor*. London: Zed Books.

Marcoux, Alain. 1998. "The Feminization of Poverty: Claims, Facts and Data Needs," *Population and Development Review*, Vol.24, no.1.

Mayoux, Linda. 1999. "From Access to Empowerment: Widening the Debate on Gender and Sustainable Microfinance," paper prepared at request of UNIFEM for the Microcredit Summit Meeting of Councils, Abidjan, Côte d'Ivoire.

_____. 1998. "Women's Empowerment and Micro-Finance Programmes: Approaches, Evidence and Ways Forward," Discussion paper, Open University, Milton Keynes, UK.

McGee, Rosemary, Clive Robinson and Arthur van Diesen. 1998. *Distant Targets? Making the 21st Century Development Strategy Work*. London: Christian Aid.

Mehta, Aasha Kapur. 1996. "Recasting Indices for Developing Countries: A Gender Empowerment Measure," *Economic and Political Weekly* (Bombay), October.

Microcredit Summit Campaign. 1999. *Meeting of Councils 1999: Final Report*. Abidjan: Microcredit Summit Campaign.

Mitter, Swasti. 1999. Online Working Group on Women's Economic Inequality, 6 September-15 October 1999; www.im.org/womenwatch.

Murray, Robin. 1998. "Three Varieties of Alternative Trade: Extending the Definition," Working paper no.1, Project on Understanding and Expanding Fair Trade, Twin/ DfID, London.

National Association of Women and the Law (NAWL). 1998. *Pre-Budget Consultations: 1999 Federal Budget. Tackling the Social Deficit – Securing Gender Equality*. Toronto: NAWL.

Neuhold, Brita. 1998. "Women's Economic Rights as Part of International Declarations and Conventions," *Women in Development Europe Bulletin*, February.

NGOs for Women 2000, "Report of Panel Discussion on Beijing +5: Setting Targets," New York, 22 November 1999.

Ocampo, José Antonio. 2000. "The Economic and Social Rights of Andean Women," speech to 8th Regional Conference of Women of Latin America and the Caribbean, Lima, Peru.

Ongile, Grace A. 1998. "Gender and Agricultural Supply Responses to Structural Adjustment Programmes: A Case Study of Smallholder Tea Producers in Kericho, Kenya." Ph.D. thesis, University of Manchester.

OECD 1996. *Shaping the 21st Century*. Paris: OECD Development Assistance Committee.

Opoku-Mensah, Aida. 1999. "Telecentres Excite Ugandans - But What About the Poor?" News Briefing, www.oneworld. org/panos/news/3aug98.htm.

Panos. 1998. "The Internet and Poverty," *Panos News Briefing*, no.28.

Pepall, Jennifer. 1998. "Bangladeshi Women and the Grameen Bank." www.idrc.ca/ reports/read_article-english.cfm?article_num=264.

Petchesky, Rosalind Polack and Karen Judd, eds. 1998. *Negotiating Reproductive Rights: Women's Perspectives Across Countries and Cultures*. London: Zed Books.

Picchio, Antonella. 1992. *Social Reproduction: The Political Economy of the Labour Market*. Cambridge: Cambridge University Press.

Pouw, Nicky R.M. 1998. *Home Economics: Developing an Alternative Perspective*. Brussels: WIDE, Network Women in Development Europe.

Quisumbing, Agnes, Lawrence Haddad and Christine Peña. 1995. "Gender and Poverty: New Evidence from 10 Developing Countries," FCND Discussion Paper no. 9, International Food Policy Research Institute, Washington, DC.

Razavi, Shahra. 1999. "Gendered Poverty and Well Being: Introduction," *Development and Change*, Vol.30, no.3, July.

Roy, Bunker. "Where Does All the Money Go? People's Struggle for Information," *Economic and Political Weekly* (Bombay), 12 July 1997.

Rubery, Jill and Colette Fagan. 1998. *Equal Opportunities and Employment in the European Union*. Vienna: Federal Ministry of Labour, Health and Social Affairs.

Rubery, Jill, Jane Humphries, Colette Fagan, Damian Grimshaw, Mark Smith. 1998. "Equal Opportunities as a Productive Factor," report for Policy and Perspectives Group of DGV, European Commission.

Ruminksa-Zimny, Ewa. 1999. "Globalization and Gender in Transition Economies." In UNCTAD, *Trade, Sustainable Development and Gender*. Geneva: UNCTAD.

Ryan, William P. 1999. "The New Landscape for Nonprofits," *Harvard Business Review*, January-February.

Saito, K. and D. Spurling, 1992. *Developing Agricultural Extension for Women Farmers*. World Bank Discussion Paper no.156, Washington DC.

Salaman, Lester M., Helmut K. Anheier and Associates. 1999. "Civil Society in Comparative Perspective." In Lester M. Salaman et al., *Global Civil Society: Dimensions of the Nonprofit Sector*. Baltimore: Johns Hopkins Center for Civil Society Studies.

Sami, Mariam. 1999. "Saudi Women Find Freedom on Web," huridocs-tech e-mail listserv, huridocs-tech@hrea.org.

Seguino, Stephanie. 2000. "Gender Inequality and Economic Growth: A Cross-Country Analysis," *World Development*, Vol.28, no.7.

Sen, Amartya. 1998. "Human Development and Financial Conservatism," *World Development*, Vol.26, no.4.

_____. 1993. "Capability and Wellbeing." In Martha Nussbaum and Amartya Sen, eds., *The Quality of Life*. Oxford: Clarendon Press.

_____. 1984. *Resources, Values and Development*. Oxford: Blackwell.

Sen, Gita. 2000. "Gender Mainstreaming in Finance Ministries," *World Development*, Vol.28, no.7.

_____. 1999. *Gender Mainstreaming in Finance: A Reference Manual for Governments and Other Stakeholders*. London: Commonwealth Secretariat.

_____. 1997. "Globalization in the 21st Century: Challenges for Civil Society," The UvA Development Lecture, University of Amsterdam.

_____ and Sonia Corrêa. 2000. "Gender Justice and Economic Justice – Reflections on the Five Year Reviews of the UN Conferences of the 1990s," paper prepared for UNIFEM in preparation for the five-year review of the Beijing Platform for Action.

Senapaty, Manju. 1997. "Gender Implications of Economic Reforms in the Education Sector in India: The Case of Haryana and Madhya Pradesh," Ph.D. thesis, University of Manchester.

Sethuraman, S.V. 1998. "Gender, Informality, and Poverty," background paper presented at WIEGO Annual Meeting, Ottawa, 1999.

Sharp, Rhonda. 1995. "A Framework for Gathering Budget Information from Government Departments and Authorities," mimeo, Research Centre for Gender Studies, University of South Australia, Adelaide.

_____ and Ray Broomhill. 1998. "International Policy Developments in Engendering Government Budgets," In Elizabeth Shannon, ed., *Australian Women's Policy Structures*. Hobart: University of Tasmania.

Singh, Ajit and Ann Zammit. 2000. "International Capital Flows: Identifying the Gender Dimension," *World Development*, Vol.28, no.7.

Snyder, Margaret. 2000. *Women in African Economies: From Burning Sun to Boardroom*. Kampala, Uganda: Fountain Publishers.

Social Watch. 1999. Montevideo, Uruguay: Instituto de Tercer Mundo.

Standing, Guy. 1999. "Global Feminization through Flexible Labour," *World Development*, Vol.27, no.3.

Stark, Agneta and Stefan de Vylder. 1998. *Mainstreaming Gender in Namibia's National Budget*. Stockholm: SIDA.

Swedish International Development Agency (SIDA). 1998. *Workshop on Mainstreaming a Gender Equality Perspective into Government Budgets*. Stockholm: SIDA.

Tzannatos, Zafiris. 1991. "Potential Gains from the Elimination of Gender Differentials in the Labour Market." In George Psacharopoulos and Zafiris Tzannatos, eds., *Women's Employment and Pay in Latin America*. Washington DC: World Bank.

UK Cabinet Office. 2000. "Women's Incomes over the Lifetime," *Briefing*. London: HMSO.

UN. 2000a. *The World's Women 2000: Trends and Statistics*. New York: UN Statistical Division.

_____. 2000b. *Review and Appraisal of the Implementation of the Beijing Platform for Action. Report of the Secretary General*. New York: UN General Assembly, E/CN.6/2000/PC/2.

_____. 2000c. "Summary of the WomenWatch Online Working Groups on the 12 Critical Areas of Concern of the Beijing Platform for Action. Note by the Secretary-General." New York: UN Commission on the Status of Women, E/CN.6/2000/PC/CRP.1.

_____. 1999a. "Integrated and Coordinated Implementation and Follow-up to Major United Nations Conferences and Summits: Report of the Secretary-General." New York: General Assembly, E/1999/65.

_____. 1999b. *1999 World Survey on the Role of Women in Development: Globalization, Gender and Work*. New York: UN Division for the Advancement of Women.

_____. 1999c. "Review and Appraisal of the Implementation of the Programme of Action of the International Conference on Population and Development: Report of the Secretary General." New York: UN General Assembly, A/54/442.

_____. 1999d. "The Role of Employment and Work in Poverty Eradication: The Empowerment and Advancement of Women: Report of the Secretary-General." New York: UN, E/1999/53.

_____. 1999e. "The Role of Employment and Work in Poverty Eradication: The Empowerment and Advancement of Women." New York: UN Economic and Social Council, Draft Ministerial Communiqué, E/1999/L.21.

_____. 1999f. "Follow-up to and Implementation of the Beijing Declaration and Platform for Action. Report of the Secretary-General." New York: UN Economic and Social Council, E/CN.6/1999/2/Add.1.

_____. 1997a. "Promoting Women's Enjoyment of their Economic and Social Rights." Expert Group Meeting, Abo-Turku, Finland. New York: Division for the Advancement of Women.

_____.1997b. "Report of the Economic and Social Council for 1997." New York: General Assembly, A/52/3.

_____. 1996a. Second UN Conference on Human Settlements: *Habitat Agenda and Istanbul Declaration*. New York: Department of Public Information.

_____. 1996b. *The United Nations and the Advancement of Women 1945-96*. New York: Department of Public Information.

_____. 1995a. *The World's Women 1995: Trends and Statistics*. 2nd ed. New York: UN Statistical Division.

_____. 1995b. Fourth World Conference on Women: *Platform for Action and the Beijing Declaration*. New York: UN Department of Public Information.

_____. 1995c. World Summit for Social Development: *The Copenhagen Declaration and Programme of Action*. New York: Department of Public Information.

_____. 1994. *International Conference on Population and Development: Programme of Action*. New York: Department of Public Information.

_____. 1993a. "Declaration on the Elimination of All Forms of Discrimination Against Women." New York: UN General Assembly.

_____. 1993b. UN World Conference on Human Rights: *The Vienna Declaration and Programme of Action*. New York: Department of Public Information.

_____. 1992. Earth Summit: *Agenda 21 Programme of Action for Sustainable Development and Rio Declaration on Environment and Development*. New York: Department of Public Information.

_____. 1990. *The World's Women 1990: Trends and Statistics*. New York: UN Statistical Division.

_____. 1979. *The Convention on the Elimination of all Forms of Discrimination Against Women*. New York: Department of Public Information.

_____. 1966. *International Covenant on Economic, Social and Cultural Rights*. New York: Department of Public Information.

UNDP. 1999. *Human Development Report 1999*. New York: Oxford University Press

_____.1998a. *Human Development Report 1998*. New York: Oxford University Press.

_____. 1998b. *Overcoming Human Poverty*. New York: UNDP.

_____. 1998c. *Russian Federation Human Development Report 1998*. Moscow: UNDP.

_____. 1995. *Human Development Report 1995*. New York: UNDP.

_____. 1990. *Human Development Report 1990*. New York: UNDP.

UNFPA. 1999. *6 Billion: A Time for Choices. The State of the World Population*. New York: UNFPA.

_____. 1998. *Southeast Asian Populations in Crisis: Challenges to the Implementation of the ICPD Programme of Action*. New York: UNFPA.

UNHCR. 1998. "Statement on Globalization and Economic, Social and Cultural Rights," 18th session, 11 May 1998.

UNICEF. 1999. *Women in Transition*. New York: UNICEF.

UNIFEM. 1999a. *Engendering the Ninth Five-Year Plan of India (1997-2002)*. New Delhi: UNIFEM.

_____. 1999b. "Capacity Building for Gender Budgets in Southern Africa," a UNIFEM Regional Workshop Report, Harare, Zimbabwe. 9-10 November.

_____. 1999c. *Globalization Gender Markers: Strategic Concerns for Women in Microenterprise and Homework*. Bangkok: UNIFEM East and South East Asia Regional Office.

_____. 1999d. Regional Study on Gender Impact of Trade in Fiji, Papua Guinea, Tonga and Vanuatu.

_____. 1998a. *Bringing Equality Home: Implementing the Convention on the Elimination of All Forms of Discrimination Against Women*. New York: UNIFEM.

_____. 1998b. *Women in a Global Economy: Challenge and Opportunity in the Current Asian Economic Crisis*. Bangkok: UNIFEM East and South East Asia Regional Office.

_____. 1997a. "ACC Task Force on Basic Social Services for All: Guidelines on Women's Empowerment," New York.

_____.1997b. *Na Molay: Primer Congreso de Mujeres Mayas/First Congress of Mayan Women*. Mexico City: UNIFEM Regional Office of Mexico, Central America and Cuba.

UNIFEM and Comision Nacional de la Mujer (CONMUJER). 1999. *Mujeres Mexicanas: Avances y Perspectivas*. Mexico City: UNIFEM/CONMUJER.

UNIFEM National Committee Singapore. 1998. Presentation to UNIFEM Conference, mimeo.

United States Department of Labor. 1999. *Issues in Labor Statistics*. Summary 99-5. Washington, DC: Bureau of Labor Statistics.

van Staveren, Irene. 1999. *Caring for Economics: An Aristotelian Perspective*. Delft: Uitgeverji Eburon.

_____. 1998. *Robinson Crusoe and Silas Marner, or Two Stories on the Gendered Monetary Economy*. Brussels: WIDE, Network Women in Development Europe.

Vander Stichele, Myriam. 1998. "Gender, Trade and the WTO: A Ghana Case Study," prepared for the Informal Working Group on Gender and Trade, Women Working Worldwide, Manchester, UK.

Wang Jaix'iang. 1991. "A Chinese View on Feminism," *Asian Studies Review*, Vol.15, no.2.

Waring, Marilyn. 1999. *Counting for Nothing: What Men Value and What Women Are Worth*. 2nd ed. Toronto: University of Toronto Press.

Warner, James M. and D.A. Campbell. 2000. "Supply Response in an Agrarian Economy with Non-Symmetric Gender Relations," *World Development*, Vol. 28, no.7.

WEDO. 1999. "A Gender Agenda for the World Trade Organization," WEDO Primer, November.

_____.1998. *Mapping Progress: Assessing Implementation of the Beijing Platform 1998*. New York: WEDO.

Williams, Mariama. 1999. "Free Trade or Fair Trade?" DAWN Discussion Paper on the WTO.

Woestman, Lois. 1998. *The Mystery of Market Worship: Report Submitted to the Diplomatic Corps of Planet Venus*. Brussels: WIDE, Network Women in Development Europe.

Wolfensohn, James. D. 1995. "Women and Transformation of the 21st Century," Address to the Fourth UN World Conference on Women, Beijing, September 15, 1995. Washington, DC: World Bank.

Women Working Worldwide (WWW). 1998. "Korean Outward Investment and the Rights of Women Workers." Manchester: Manchester International Centre for Labour Studies.

_____. 1996. "World Trade is a Women's Issue. Promoting the Rights of Women Workers in a Changing World Economy," Women Working Worldwide Briefing Paper, Manchester, UK.

World Bank. 1998. *Global Economic Prospects*. Oxford: Clarendon Press.

_____. 1997. *World Development Report*. Washington, DC: World Bank.

_____. 1995. *Toward Gender Equality: The Role of Public Policy*. Washington DC: World Bank.

World Health Organisation (WHO). 1999. *The World Health Report 1999: Making a Difference*. Geneva: WHO.

Zohir, Salma Chaudhuri. 1998. "Gender Implications of Industrial Reforms and Adjustment in the Manufacturing Sector of Bangladesh." Ph.D. thesis, University of Manchester, UK.